I am within you always - and
you within me - gaze upon
the light of the sun for
there you will find me -
always within your heart -
at night I talk to you in
your dreams - whispers
like a gentle breeze passing
through - one heart within
the merging of souls. Floating
through the universe - through the
portal of divine love -
oneness - show my light -
my love to flow through
you to fill you with joy
like a million rose petals
blossom to eternity.

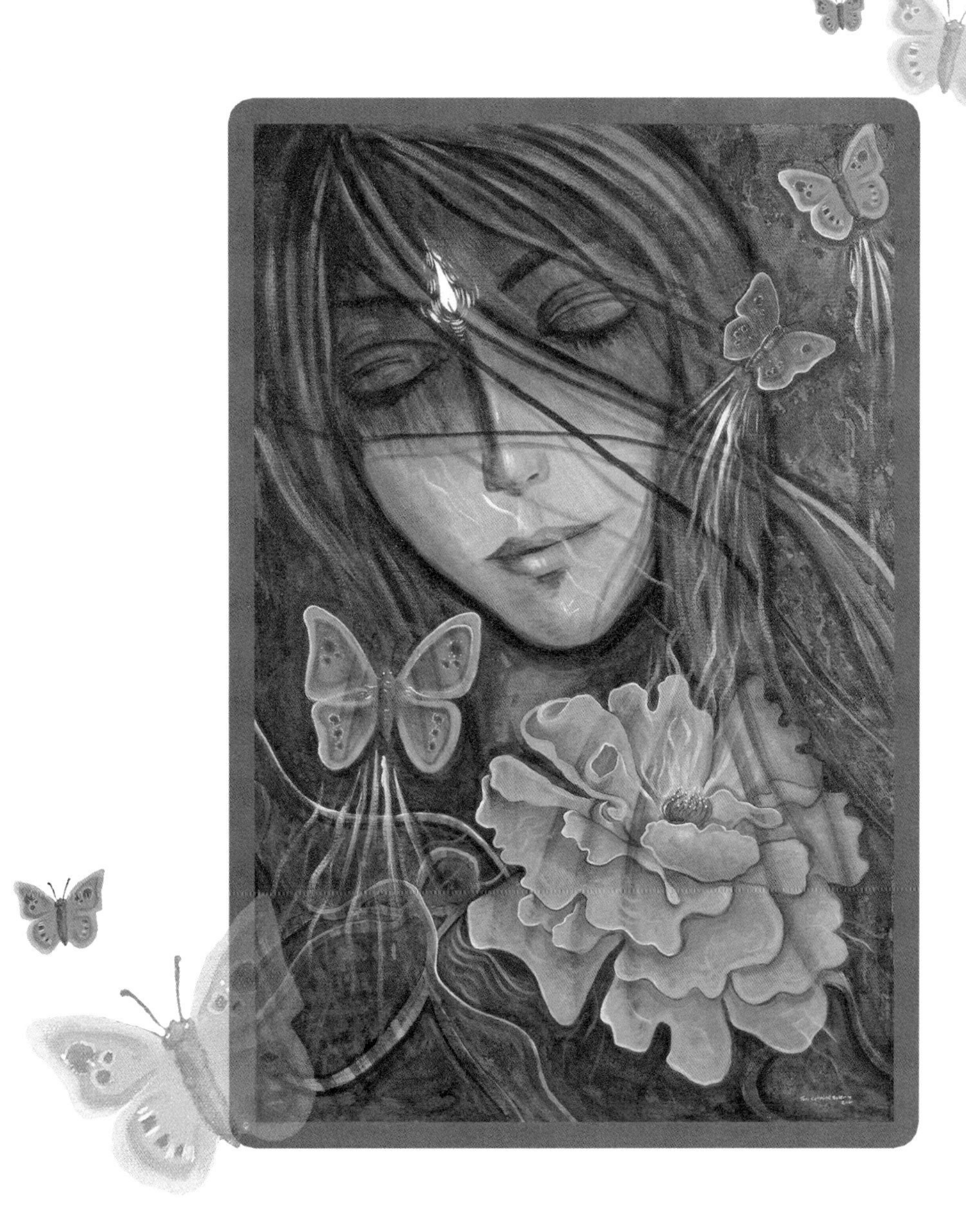

TONI CARMINE SALERNO

Art... Life... Reflections...

BLUE ANGEL GALLERY
AUSTRALIA

"Toni Carmine Salerno:
Art, Life, Reflections"

All paintings and text: Toni Carmine Salerno
Design: Kiddiepunk Graphics
Editing: Tanya Graham

Published in 2005 by :
Blue Angel Gallery
80 Glen Tower Drive
Glen Waverley, Victoria 3150
Australia

Phone : 61 3 9574 7776
Fax : 61 3 9574 7772
E-mail : tonicarmine@optusnet.com.au
Website : www.tonicarminesalerno.com

ISBN : 0-9579149-4-6

Contents:

PART ONE:

LIFE & REFLECTIONS

The following extract is taken from an interview conducted by Paul M. Segal with the artist and author Toni Carmine Salerno.

Part of this interview was aired on the 'Write Now' radio program.

Winds of Change

What factors led you to produce your unique style of art?

I have always known that I would paint regardless of whether I ever sold a painting or not. Painting has been a part of my life since I was eleven years old.

The beginning of the 1990s ushered in a period of major change in my life, which turned my existence upside down. The business I was running was struggling and eventually my business partner and I had no option but to appoint a receiver. As a result we were both declared officially bankrupt.

Just prior to this, my twenty year marriage had ended in divorce. Separating, especially since my wife and I had four children, was heart-wrenching. It's an experience I have perhaps still not completely reconciled within myself, though I now realise that there is never a gain without a loss and never a loss without a gain – that's life!

I found myself on my own, without work and with no clear direction for my life.

How did you manage to turn your life around from such a challenging position?

Somehow, within all of my struggles, I developed a kind of new found excitement and enthusiasm for the possibilities that my new life might hold.

Old friends and acquaintances drifted away while new friendships formed. My new circle of friends and acquaintances seemed to hold fundamentally different beliefs and attitudes to the people I had previously known. They also were predominantly women, which was a welcome change in itself.

For most of my life I had never really felt that I had much in common with most of the men I knew. I felt that women operated more on an emotional level and I was able to be more of who I truly am in their company.

I began to find my new circumstances both stimulating and challenging. To be quiet honest, I never really had much of a connection with many of the people I previously associated with, apart from my four children and a few close family members.

I had changed over the years and was now looking for something new which would give my life some kind of deeper meaning and purpose.

Did you find any assistance or guidance to help you discover your purpose and meaning?

I met Martine. She was perhaps the first person I'd ever come across who encouraged me to question my beliefs, or rather, my lack of belief in myself. At this stage, she was my main source of support.

Prior to my separation and bankruptcy I had largely come to accept that my underlying unhappiness was simply part of life. I had resigned myself to believing that life was just that way. Martine helped awaken me spiritually and emotionally. She suggested I see a counsellor.

She believed that talking about my life with a counsellor was something that would help me. Prior to this I knew nothing about counselling. I had never even considered it as an option.

It was Martine's encouragement, as well as her sometimes blunt statements and strong opinions, that set me off along the often torturous path of self-discovery through which I would eventually discover a greater purpose to my life.

Looking back, I now clearly see that everything in life happens for a reason and that all events in my life have been a blessing, even though at the time I experienced them they seemed to be quite the opposite.

Martine has obviously played an important, pivotal role in your life. How did you meet?

Was it random fate or something predestined? I believe it was destiny. I need to go back a few years to tell the story of how Martine and I first met.

I arrived home from work one Saturday afternoon, walked over to the kitchen counter and opened the newspaper. As I reached for the newspaper, I truly felt that I'd had enough of my boring and depressing outlook on life. A voice ran through my head, which I think stemmed from deep within my soul.

The voice said, "I've had enough of this! I'm not going to accept it anymore. I'm going to do something about it." These thoughts and feelings all echoed simultaneously.
As I opened the paper, I was immediately drawn to a tiny advertisement for Tai Chi classes. I had been wanting to do Tai Chi since having visited Hong Kong some years earlier but I had always put it off, inventing one excuse or another to myself.

While I was in Hong Kong, I saw a group of elderly locals practicing Tai Chi in a tiny courtyard just outside my hotel window. As they went through their practice, I thought that the movements were the most beautiful and graceful I had ever seen. These people seemed so peaceful and serene as they practiced their gentle movements. It seemed as though they were somehow at one with the flow of life itself, in body, mind and spirit. So, without hesitation, I picked up the phone, rang the number in the advertisement and enrolled in a ten week Tai Chi class that was to be held every Tuesday night at the Mount Waverley Civic Centre.

To my surprise, immediately after each Tai Chi class, David, the instructor, conducted a meditation. I also sat in on the meditation and quite enjoyed it.

After the first term, the class took a two-week break before commencing a new term. A few nights before the class was scheduled to recommence, I had a phone call from David who said that he didn't have enough people to hold the Mount Waverley class any longer and he invited me to attend his Wednesday night class in a nearby suburb. I did.

Martine, who was a member of one of David's other classes, had also been asked if she would like to attend the Wednesday night class. She agreed to attend the class which would be held straight after the Tai Chi class at the Nunawading Civic Centre.

So, one cold Winter's night, I met Martine for the first time – in this life at least. I say this because from the moment I first saw Martine, I was struck by an inexplicable feeling which I cannot adequately verbalise. I wouldn't describe it as love at first sight, but rather, a kind of mysterious and profound fascination and attraction.

Perhaps a more accurate way to describe our first encounter was that it triggered an inner recollection of somehow, maybe, having known this person before. I don't think I had ever heard of the concept of past lives at that stage.

So once you met Martine, was it obvious you were going to end up together?

No! Over the coming months, through meeting once a week at David's meditation class, Martine and I slowly formed a bond. It was not romance as such, but it felt more like a brother-sister relationship.

Some months later, the person who had originally brought us together looked set to cause our separation. David informed the group that he was moving to New South Wales, so there would be no more classes after the end of the term. My heart sank at the thought of not being able to see Martine again. Luckily, Martine and another lady, Heather, suggested that we try to find another meditation class and attend together.

My friendship with Martine grew stronger, though romance was still not on the cards. We explored different meditation techniques and healing modalities which eventually lead us to participate in a Reiki One course at the Usui Reiki Centre in Camberwell.

Over time our friendship deepened, along with our spiritual awareness, as we discovered a whole new spiritual dimension to life – a whole new world to be explored and experienced.

I began to believe that maybe there really was a greater purpose to my life.

The next few years brought many changes. On a physical level, the changes were most notably bankruptcy and divorce, however it was on a spiritual, heartfelt level that even more profound changes occurred. My painful experiences have since largely faded in the mists of time, yet the spiritual changes remain forever present.

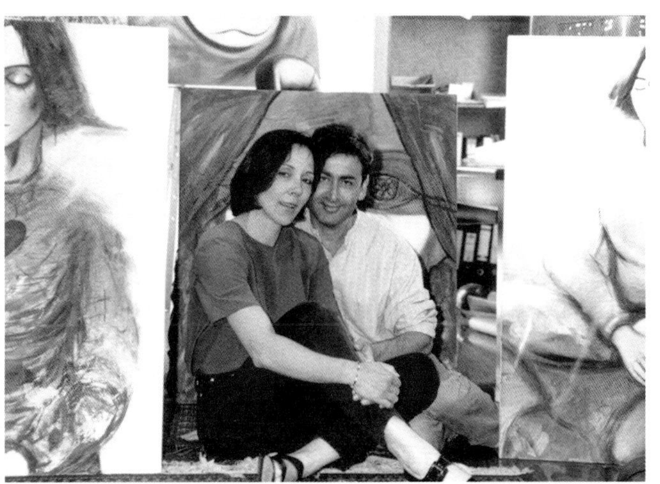

THE PHYSICAL EVENTS OF LIFE ARE TRANSIENT, ONLY THE SPIRIT IS ETERNAL.

THE EARLY YEARS

Could you share some of your memories of childhood?

I was born in Melbourne, Australia, on the 20th of October 1954. My parents Emma and Eugene, had migrated to Australia from Calabria in southern Italy, several years earlier.

My parents had known each other for about five years prior to arriving in Australia. They were both teenagers when they were engaged, back in Italy. They married shortly after my mum arrived in Australia with her family.

Dad had arrived in Melbourne a year earlier. Having travelled by boat, he arrived at Victoria Docks one cold Winter's day in July 1952, after a thirty-four day voyage on an Italian ocean liner, called 'Napoli'.

My father was barely twenty years of age when he left his place of birth and set off to an unknown, mysterious land on the other side of the world.

A gentleman named Luigi Stelato, an Italian who had migrated to Australia in the 1920s, sponsored my father, who had no relatives or friends in Australia. Luigi sponsored many southern Italians and helped them find employment after they arrived.

It was arranged that Luigi would come to collect Dad when he arrived. So Dad was waiting on Victoria Docks, while all the other passengers were greeted and picked up by their friends and relatives. Luigi Stelato was nowhere to be seen. By late afternoon my father was still alone and helpless, not knowing what to do. Finally Luigi arrived and drove Dad to a home in Oakleigh, which housed seven other Italian men who had also migrated to Australia with Luigi's help. The next morning Dad woke up to find himself home alone. The other men had gone off to work. Later that morning he decided to go for a walk around the surrounding streets. As he wandered through a world which would have been completely foreign to him, he must have surely wondered if coming to Australia had been such a great idea after all. He walked around and eventually ended up getting lost, with no way of communicating with anyone as he didn't speak a word of English.

When we get together at the family lunches and dinners my mother lovingly and passionately prepares, my father still tells us many wonderful and intriguing stories of his early experiences in Australia.

What about your parents' life in Italy, before they came to Australia?

Back in Italy, both Mum and Dad's families had lived in country areas on small farms and were practically self-sufficient. They picked, cultivated and made everything they needed to survive. They owned land, which they still own today.

Apart from beer and chocolate, my father, who has a delicate stomach, will not eat anything he hasn't grown, prepared or supervised the manufacturing of – in fact, if Mum hasn't cooked it, he probably won't eat it!

My parents, like most of the people of their generation and background, were true organic farmers

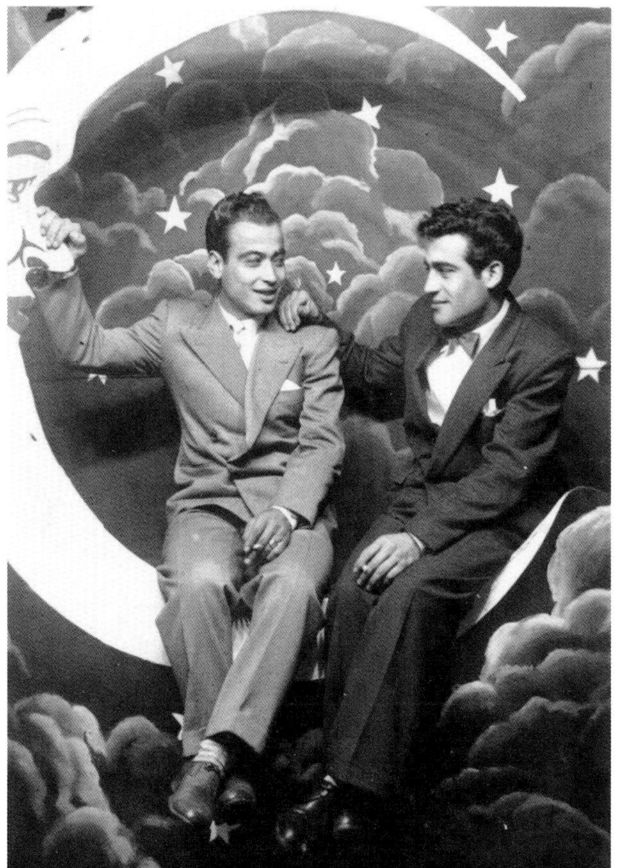

Toni's uncle and Toni's dad, Eugenio (right). Luna Park, Melbourne, 1953.

long before the term was invented. Moving to a distant land on the other side of the world was an amazing experience for both of them. Dad had never even seen the ocean until he was about fifteen years old and all of a sudden he found himself surrounded by nothing but sea as he headed towards Australia.

Would you describe the place where your parents lived in Italy?

Castrolibero, my dad's birthplace, is a small old town which, like many old Mediterranean villages, is perched high on a hilltop. The closest coastal town is Paola, a quaint ramshackle town overlooking the azure blue of the Mediterranean Sea.

Paola was the home of the region's patron saint, Saint Francis of Paola. There are several different stories as to who Saint Francis was. Many people believe he was French and that he travelled to Paola, gliding over the sea on his brown woollen cape. He then lived in a cave (which still exists today) for several years and performed many miracles by healing people. Today, Paola is less than a twenty-minute drive from Dad's old village. However, back in the days of his childhood, when the vast majority of people did not have access to a car, it must have seemed like a whole world away. Tunnels now replace much of the steep winding road that led to Paola.

One day Dad, along with some of his young friends, decided to disobey their parents' orders and set off on foot to Paola. They walked, climbed and cut through the steep hills and mountains for ten hours, until they stood high upon a cliff. Before them lay the Mediterranean Sea.

When Dad tells this story, we still feel the awe and wonder he felt when he first looked out over the vast expanse of the Mediterranean Sea from that cliff.

So, back in Australia, what was your early life like?

I was born into a family with a very different culture to the existing culture in Australia at the time. And, just like my parents, it took me a long time to adjust.

I was seven years old when my parents finally realised that it might be a good idea to send me to school. One day, Dad drove me to

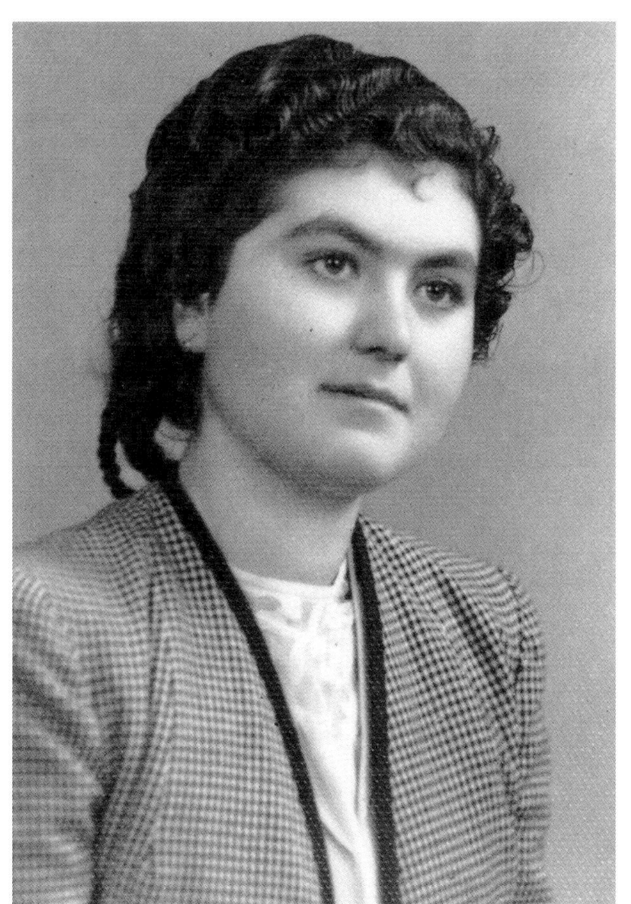

Toni's mother, Emma. Italy, 1951.

South Oakleigh Primary School, parked out on the street and let me out. It was my first day of school.

I had experienced no kindergarten or preschool, I couldn't speak English and had no clue where to go or what to do or expect. I walked towards the school building, feeling terrified. I felt like an alien. A few kids were looking at me and talking amongst themselves. I felt sure they were talking about me. I panicked and ran straight back home. Half an hour later, as I walked up our driveway, Dad and an Australian friend of his, a police officer named Norm Nash, were outside to greet me. I explained what happened in a teary voice and told Dad that I did not want to go back to school.

"No worries," Norm told my dad. "I'll drive young Toni back to school." So Mr Nash kindly took me back to school. Like my father, he parked out on the street and told me to get out of the car and go to school. That morning marked my introduction to both school and to the emotional trauma that can be part of one's learning.

In spite of this traumatic start, I managed to assimilate reasonably well at school, even though I always felt like I was different to the other kids. When I look back at my early school photos it is obvious why. I'm the only Italian-looking kid in the class. I'm still not quite sure why my parents sent me to South Oakleigh Primary, when most kids of Italian background were sent to the nearby Sacred Heart Primary School, where I probably would have felt more at home.

After you settled in at school, were there any other major dramatic events in your childhood?

A few years later, just as I was starting to feel a sense of belonging, Dad decided that we were moving to Italy – for good. The next thing I knew, I, along with my brother, two sisters and parents, were on a boat headed for Italy.

We cruised aboard an Italian liner through Fremantle, Western Australia, then on to Singapore and Bombay. Then we travelled through the Suez Canal and Malta, eventually disembarking at Naples. The voyage was a wonderful experience and a refreshing break from the boredom of suburban Melbourne. It was definitely life-changing.

After arriving in Italy, we caught a taxi from Naples to Dad's hometown in Calabria. My father negotiated an all-up deal with the driver, who agreed to take us on the six-hour journey to my grandparents' house. It was the same house Dad had grown up in before coming to Australia.

After getting over the initial shock of discovering that my ancestral home had no running water or electricity, even though the year was 1964, I quickly acclimatised and started to enjoy the experience.

I loved Italy and still do. Everything is so old, earthy and wonderful; a rich and wondrous tapestry of colour, history and flavours that make me feel alive.

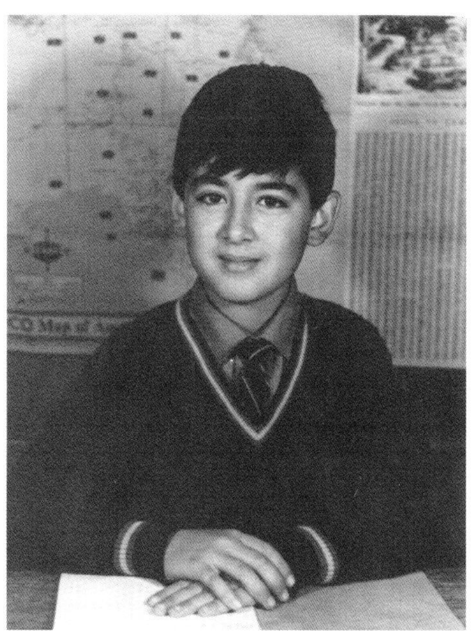

Toni at Sacred Heart Primary School, Oakleigh, 1967.

Had Italy changed much in the time your parents had been in Australia?

Everything in my Dad's hometown was pretty much as he had left it, twelve years earlier. My aunt and grandmother still cooked on an open fire. Water was collected from a running stream which filtered down from the mountains and the only source of light at night was a small lantern in each room.

We were surrounded by little vineyards, and hills covered in chestnut trees, beautiful old oak trees, fig and olive trees. There were also numerous fruit trees, beautiful wild flowers and green grassy fields everywhere you looked.

Italy ignited something within my soul and I felt at home there. It felt familiar. It was the same kind of feeling I experienced many years later when I met Martine.

Our anticipated permanent stay in Italy was short-lived. Four months later, Dad decided we were returning to Australia. He has a habit of changing his mind and is very impulsive. So the next thing I remember is being on a plane flying back to Australia.

So you had another big move. Was life in Australia different this time around?

We settled down in Melbourne once again and I attended Sacred Heart Primary School. There I was indoctrinated into all the mysteries of the Catholic Church. The Sisters of the Sacred Heart ran the school and lived in the convent next door.

I WAS BORN INTO
A FAMILY WITH A
VERY DIFFERENT
CULTURE
TO THE EXISTING
CULTURE OF
AUSTRALIA
AT THE TIME
AND, JUST LIKE
MY PARENTS,
IT TOOK ME
A LONG TIME
TO ADJUST.

During the next two years, I was to learn lots of interesting things. For example, I learnt that if I missed Mass one Sunday and died before I had a chance to go to Confession, I would burn in hell for a really long time, no matter what the excuse was. I learnt that God sent his Son down to Earth and allowed him to be crucified in order that 'we' could be saved. God was an all-loving guy but he was not someone you messed around with, especially if you were just a lowly sinner.

How do you relate to those teachings now?

Looking back on it all, I realise that even though it was all so stern, cold and fear-based, my experience at Sacred Heart School gave me a deep sense of spirit. The Catholic Church is steeped in spiritual mysteries and myths.

My experience at Catholic School added yet another dimension to my life – the awareness of spirit. And just like Italy, it would later help fuel my imagination and future work as an artist. For a while I even contemplated becoming a priest. I wanted to be on God's good side and do all I could to avoid the eternal fires of hell.

My time at Sacred Heart Primary School came to an end two years after arriving back in Australia. My dad, (yes, once again) spontaneously decided we were going back to Italy. This time, according to Dad it was definitely for good.

This sounds like a comedy. Did you believe him after the last experience?

Yes, I did, because he was very determined. He purchased about half a dozen enormous wooden crates from the Volkswagen factory in nearby Clayton. He packed practically everything we had in the house. He even included the 'Hills Hoist' clothes line, an Australian invention that he thought might be a wonderful thing to introduce to southern Italy. Dad did not realise that most Italians live in apartments and have neither the room nor inclination to erect a rather hideous galvanized-steel rotating structure on which to dry clothes. In any case, we would be the first family in southern Italy to erect an Australian clothes hoist on their property.

So, the next thing I knew, we were back on a beautiful Italian liner headed for Naples. The 'Achille Lauro' was a brand new boat setting out on its maiden voyage. My mum, who always gets seasick, was feeling ill even before our boat left the harbour. She spent most of the voyage in bed, being looked after by a nice young Italian steward named Colombo. The rest of us had a pretty good time exploring the boat.

What was life like in Italy, the second time around?

When we arrived in southern Italy, we rented an apartment within an old fortressed castle, called The Casino, in the little town of Santa Lucia, just up the road from my grandparents' house. The original occupants of the now rather delapidated castle were once very wealthy; they owned large tracts of land that surrounded the Casino.

The Casino was surrounded by high stone walls. Flanking the huge front gates were two towers where guards once stood watch, in case of invasion. Buildings, which once housed servants, formed part of the walls. Also built within the fortress walls was a small private church and on one side of the oval enclosure, there was a blacksmith's workshop. During our stay, an old blacksmith still worked there.

The main part of The Casino was a three-level building, which, like everything else, was built of stone. The ground floor of the main building housed an olive oil distillery. At one point in its history, the ground floor had housed horses, farm animals and produce derived from the land.

The top two floors were the living quarters. We rented two huge rooms, plus a galley-style kitchen on the second level, which was at some stage set up over a large old balcony area. The rooms were so large and old that they sagged slightly in the middle. If you jumped up and down it felt as though the floor might give way.

The owners at the time, who were the descendants of a once aristocratic and powerful family, were almost bankrupt when we met them. The owner, Don Ciccio, as we knew him, was a slightly eccentric man in his late fifties. Apparently Don Ciccio was a gambler who, over the years, had gambled away most of the family fortune, including most of the land surrounding The Casino.

IT WAS WHILST DRAWING THIS PICTURE THAT A FEELING STEMMED FROM WITHIN ME AND I DECIDED I WANTED TO BE AN ARTIST.

The Casino sounds like an interesting place. Did you enjoy living there?

Life at the Casino was fun! My brother, sister and I would visit the blacksmith, who was a kind, warm-natured man with a crooked neck that leaned towards his left shoulder. We would look through the old workbenches while he told us stories about the place. He would show us what he was making.

Among the old bits of metal and tools we would find amazing old coins that dated back to before Italy became a Republic. It was at the Casino, at eleven years of age, that I realised I wanted to become an artist. I remember gazing through a window which looked out to a nearby village. Perched high on a hilltop, looking out across the valley, I drew a picture of the town with crayons.

It was whilst drawing this picture that a feeling stemmed from within me and I decided I wanted to be an artist.

A few months later we purchased a house of our own, a quaint pink rendered house, set on a few acres of land. My brother, my eldest sister and I went to school and learnt to read and write in Italian.

So, finally, everything was going well for you?

Yes! Everything was going well. I liked Italy and I was happy that my family had finally settled down. Then it happened again. Dad decided, out of the blue, that we would all return to Australia. I was very upset.

You must have felt like a yo-yo. So, what happened when you returned to Australia?

Painting and drawing became my obsession. When I wasn't at school, nearly all my time was spent painting. I would go to the local library and borrow countless books on art. Through books, I was able to explore the history of painting and sculpture.

I was fascinated and inspired by the painters and sculptures of every period of history: the genius of Michelangelo, his wonderful sculpture and frescoes; Leonardo da Vinci's ethereal and magical works; the beauty of Botticelli's 'Springtime' and 'The Birth of Venus'. I loved the French impressionists: Monet's light-infused landscapes and the water-lily paintings of Giverny. I could not get enough of Pissarro's lush green fields and Van Gogh's beautiful sunflowers, starry nights, swirling clouds, poplars and irises. I loved exploring Gauguin's work, reading about his adventures in Tahiti and his torturous encounter with Van Gogh. I began exploring Picasso's vast body of work. He embraced so many different styles and moods and I enjoyed reading about his amazing life. I was moved by Jackson Pollock's action paintings.

Modern or classical, every artist I came across and the art of every period inspired me in different ways.

As a teenager, did you become side-tracked, or did your focus remain on painting?

My passion for painting and my desire for self-expression grew stronger. I produced hundreds of drawings and paintings. I would paint on anything I could get my hands on, any kind of paper, cardboard, wooden panel or canvas.

My father would often come home with old canvas blinds he picked up for a few dollars at a second-hand furniture store and I would prime them, then paint pictures on them. I even painted a few murals on our walls at home.

I also wrote poetry, even though I never really showed anyone. My writing at the time revealed a certain loneliness and melancholy. I wrote a type of psychedelic, surreal style of poetry, in keeping with the hippy-culture of those times.

Did you enjoy high school, this time around?

I couldn't wait to finish high school, which I hated, except for the art subjects. I wanted to go to art school. However, that's not what happened. Instead, I ended up leaving school halfway through Year Ten.

I married young and had a family. Basically, my life took on a whole new direction.

Did you continue with your art?

I continued to be fascinated by art and I continued to paint and draw in my spare time. I never thought about having an exhibition or trying to sell anything. Art was simply part of who I was, something I just did, and did not want to live without.

People often say, 'Painting must be so relaxing'. I wish that were true, but it often is not. Painting, for me, has always been an emotional experience, through which I express my feelings. At times, painting pictures is quite challenging emotionally, even tormenting. I now realise that my painting has always been a kind of psycho-emotional analysis.

So how do you learn about yourself through your painting?

Art has always been a kind of therapy for me. It has enabled me to keep a connection to the spiritual world of the imagination, without which I don't think I would be able to function.

I remember feeling a sense of sadness and regret in my twenties and early thirties, at not having attended art school and not pursuing an artistic career. I held some unexpressed resentment towards my father for many years, because I falsely believed that the reason I did not go to art school was because of his lack of encouragement. Dad, like many others, believed that pursuing an artistic career would lead to poverty. Later in my life, I finally realised that this distorted view was simply a myth. I finally admitted to myself that if I had really wanted to go to art school, nothing would have stopped me. Looking back, I see that everything that happened was meant to happen exactly as it did. I have four beautiful children and experienced so much in life as a result.

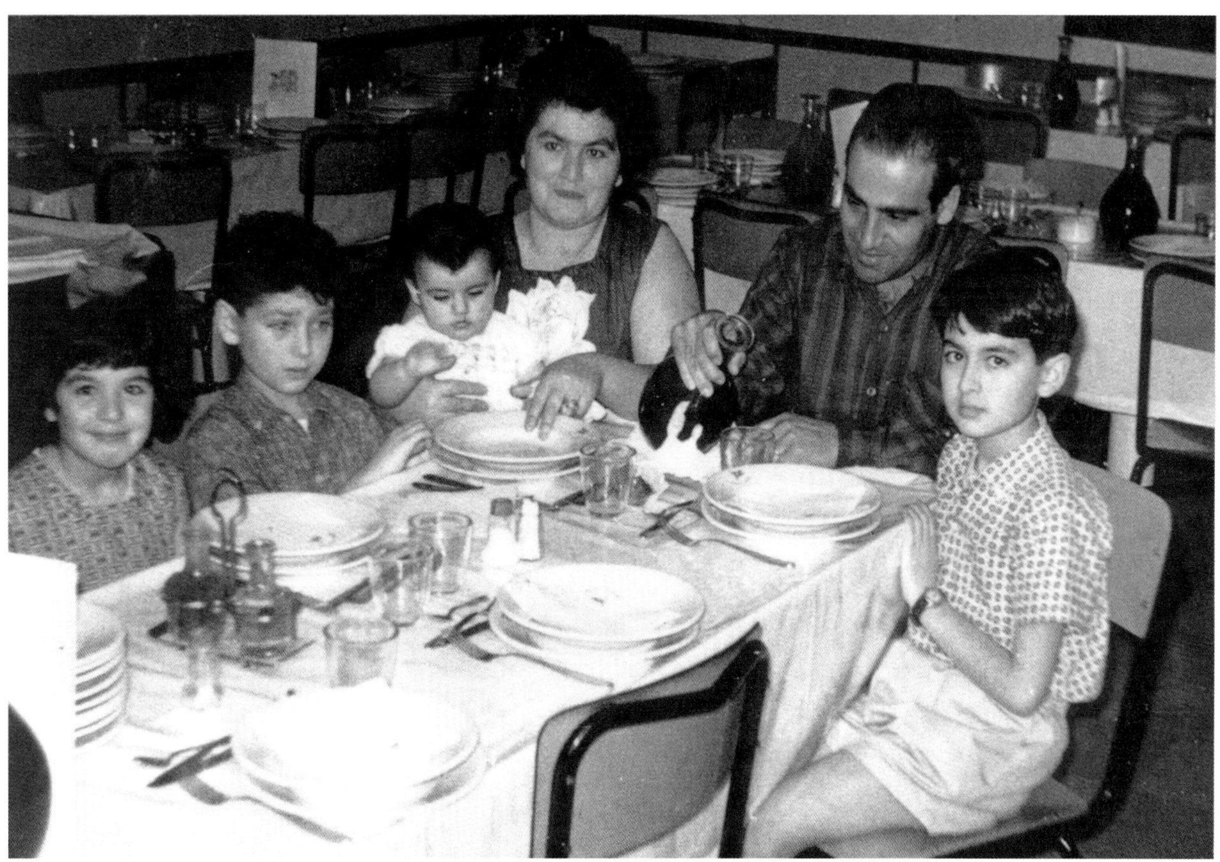
Toni's family in 1964 on board a ship to Italy.

I continued to be fascinated by art and I continued to paint and draw in my spare time.
I never thought about having an exhibition or trying to sell anything.
Art was simply part of who I was, something I just did, and did not want to live without.

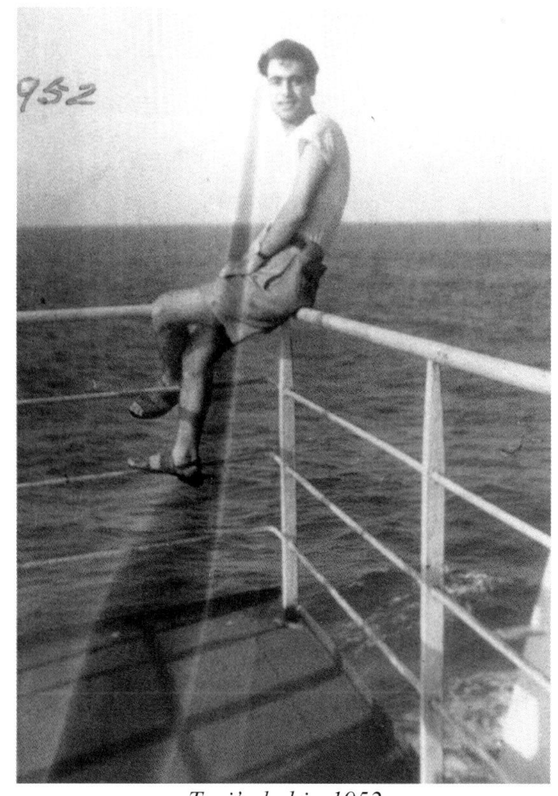

Toni's dad in 1952,
coming to Australia for the first time.

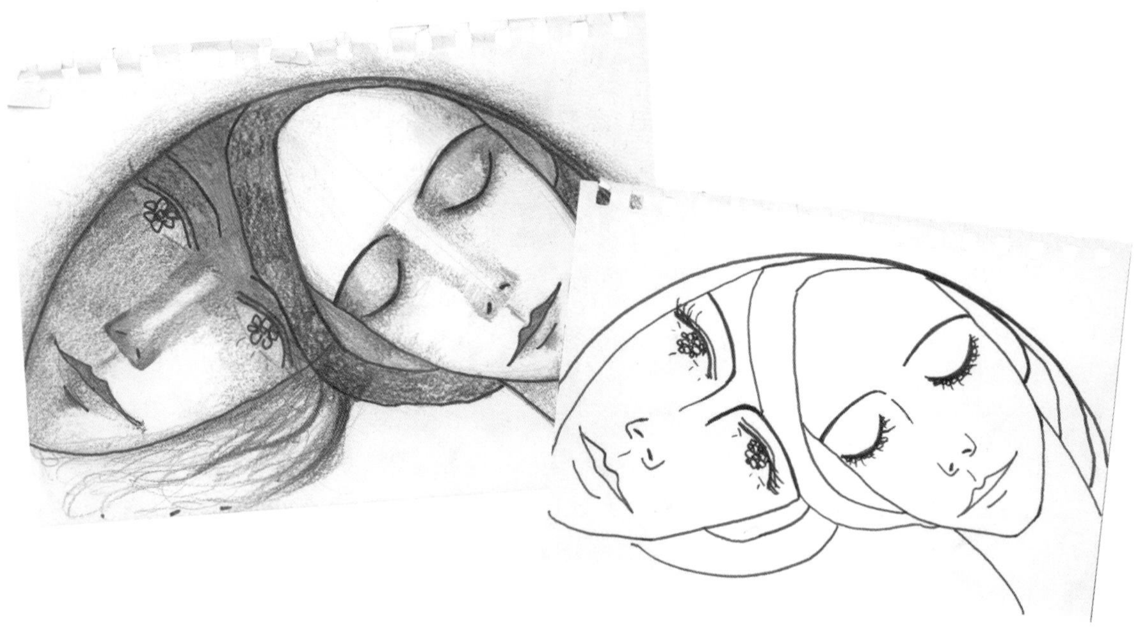

REBIRTH OF AN ARTIST

You paint a lot of beautiful female images. Do you use models?

Yes, for some of the work. I've used several different models, mainly for the nude work. It is difficult to memorize the human body in such a way as to be able to paint it from every angle and position. I only use models as a basis for the drawing, but the painting is always done at a later stage, alone and in private.

At what point did you start to believe in yourself as a professional artist?

After my business partner and I were forced to close our business and appoint a receiver, I spent most of my time dealing with the receivers, accountants and lawyers. While Martine went to work each day, I started to think about how I would now earn a living.

In my life, I have never really worked for anyone, so it was only natural for me to think about starting some new business venture. I had no formal qualifications of any kind but I was not short of ideas. However, every time I came up with an idea for a new venture, I could not bring myself around to taking the action required to bring it all about. Nothing I came up with felt right. I simply wasn't inspired or excited by any of my ideas, but I had to earn a living somehow.

At this point, had you even contemplated becoming a professional artist?

The possibility of painting for a living did not enter my mind, simply because I did not believe it was possible for me to make a living from painting.

This saga of trying to work out my career went on for months. In the meantime, Martine encouraged me to spend time at an art studio, 'Art Central,' in Malvern. Martine thought it would be good for me to be around people who shared similar interests. At first I was reluctant to go. I figured, I have four children to support, so I really should be working, not indulging in fantasies.

However, I finally decided to go to Art Central. On Tuesdays and Wednesdays I used the Art Central studio to paint and on Thursdays I attended life drawing class. A guy named Tom Fantl ran the place. Unlike me, he had been a professional artist all his life. He had lived in Europe and England for many years and had achieved reasonable success as an artist. At the time I met Tom the economy was in depression and as a result, things didn't seem to be going very well for him, apart from his art school.
Tom supplied me with a couple of stretched canvasses. My first painting was the blue 'Universal Christ' which has since become a fairly well-known piece. It is also one of the few paintings I have been reluctant to sell because of its personal significance to me.

The personified image of universal love and compassion that permeates both the spiritual and the physical universe has been my driving force.

Looking back on the 'Universal Christ' painting, it almost seems as though that painting was a prediction of all that has unfolded in my life in the past ten years.

I kept on painting at Art Central and enjoyed it greatly. It was really nice, for the first time in my life, to be surrounded by people who were as passionate and interested in art as I was.

Meanwhile, I also continued the horrible cycle of contemplating new business ventures that I could not bring myself to start. I was happy painting, but I needed to earn an income. This situation caused much turmoil and frustration in my life, that at the time bordered on despair.

Martine would often say, "You're an artist. That's what you love to do, so just do it." I would say, "Martine, you don't understand. You can't make a living from being an artist, unless you're famous." Looking back now, I realise that I was mimicking my father. That is exactly what he believed when I was a teenager wanting to go to art school.

So, how did you resolve the dilemma?

I continued painting and searching until one day it all came to a head. At the time, I was painting a picture in my studio at home. I remember taking a break and going to sit on the front porch. Tears came to my eyes. I had to earn an income but had lost interest in everything except for painting.

As I sat there feeling sorry for myself in the warm afternoon sun, I reflected on my life. I remembered all the different things I had done and experienced. I realised, of the many things I had tried and done, painting was one of the few things in my life I still loved and continued to do. As I was wondering why the world sucked, I began to look at the whole thing from a spiritual perspective.

Why would God give me this deep urge and need to paint, but not enable me to use it as my life's work? I sat there thinking, "There must be a reason why I paint and why this desire in me is so strong." So as I sat there, for the first time in my life, I really looked at the whole thing objectively. I decided – stuff it, for better or worse, I am going to be an artist, no matter what. I would at least give it a real go.

At that moment, I faced my doubts and fears and decided to trust. I gave the universe the benefit of the doubt. Maybe God wasn't a cruel joker after all. Maybe all I needed to do is honour the gift I'd been given. For once in my life I was going to be what I had always wanted to be.

I suppose there was also a part of me that figured, "I'm already bankrupt, so what have I got to lose?"

How did your life change after you made that decision?

I placed my trust in the universe and prayed that somehow it would all work out. I have since seen this same scenario being played out time and time again in other people's lives.

The universe will give us what we want, provided we are true to ourselves and honour the gifts nature has bestowed upon us. When we neglect what is truly in our hearts and neglect to honour that which we truly are, the universe will step in eventually and bless us with some form of crisis through which we are forced to re-evaluate our lives.

Having made the decision to be an artist, it was only natural for me to assume that in order to make a living from my paintings, I would have to get my work into art galleries. I envisioned the opening night of my solo exhibition – everyone sipping wine and champagne, with me being the trendy artist in a dark jacket, blue jeans and a white T-shirt. However, that's not what happened. There was only one solo exhibition and it wasn't in a trendy art gallery but in a place called Angels Bookshop Gallery in the not-so-trendy suburb of Frankston.

Even though it was a beautiful event and I received lots of encouragement and praise, I did not sell one painting.

How did you handle the setback of not selling your art?

I continued to ask the universe to manifest a gallery that would sell my work, but the type of art gallery I envisaged never came. It was over the course of the next few years that I learnt a valuable lesson about manifesting your dreams. A gallery did soon come – my very own gallery. Though not in the form I had envisaged, it would eventually prove to be much more than I had ever dreamt possible.

What was happening in the other areas of your life, while these developments took place?

Martine and I married and settled into a 'Brady Bunch' type of situation, which was colourful, to say the least. Trying to get my children to get along with Martine's two children was no easy

WE EMBARKED ON A SPIRITUAL JOURNEY, EXPLORING THE NATURE OF LIFE AND THE HUMAN SPIRIT.

task. Life was anything but boring.

A few years earlier Martine and I had completed a Reiki One course together. Reiki is a vibrational healing modality, which works on an emotional level. It works on the theory that all illness stems from an emotional imbalance that one has been unable to resolve. Reiki is also used to enhance vitality and leaves one feeling calm and at peace with life, thus creating a general feeling of wellbeing. The word Reiki means Universal life force or energy.

Martine went on to do Reiki Level Two, which deals primarily with Absent Healing. Reiki Two works on the principle that thoughts, feelings and emotions are energy frequencies which we can tap into to send Reiki to anyone anywhere in the world. It also helps you understand the power of your thoughts and the importance of having loving, positive thoughts.

Martine and I were both interested in all forms of natural healing, as well as counselling, psychology and meditation. We explored everything we came across that pertained to the wellbeing of mind, body and spirit.

We embarked on a spiritual journey, exploring the nature of life and the human spirit. We loved spending our time browsing through new age bookstores. We often left the shops with a bag full of books, tapes and compact discs.

We dreamt about one day opening our own bookshop and natural healing centre. At the time, Martine had a part-time job, which entailed demonstrating the virtues of facsimile machines and photocopiers to prospective buyers or clients who had just acquired one. A job, needless to say, she did not find very inspiring. In fact, she was starting to hate her job and feel trapped in it.

Finally, we reached a point where we decided we would turn our dream into reality. This decision coincided with my recent decision to be an artist. We started to look for a place to rent where we could set up a bookstore and healing centre. We decided to look for a place large enough to also have an art gallery where I could exhibit my paintings.

How did you manage to set up your new art gallery?

Between Martine and I, we have six children. At the time, most of them were still at school, so we decided we would look for commercial premises close to our home in the suburb of Glen Waverley.

We both knew that it would probably have made more commercial sense to look for a place in one of Melbourne's more alternative inner-city suburbs, however we decided that our family was a priority and so we looked for something close to home.

I remember lying in bed one morning, having just woken up, still half-asleep and having a strong feeling, more like a voice speaking to me through my thoughts.

My intuition told me that the perfect place for our bookstore and gallery was a two-level building near the railway station in a shopping centre.

I showered, had breakfast and drove to Glen Waverley shopping centre, sure of the fact that I would find a vacant, two-storey building for lease near the train station.

I drove and walked around for an hour or so but couldn't find anything that fitted that description. In fact, I couldn't find anything for rent at all. I walked around the station and around every shop and building in the entire place but with no luck.

I returned home in frustration, thinking, "So much for the inner voice of intuition." Over the coming days, I started to doubt my new approach to life, especially my intuition. The disappointment of this recent event may seem trivial to some, but to me it was quite shattering at the time.

I had put my trust in the fact that there was a spiritual element to life that communicated to us through our heart and soul and that we could be guided by this inner voice. I was living intuitively, in the belief that my intuition would guide me towards fulfilling my dreams.

Were you able to keep your faith at that point?

About a week went by and once again I found myself questioning the existence of God and feeling disillusioned. "Maybe all this spiritual stuff is just crap", was the thought silently going around in my mind. "Perhaps all these new age theories are simply an illusion."

Martine came home earlier than usual one day and found me feeling sorry for myself, so she said, "Why don't we both go and take another look?" We jumped into Martine's car and set off for the Glen Waverley shops. A moment later Martine said, "Let's go and take a look at Mount Waverley Village Shopping Centre instead."

For those of you who know Melbourne's south-eastern suburbs, you will probably know that Mount Waverley borders with Glen Waverley. The Mount Waverley shops are only a fifteen minute drive from where we live and I wondered why that thought had never entered my mind.

So we drove to Mount Waverley Village and the first thing we saw was a two-level building with a big "For Lease" sign on it. And, would you believe, just behind it was the railway station.

We rang the real estate agent, whose phone number was on the sign and he promptly met us at the premises and showed us around.

The moment we walked in we knew it was the place. It was big, light and airy. The upstairs was a perfect space for an art gallery and the rent was within our price range. We also discovered that the place had been vacant for over a year, even though shops in that area usually get leased very quickly. We made an offer to rent the place and signed the lease.

It is interesting to note that the building had been vacant for about a year, which was roughly the same time we originally had the thought to one day open a bookstore and natural healing centre.

One of the most significant things I have observed since then, is that often when we make a wish that is aligned to our true purpose and destiny, the Universe answers or provides what we want very quickly. We are the ones who usually delay things, not the Universe.

This episode restored my faith in intuition and was a valuable lesson in the importance of remaining open-minded and flexible. It was only my fixed expectation that the bookshop had to be in Glen Waverley that prevented me from finding the shop sooner. We are always intuitively guided. It is simply our preconceived ideas and rigid expectations that hinder us. There are always infinite possibilities and the Universe will always provide that which is in our highest good.

You seem to get your answers after going through a struggle. Why do you think that happens?

Often the low points in our life can be a blessing in disguise. They can turn out to be new beginnings and herald a period of positive change. Through crisis and struggle we can emerge with renewed hope and direction for our lives. Often we need to be humbled first, before we discover our true inner strength and purpose.

Through inner turmoil, you discover your soul. We are forced to look within, and in the process, we discover the suppressed parts of ourselves.

Healing occurs when we embrace all of who we are and love and accept ourselves as we are. As I began to acknowledge and honour who I really was, my life underwent a period of positive transformation. Now, years later, I realise that there's nothing in our lives to fix; there are only disowned parts of our Self, wanting to be acknowledged and loved. During this process we discover the voice of intuition; a voice which stems from our soul. As we listen and pay attention, we discover that our intuition is simply trying to guide us towards our highest truth, which is love.

Intuition always points us towards the heart and asks us to look inside our heart for guidance, instead of looking for guidance in the outside world.

When you follow your intuition, you discover the wisdom of your soul.

We are not merely a body, we are living energies. The real you is part of a universal energy field. Within this unified field, all in creation is energetically linked and therefore, we can communicate energetically with all living things.

We are part of a wondrous and magnificent universe, which appears to be both tragic and magic. To feel more of the magic, we must trust and open our hearts. It was through trust and through opening my heart that I discovered a deeper meaning for my life.

What about when you experience fear? How can you get to a point of trust?

Many people believe that we have free will and to a large degree I think we do, even though I believe that in the grander scheme of things, much of life is predestined by our own soul.

The free will we have is the will to choose love or fear in any given moment or during any given event in our life. This choice has an enormous impact on us for it changes the way we experience and perceive life. The way we experience a particular event depends on whether we view it through love or through fear.

THROUGH INNER TURMOIL WE OFTEN DISCOVER OUR SOUL. WE ARE FORCED TO LOOK WITHIN AND IN THE PROCESS WE DISCOVER THE SUPPRESSED PARTS OF OURSELVES.

Two people may be confronted by the same situation, yet have a completely different experience of it. For example, two people may be in the same house. It's a stormy, cold, dark night. There's thunder and lighting. One person fears the thunder and sees it as a horrible experience. The other person loves thunder and lightning. To them it's an awesome display of majestic power and beauty. One person is in a state of fear; one in a state of love and this affects the way they each experience the same event.

The first step to overcoming fear is to acknowledge it. Identify the fear, acknowledge it, look at it, then surrender it. Place your faith in love, bathe yourself in love and light and see the world as a loving place where nothing is ever truly lost.

Love is the only thing that will help you overcome fear. Fear is simply a projection which, from a spiritual viewpoint at least, is simply an illusion.

So what is the meaning of life?

There is obviously some form of intelligence inherent within the universe and this intelligence, though at times appearing chaotic, also has a natural order to it.

When we look out into the far-reaching corners of the universe with our space shuttles and telescopes, we see amazing pictures of planets, stars, endless galaxies and solar systems that are breathtaking in their beauty.

We have probably all seen snapshots of space that are awe-inspiring and wonderful. From a distance, all seems elegant and beautiful; timeless and serene. Yet if we were able to get

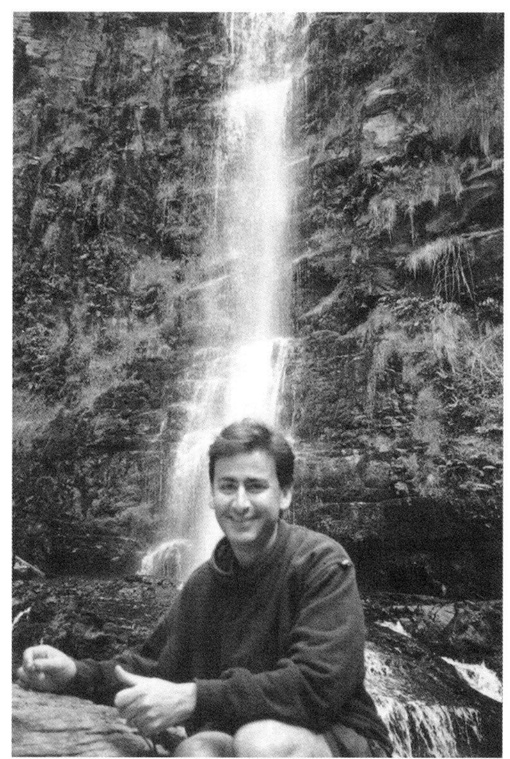

Toni

close to some of these planets, stars and galaxies, we would find that what seems elegant and beautiful from afar appears violent and chaotic from up close.

From a distance we see beauty and order. From close up we perceive chaos. This is also true in our lives. We can view many of the unpleasant events in our lives as disorder or disease or, we can view them with ease and look for the order. Behind conflict and disease there is peace and tranquillity.

The only reason that we are unable to see the order is because we have inner conflict. The conflict between what we feel in our hearts and what our mind says. In our heart we know what we would love to do and experience in life, but our mind often convinces us not to pursue our dreams, through fear.

This struggle between what we feel in our heart and what the mind tells us, is the primary cause of stress in our lives. Stress is part of the human condition - we live in duality.

Our intuition is the bridge between the physical and spiritual. Intuition links the finite with the infinite. To fully appreciate the value of our intuition, we must realise that the logical mind and human reasoning are contained within the mental parameters of time and space. That is, we are mentally locked into a three-dimensional world, which appears to us as solid – a world of duality where everything is separate, separated by time and space. We believe that we exist in this three-dimensional reality, yet this is an illusion and a limited view of life.

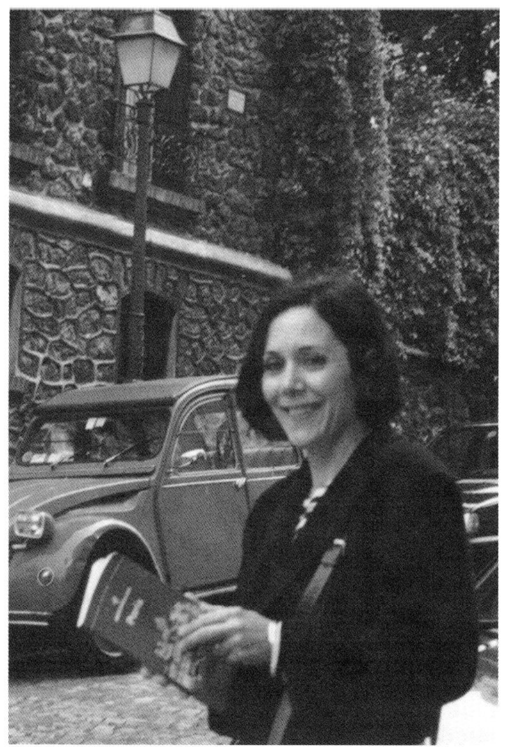

Martine in France

In our 'reality,' we see ourselves as a physical body set within the dimensions of time and space. In 'actuality,' we are timeless and spaceless. By 'we,' I mean spirit – the actual 'you' that is timeless and multidimensional. We encompass both the physical and spiritual realms of awareness. So all we truly desire in life can be found, manifested and achieved by connecting to what we truly feel in our hearts.

Within all matter, billions of negative and positive wave particles rotate around each other. Within what appears to be dense and structured matter there is mainly empty space. At the heart of matter there exists only energy; waves of energy and motion that can also be described as spiritual energy.

Spirit is timeless and eternal, it is able to see the bigger picture of life. Our spirit is not limited or affected by fear, therefore it is not restricted in any way. To the spirit, all is possible, provided you are aligned to your soul's will and purpose. Your true purpose can only be discovered when you look within your heart.

Why did you decide to call your centre Blue Angel?

I had painted a picture, which I called Blue Angel. The Blue Angel symbolically represents Archangel Michael, who is sometimes referred to as the 'blue ray.'

Martine suggested we use the same name for our centre. It felt right, so we registered the name and our solicitor nominated Blue Angel Bookshop Gallery as the tenant. Our centre would be dedicated to Archangel Michael.

Martine and I signed the lease and our solicitor sent it off to Australia Post, who were the landlords. A few days later I received a phone call from a manager of Australia Post Property Division who wanted to know what kind of books we planned to sell in our shop. I answered that we would stock books on spirituality, different religions, psychology, self-awareness, art and health. He wasn't convinced and asked if we intended to sell R-rated books or sexually explicit material in our bookstore. I was shocked and asked why on Earth he would think such a thing. He answered that The Blue Angel was a famous movie made in the 1930s starring Marlene Dietrich, who plays the role of a prostitute. I laughed, yet at the same time wondered whether we had made a big mistake by calling our place Blue Angel. I hoped nobody else would think Blue Angel was some kind of brothel, it really wasn't the image we were hoping to project!

We were planning to have therapeutic masseurs work from our centre, along with a range of other therapists. What if, like the Australia Post Property manager, others thought the Blue Angel was a brothel? I don't think I fully convinced the guy from Australia Post. He approved the lease but only on the special condition that we were not to stock or sell R-rated or pornographic material.

How did you feel, finally having the business you wanted?

We were excited that our dream was set to become a reality, though neither Martine nor I had any prior retail experience. We had not done any research and didn't have a clue about where to buy books and stock. But somehow everything fell into place.

For example, I saw an advertisement in the Melbourne Trading Post. A lady in Portland, which is about a four-hour drive from Melbourne, advertised some bookcases, card stands and a counter. I rang her and purchased the lot over the phone, sight unseen. A few days later a truck arrived and delivered a number of old bookcases and card stands. I set about cleaning and painting them and the bookstore started to take shape.

What was the early response to your new venture?

There were some interesting signs. Like the time I was standing outside the front of the shop painting the verandah posts, when a couple of elderly gentlemen strolled past. One remarked to the other, "I'll give them six months before they close." This was not a very encouraging comment given that we hadn't even opened yet!

I told my accountant that Martine and I were opening a bookstore, natural healing centre and art gallery in Mount Waverley. I excitedly told him how I thought it would be great because there was no such centre anywhere nearby. To this, he coldly replied, "Maybe there was nothing like it in that area because there is no need for it." Obviously I hadn't looked at it from that perspective – I wanted to see the glass as half full and not half empty.

What about after you opened for business? Did you start off well?

The first week we were open a gentleman walked into the premises and asked in a rather scholarly voice, why we had named our shop after a brothel. Once again he cited the Marlene Dietrich movie called, 'The Blue Angel'. He picked up a copy of Julia Cameron's, 'The Artists Way' and I began to tell him what a wonderful book it was, when he abruptly told me, after reading one sentence in the book, that he had come to the conclusion that it was basically crap. He told me he was a university lecturer, his speciality was literature and the one sentence he read in 'The Artists Way' was wrong.

We had only just opened and due to my fear of failure, I decided I would be nice to all the customers, so I didn't say anything to this guy, I just smiled and probably mumbled, "Come back again," even though I felt like telling him to get stuffed.

Blue Angel took off. As it turned out there was a need for a place like ours in the area after all. Blue Angel quickly became the 'talk of the town' in new age circles and though we struggled a bit at first, in time Blue Angel became a small success story.

CREATIVITY DOES NOT RELY ON ARTISTIC TALENT – CREATIVITY IS UNIVERSAL, REGARDLESS OF WHETHER YOU THINK YOU HAVE ARTISTIC TALENT OR NOT.

Were you able to continue your interest in healing and consciousness, while running a busy centre?

Through Blue Angel, Martine and I met many weird and wonderful people and formed many friendships. Blue Angel gave us the opportunity to continue to further explore the nature of healing and creativity.

Martine studied to become a Reiki Master-Teacher and has since gone on to practice Reiki and teach the principles of Reiki to hundreds of people.

I began to hold Intuitive art and writing groups in our gallery. I set up a process where people could express what they felt through love rather than create through their logical mind. Through these workshops, which I have conducted for many years now, I realised that everyone is creative. Creativity does not rely on artistic talent – creativity is universal, regardless of whether you think you have artistic talent or not.

So, what is the key to unlocking this creativity for those of us that don't believe we have it?

We all have an endless stream of creativity inside us. The simple secret to unlocking your creativity is love. When you create a loving environment where people feel that it is safe for them to express their feelings and fears, their creativity automatically flows out.

We each have a story to tell and as we share that story and express what we feel inside our hearts, we heal. I realised that the only things that block creativity are fear, and the false belief some of us have that we are not creative.

The more I observed people, the more I came to see the awesome beauty and potential that lay inside everyone. I noticed how one's beauty and potential are often hidden behind layers of fear and guilt. Many people believe they are somehow not good enough, yet I have seen how easily these misconceptions dissolve when you make them feel safe, accepted and loved.

When you know that you are not being judged and don't have to measure up to somebody else's expectations or standards, your fears dissolve and your inner light shines through.

What do you believe attracted people to Blue Angel?

Blue Angel grew to have a magnetic attraction for many people who were searching for something that would bring a greater sense of meaning and purpose to their lives.

We were fortunate to attract a wonderful team of consultants. The services we provided included Tarot Readings, Numerology, Past Life Therapy, Massage, Counselling, Psychology, Reiki, Art Therapy and Astrology, to name but a few.

Blue Angel was open seven days a week and almost every night the gallery was full with people attending our various courses and workshops.

What about your artwork? Did it begin to sell?

I continued painting at home, in my studio, as well as helping out, teaching and consulting at Blue Angel. It took me a while to start to really believe in myself.

Occasionally I sold a painting, however, I continued to believe that I needed to find a way of getting my work into galleries in order to make a reasonable living from my work. I was always trying to envisage ways of making my work fit in and get accepted by the traditional art galleries, even though deep down it didn't feel right.

My paintings were closely linked to my spiritual beliefs.

Many people who came to Blue Angel seemed to love my work but most did not have the money to purchase paintings.

In those early years, my self-esteem was low when it came to my work. Several months after we opened Blue Angel, Martine and I realised, as we came down from our meditation one night, that one of my oil paintings, which used to hang in the stairwell was missing. The painting had been stolen while we conducted our meditation. Instead of being upset, I somehow felt honoured that

someone would consider one of my paintings worth stealing.
Martine looked at me in amazement, I'm sure in her mind she was saying, 'What am I going to do with this guy?'

I continued sabotaging my success as a painter, both through my attitude and by underselling my paintings when I had the chance to sell them.

Each time someone enquired about a painting, the price they were quoted depended on whether I gave them the price or one of our staff quoted them. Each time one of our staff or consultants sold one of my paintings I ended up with a reasonable sum, usually the asking price or close to it. Whereas each time a prospective buyer approached me about one of my paintings, my first reaction was to discount it, even though they often made no such suggestion.

So it got to the stage where I was banned from dealing with the public, when it came to my artwork.

Besides selling your paintings, did you succeed with any other means of promoting your work?

It seems that the universe noticed that I needed some help.

A young man named Paul Newman (no relation to the actor), entered my life and became, for a while, the self-appointed promoter of my work. Paul was a bright young man, with a lot of charisma. At that time, though only in his early twenties, he had considerable experience in marketing. We had come to know him through his occasional visits to Blue Angel. He would come in every once in a while and purchase candles and incense.

Paul asked to see me one day and enquired, "Would you like some help to promote your work?" Paul noticed that I was producing prints of my artwork and thought they could be successfully distributed and sold through other retail outlets apart from Blue Angel.

I wasn't really excited at first, probably because I didn't believe people would be that interested in my work. However, Paul persisted, discussing the possibility during other brief meetings we had over the coming weeks, and I finally agreed to give it a try.

Paul and I spent many hours thinking of ways to display and sell my art prints. Together we designed stands and worked out how the prints would be packaged. We also decided to produce greeting cards featuring some of my work.

We came up with the trading name, 'Just Imagine Arthouse' and created a web site so that my work could be seen on the Internet. I also employed the services of my second eldest son, Michael, who had, unbeknownst to me until then, developed quite a talent in graphic design.

Michael designed our greeting cards, signs and business cards. He helped set up Just Imagine Arthouse and helped in the day-to-day running of the business.

The turning point for me came when we decided to hire a stand at the Sydney Mind Body Spirit Festival, which was a four-day event frequented by over ten thousand people. We simply arrived the morning the festival was about to open and stapled samples of my art prints on the black felt walls of the stand. Until that point I had only shown my work at Blue Angel so I was quite nervous and not sure what to expect. I had the belief that the primary reason many people made positive comments about my work was because they knew me through Blue Angel. In Sydney, most people had never heard of me, or ever seen my work, so I was understandably nervous.

To my amazement, my art prints evoked a similar reaction in hundreds of people in Sydney, to those people who had seen my work at Blue Angel.

Did everybody react positively?

Some people would walk straight past my stand. The stand was hard to miss since it was filled wall to wall with prints, yet to some, it seemed as though my artwork was invisible.

However, many people seemed to be overwhelmed by the sight of my work. These people seemed to be touched emotionally by it.

There were people at that festival from England, Europe and many other countries that all had a similar reaction.

This gave me enormous encouragement. From that moment on, I began to value my work and myself more. I was inspired to continue my journey and I came to accept that my work was, in its own unique way, inspiring, at least to some.

Until that time I had often felt that my work was peculiar. My art did not really seem to fit into any category; not modern enough for the contemporary art scene, nor did it fit easily into the concept of new age art.

The Sydney festival helped me realise that my paintings did not have to fit in with existing categories or styles in order to be valid. My paintings and writings are simply my expressions. I accept that they are not for everyone and that not everyone will resonate with them. Above all, I realised that my work does have a place and does serve a purpose.

In sharing the journey your life has taken, do you realise anything in a different way than you had before?

I am beginning to see a rhyme and reason for all the events of my life. Many of the things I once thought were a mistake or an unfortunate set of circumstances, I now see as a necessary and precious part of my life.

Once I was able to set aside the limiting and false beliefs that I held about myself, I found that I could then express and be more of who I truly am. The true purpose of my life became apparent and an amazing transformation, one I previously never thought possible, began to occur.

ONCE I WAS ABLE TO SET ASIDE THE LIMITING AND FALSE BELIEFS THAT I HELD ABOUT MYSELF, I FOUND THAT I COULD THEN EXPRESS AND BE MORE OF WHO I TRULY AM. THE TRUE PURPOSE OF MY LIFE BECAME APPARENT AND AN AMAZING TRANSFORMATION, ONE I PREVIOUSLY NEVER THOUGHT POSSIBLE, BEGAN TO OCCUR.

Through my life experiences, I have come to realise that we are restricted, primarily, by our own beliefs and by our lack of faith in the Universe. Much of what I previously believed now feels like such a limited and narrow way of viewing things.

I now know in my heart that there is a spiritual force driving the events of our lives as well as the events of our world. I cannot prove many of my theories, nor do I wish to. All I know is that life is what it is and that whether we agree or not, life has its own agenda. All is ultimately perfect as it is.

We each have our path in life, a path chosen by our soul. From our soul's perspective, no path is the wrong path, everything is simply an experience. The more we try to learn about life the less we really know about it. Ultimately all that matters is love; that we love and know we are loved.

Life is a great mystery – far grander and more beautiful than we probably can ever imagine. Life simply invites us to live.

All the events in our life are transient, however nothing is ever truly lost. When we feel we have lost something, it has merely transformed, leading us closer to love and God and closer to fulfilling our purpose. Only the mind believes in the illusion of loss. From a soul perspective, all is eternal and a necessary part of the whole.

The human mind is like a computer. We have been programmed in a particular way, for a particular purpose. Often we are not aware of the purpose, nor are we able to logically understand it. As a result of our programming, our mind interprets life through its own limited understanding.

Our thoughts, like our language, stem from our illusions. We believe that we exist in a concrete three-dimensional world and often cannot feel the presence of the great spiritual force which lies at the core of our being. It is only when our mind aligns with our spirit that we discover the hidden dimensions of life.

I have realised that stress and frustration are simply the result of the conflict that exists between the heart and the mind – between being and doing what we would truly love and doing what we think we have to.

The conflict between heart and mind clouds our ability to see situations clearly. It is difficult to have clarity whilst thinking thoughts like: "I should...", "I have to...", "I need to..." It is only by thinking about what you would love to do that you find balance and harmony.

What can a person do to gain this understanding themselves, if they don't have it already?

Being aware of what you would truly love is the first step. However, being aware has little effect on your life unless you follow it up by taking action. Doing what we love is very different to thinking about what we love.

When you put your energy into doing what you love, rather than what you think you should do, your life will transform. Start to listen to your heart and you'll discover that your heart is yearning for you to be and do all that you truly love.

Everything that you would love to be, do and have already exists inside you in the form of creative energy. Your heart is simply waiting for you to accept it.

What about on a larger scale, the state of the world?

On an energetic level, all of creation was present within the original point of oneness prior to the Big Bang. All existed in a spiritual abstract form.

The beginning of the physical universe was like the start of a movie; the story and characters already existed prior to the start. When watching a movie, we get to experience the story which has already been scripted and the same goes for life - it is merely our experience of the story, which already exists.

The oak tree already exists inside the acorn. It simply exists in another form. So it is with people and the world. All we truly desire already exists in the spiritual world of our dreams. In order to fulfill our dreams we must learn to love, accept and believe in ourselves, and to surrender 'our will' to the will of 'our soul'.

You said that all that matters is love. How can people live this experience in a day-to-day, practical sense?

Love helps us to surrender our fears and trust in the infinite light of creation, to reveal our infinite possibility. Love connects us to the wisdom of the soul. As Plato said, "All learning is simply recollection." All knowledge already exists within you.

All of creation is made up of opposites, which together form a whole. In order to be 'wholly you', you must embrace both the negative and positive parts of yourself. When you realise that there are no mistakes and that everything that happens serves a purpose, even though we may not understand it at the time, you begin to see that there is a divine order to your life.

Our ability to see the divine order depends largely on our ability to accept. When we try to fix things, instead of transform them, we interfere with the natural order. In order to want to fix something we must first have judged that it is wrong or bad.

Transformation occurs through love. It does not stem from the belief that something is wrong and needs to be fixed.

When we stop wanting to change the world and accept everything in our reality as a valid and necessary part of the whole, life seems more balanced and we begin to realise that everything makes an equal contribution to this wondrous tapestry of life. In turn, this frees us from our own restrictions and we begin to realise more of our unlimited potential.

So, how can people find this awareness, this balance?

Balance stems from love and acceptance. You are, in essence, the light of your soul and the more your perceptions are brought into balance, the more the purpose of your life becomes apparent.

When we find the balance within ourselves, we see more balance in the world around us. What we search for externally is simply what we fail to see inside ourselves. We will not find what we seek in the outside world, until we realise that what we seek already exists spiritually inside us.

There is a rhyme and reason for all things in this world, even though the reasons may not always be clear to us. Remember, it is not always what you know but who you know that is important. The most important person to get to know is you.

How can a person get to know themselves?

Often, before you can truly know yourself, you must let go of that which no longer serves you – mainly fear – and embrace the healing light of love. At the same time it is important to be willing to embrace change in the knowing that there is never loss without gain. From a soul perspective nothing is ever truly lost; it is simply transformed. Embrace those aspects of yourself that you try to hide or are ashamed of, love and appreciate every aspect of yourself and learn to see that everything about you serves a purpose. Ask yourself, "How does this trait which I perceive to be negative serve me and others?" Look honestly and you will discover that every perceived negative trait comes with a positive trait attached to it. You can only come to truly know yourself when you embrace everything about you in its totality.

WHAT WE SEARCH FOR EXTERNALLY IS SIMPLY

WHAT WE FAIL TO SEE INSIDE US.

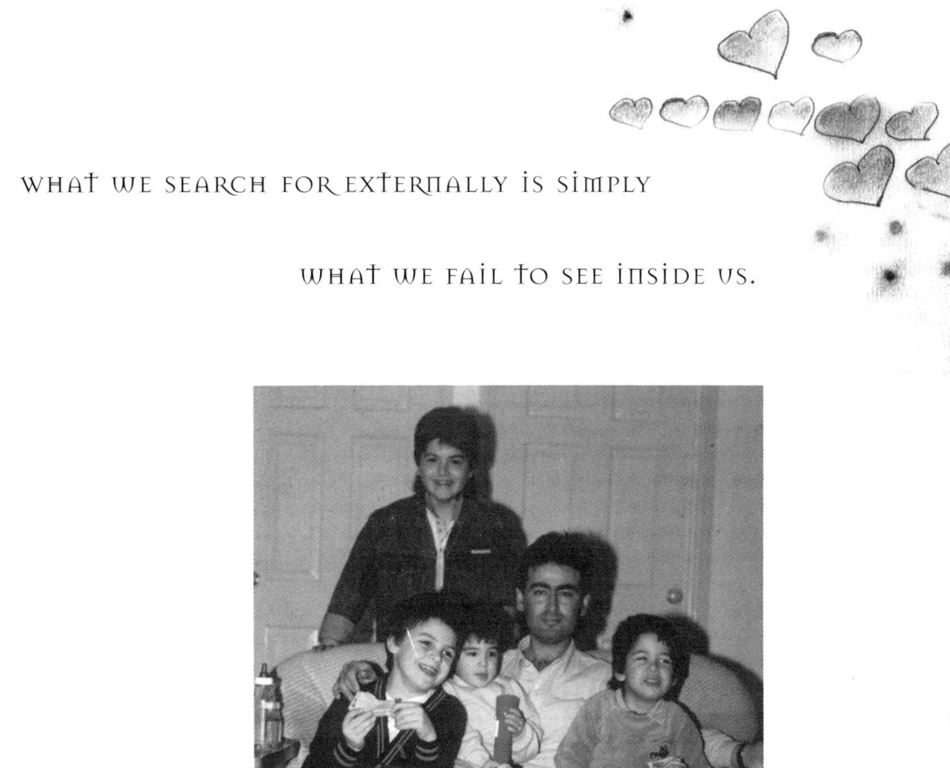

Toni and his children 1988

THE ORACLE CARDS

To date, you have produced many oracle card sets, featuring your artwork and writing. Could you tell us about your Oracle cards and explain what an Oracle is?

The use of the word 'oracle' stems from ancient Greece and Rome – it was a shrine used to consult the gods.

Ancient Greeks and Romans would seek prophetic advice from the Oracle, which was usually symbolically represented by a statue of one of their many gods and goddesses.

Contrary to popular belief, the ancient Greeks and Romans were very spiritual people, though their spirituality seemed to be mostly driven by the fear of upsetting the gods and goddesses who reigned supreme over 'sky, earth and water'.

To appease the will of the Gods, they sought advice from the Oracle before undertaking any significant course of action. However, as statues do not speak, guidance had to be delivered through a sign or event, which would in turn have to be interpreted as either a good or bad omen.

The ancients, especially the Romans, believed in an endless array of superstitions. Whether something would be interpreted as a good or bad omen depended on one's personal beliefs and superstitions. The Roman emperor Augustus, for example, would not set off on a scheduled military mission if he accidentally put his slippers on the wrong way that morning. He interpreted this as a warning from the gods.

In recent years, our interest in the Oracle has resurfaced, mainly through the use of Oracle card sets. There are currently many decks on the market, usually comprising an image plus a written message of guidance for each card. While this makes the current day Oracle a lot easier to comprehend, like everything else in life, it remains coloured by our individual beliefs.

We all view life from our own perspective and we each live life through our own individual truths.

What is truth?

Apart from unconditional love, the only truth I have discovered to date is that there is no one single truth.

In physical life, there is no such thing as 'The Truth' for we all see the truth differently. For example, a group of people may be all against war. They want peace, but if you get them together in one place to discuss ways of creating peace, without a doubt they will all have a different view on how it should be achieved. They may even fight about it.

Someone may think that a certain person is beautiful while someone else may be of the opinion that the same person is unattractive. Who is right and who is wrong? Who can make that judgment?

Someone we may consider physically beautiful now will one day grow old and perish.

Physical beauty is transient and subject to change. If we look carefully we discover that only temporary individual 'truths' exist, not universal eternal ones.

Life is forever changing, all is in a continuous state of flux and transformation. There can be no ultimate truth within the context of space and time because everything within the realm of time and space is forever changing.

In order for a universal truth to exist it must be unchanging and not affected by space and time; it must stem from the eternal, spiritual heart of creation.

Perhaps the only truth that fits these criteria is unconditional love. Unconditional love is unchanging, it accepts all as it is and flows with change rather than trying to resist it.

How does this relate to the Oracle Cards?

I believe we are drawn to things like the Oracle Cards because we want to make sense of life, we want balance, health, fulfillment and peace.

I believe that we will never find these things while we have an "I'm right and they're wrong" attitude, or believe that everything in the world should be the way we think it should be. To get what we want out of life, we need to accept that there is no single truth that applies universally.

The most popular Oracle Card sets seem to be those that touch a place deep inside our hearts – they contain messages and imagery that encourage us to be who we truly are. They encourage us to let go of the many masks we put up to hide from ourselves and from those around us. They have a way of infusing us with inspiration and love.

We are instinctively drawn to what brings us balance and love. There is a yearning inside all of us for love.

WE ARE INSTINCTIVELY DRAWN TO WHAT BRINGS US BALANCE AND LOVE. THERE IS A YEARNING INSIDE ALL OF US FOR LOVE.

How does the Oracle work?

Sometimes one kind word is all it takes to change our lives. If a picture speaks a thousand words, imagine the potential power of an image.

Within an image, it is not so much the subject matter that is important but rather the energy infused within it. This is also true with words. It is not so much what we say but rather the intention behind our words that matters.

How did you create the cards?

All of my work is created intuitively, that is, I give no conscious thought to the creative process. Nothing is planned or worked out, everything is immediate, stemming forth from within each moment, each word or brushstroke. I simply set aside the restrictions of the conscious rational mind and enter the abstract world of feeling.

How do people know which pack of cards is best for them?

Simply by using their intuition. They can just go with whatever they are drawn to.

Oracle cards are very personal as people can interact with them and pick their own card for that moment. You can just pick a card, or ask a question and pick a card – either way, you will pick the card that is the most beneficial for you at the time. It will have a balancing, healing effect on you, or provide an answer to your question. You can also pick a card for the past, the present or the future, as within the realm of spirit, time does not exist as it does in our way of thinking.

Can you elaborate about the nature of time?

One of the most interesting ways I have heard time described comes from Plato. For Plato, time was "The moving image of Eternity." Perhaps time is simply our way of perceiving the journey of our lives. We could also perceive life as a journey through something that already exists. Like reading a book, the story is already written before we start reading it.

How can people best use your Oracle cards?

I often get feedback from people who have used my Oracle cards, telling me how accurate a message was for them, inferring that I have some kind of magical power that gives people the right answer to their questions. However flattering this might be, it is simply not the case.

As I often explain, it is not the creator of an Oracle set that has the power of prophecy but the individual user. Each time you pick a card, you are intuitively guided by your own energy field or soul to pick the most appropriate card for you at that given moment. It is your own spirit which, through the medium of the Oracle, helps you see, hear or feel that which will be of greatest benefit to you at that time.

Would you expand on the concept of soul, spirit or energy field?

Sure, let us go back to the beginning.

Try to imagine what things were like the moment the universe was born. At some point, far back in time, a tiny point of light within the underlying fabric of creation exploded, causing what we now know as the 'Big Bang'. Unimaginable heat and radiation expanded from a point smaller than the size of one atom, to become the enormous and ever-expanding universe of today.

This mysterious super-luminous event triggered the seemingly endless cycles of creation and transform-

EACH TIME YOU PICK A CARD, YOU ARE INTUITIVELY GUIDED BY YOUR OWN ENERGY FIELD OR SOUL TO PICK THE MOST APPROPRIATE CARD FOR YOU AT THAT GIVEN MOMENT.

ation responsible for the present day universe. We – the universe – continue to expand and evolve through time and space. We are part of this beautiful planet Earth, surrounded by a sea of stars and galaxies spanning trillions of light years through space.

It is easy to get caught up in our everyday 'reality' full of worldly concerns and forget that we form part of the Earth, which in turn forms part of an incredible and unimaginably vast universe.

If we could view our life from a broader perspective, we would realise that our individual lives are but a grain of sand continuously moved by the one great cosmic ocean – the universe.

We all stem from the one place. We are all infused with the same universal energy and life force. We are not solely our bodies, but part of an energy field or spirit that is universal in nature. All is interconnected energetically throughout the fabric of space-time. We are all part of one creation, which is infinite, innately intelligent, all-powerful and all-knowing.

Another word for this energy or spirit is the Oracle. From the perspective of the Oracle, which exists outside the realms of time and space, past, present and future all exist now – they are all one.

Furthermore, the laws of physics state that energy can be transformed but never destroyed. Energy simply changes from one form to another. This concept is one of the underlying principles that govern the universe and if it is true in physics, then, I think it logically follows that the same principle is also true in our lives.

Viewed from this perspective, death is simply a transformation from one form, 'physical,' to another form, 'spiritual'. So if past, present and future are all one and nothing is ever lost, but merely changes state, it should come as no real surprise that people can communicate with the spirits of those who have passed away. And if we can communicate with spirits who have passed on, then we can surely communicate with our own spirit while we are still in physical form – it is simply a matter of finding a way to access that information.

This process is known as 'intuition' and Oracle Card sets can be a powerful tool for accessing that inner wisdom.

Do you believe that life is a self-fulfilling prophecy?

We live in a world of duality, where there is a constant clash between the logical mind and the heart – between love and fear. Love resides in the heart and stems from our spirit.

When we listen to and are guided by what we feel in our hearts, we are intuitively guided towards fulfilling our highest potential.

To do this we must learn to listen, not to the often negative, fearful and restricted views of the mind, but to the intuitive, loving and gentle voice of the heart.

We must listen to the voice of love. Love is the voice of balance; it is the positive voice of acceptance and grace. To love is to flow with the great golden river of life, not to struggle against it. The great golden river is the spirit of life. The desire to swim against the current stems from fear and a need to control.

The stress, pressure and fast pace of modern-day life are enough to overwhelm all of us at times. During stressful periods our ability to think and see situations clearly is often clouded in a haze of confusion.

It is hard to regain clarity and balance while thinking, "I should...", "I have to...", "I need to…". Watch your thoughts and consciously switch your focus from "should", "have to", and "need to", to "I would love to...". Think of the things you would love to be doing rather than the things you think you should do. Bring your focus to the feelings inside your heart… Listen.

Your heart never says "should" or "need." The heart only says, "I love you."

Love allows us to express the wonder and unique beauty we each hold inside us. Love allows us to follow our hearts and pursue our dreams. Love allows the light of infinite creation to flow through us, which can show us infinite possibilities for our life. Love allows the wisdom of the soul to shine through.

The purpose of an Oracle is simply to point you in the direction of love – to help you fulfill your soul's deepest desires and inspiration.

An Oracle can be a paragraph in a book you open randomly, a butterfly fluttering by to lift your spirits, or it can come in the form of a card set, designed to put you back on your course or align your dreams and aspirations with divine time and synchronicity.

An Oracle can be a chance encounter with someone you bump into on the street, it could be a loving act of kindness from a friend or stranger, it can be the words of a song on the radio. An Oracle helps us tap into our intuition, always pointing us in the direction of the heart, where we discover the prophecy of love.

WE ALL
STEM FROM THE
ONE PLACE.

WE ARE ALL
INFUSED WITH
THE SAME
UNIVERSAL ENERGY
AND LIFE FORCE.

What was your intention with your CDs, 'Meditations for Inspired Creativity and Healing' and 'Meditations for Inner Peace'?

The meditation CDs are a verbal, poetic interpretation of my work and paintings. Writing and images are one and the same thing – just using different mediums.

Meditation is another tool for people to tap into their own creativity and intuition. It helps us transcend our daily reality and connect us with the spirit of life. Meditation can help us find inner peace.

There is ever-increasing interest in your work internationally. What direction do you feel your work is heading towards in the future?

The first thought that came to my mind is a phrase from a John Lennon song, "Life is what happens to you while you're busy making other plans." I am always mindful that there is a higher force at work in my life, so I try to remain open, rather than have fixed expectations or goals for the future.

However, having said that, I would truly love to continue to expand my work in ways that will empower others and assist them to recognise their own magnificence and beauty.

... end

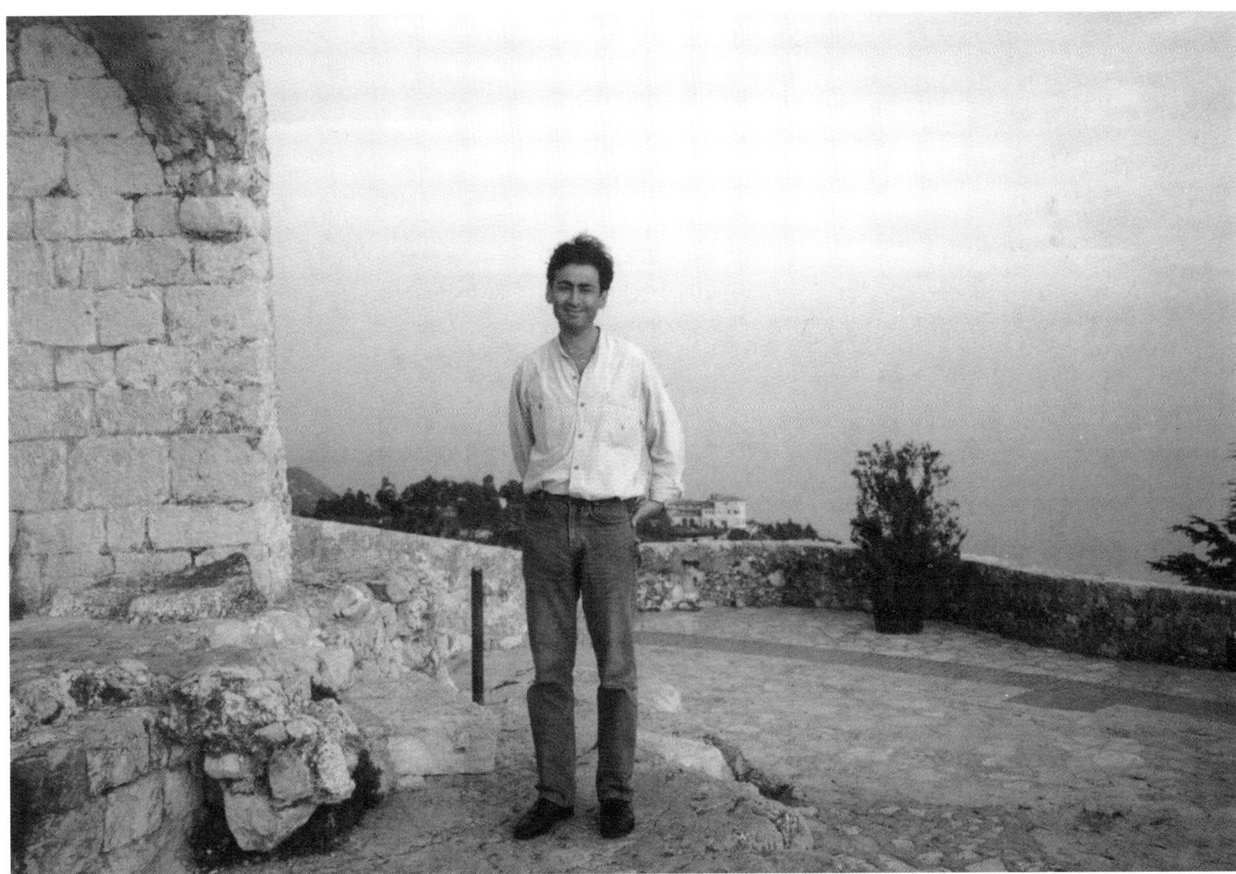

Toni at Eze Village in the south of France

Paul M. Segal *is a photojournalist who has interviewed many leading figures in the human potential movement, including Neale Donald Walsch, author of 'Conversations with God;' Caroline Myss, author of 'Anatomy of The Spirit;' Robert Kiyosaki, author of 'Rich Dad Poor Dad;' and Doreen Virtue, author of 'Healing with the Angels'.*

Paul is the co-founder of Inner Power Training. As well as being a host of 'Write Now' radio and 'Visions' television show, he is a professional speaker and co-author of 'First Kiss and Laugh Now'.

Believe in yourself – you are a wonder of creation.

Wash away all fear – you will discover a shining star.

Allow all around you to just be – let go and trust.

Remember, you are an ocean of light

and 'we' are a reflection of one another.

Remember also the sacred power of Mother Earth,

of Father Sun, the universe and stars.

Let there be always a flame in your heart.

May your passion engulf the earth.

As each new moment unfolds, a new star is born

– through an explosion of love.

Let us be in sacred union with one another,

for there is no greater love than this.

Love shines beyond all that is luminous,

through the merging of our souls –

it moves the ocean's tides.

one eternal heart,

forever yearning creation, miracles and magic.

rest and bathe in my light.

as I glitter the night with jewels,

then at daybreak, shine upon creation.

as dew drops form,

they become a river that flows towards an ocean of infinity.

may the stars fill your heart,

like the rays of an ancient sun

through all of life's mysteries.

Toni Carmine Salerno

PART TWO:

THE PAINTINGS

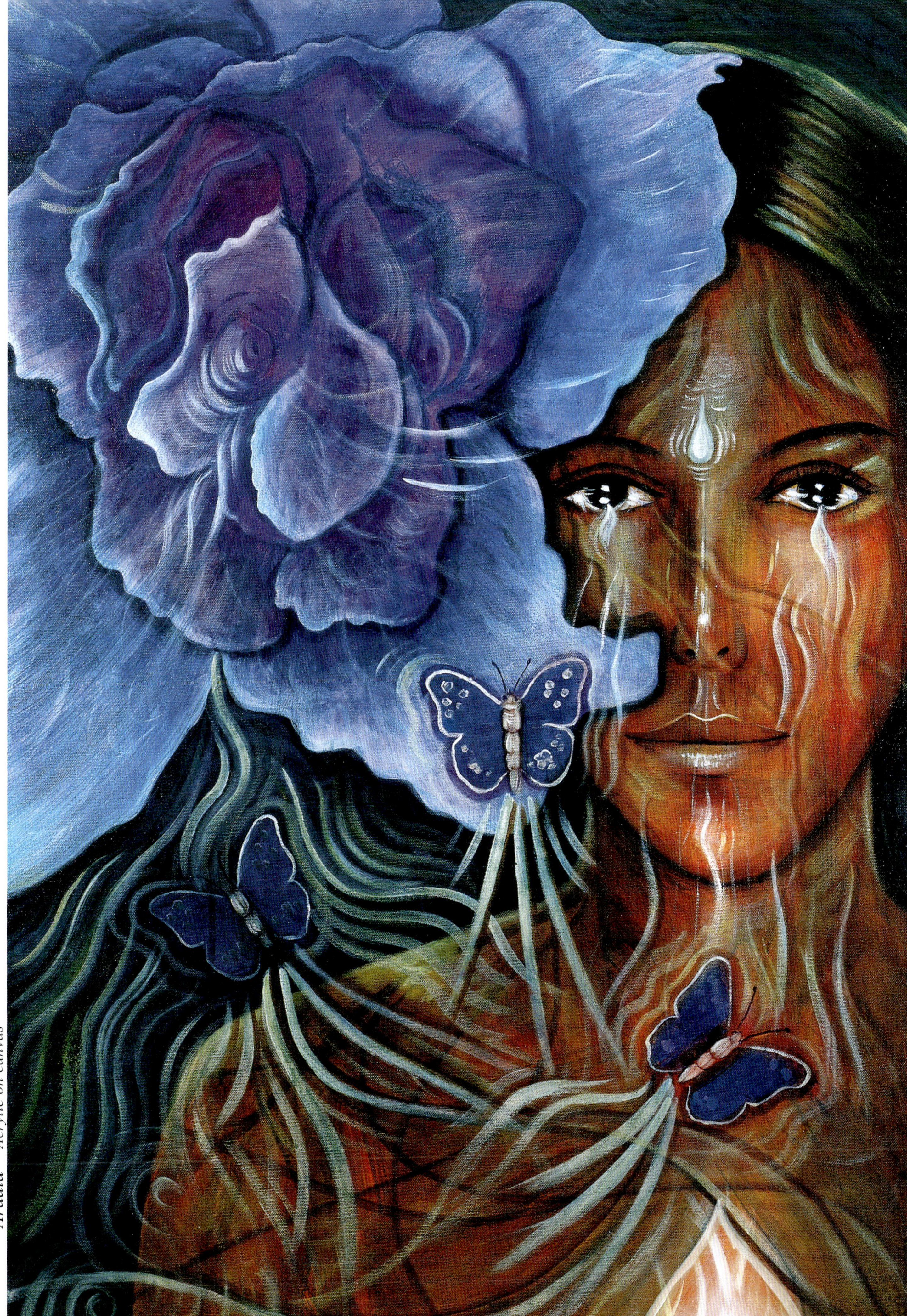

"Aradia" Acrylic on canvas

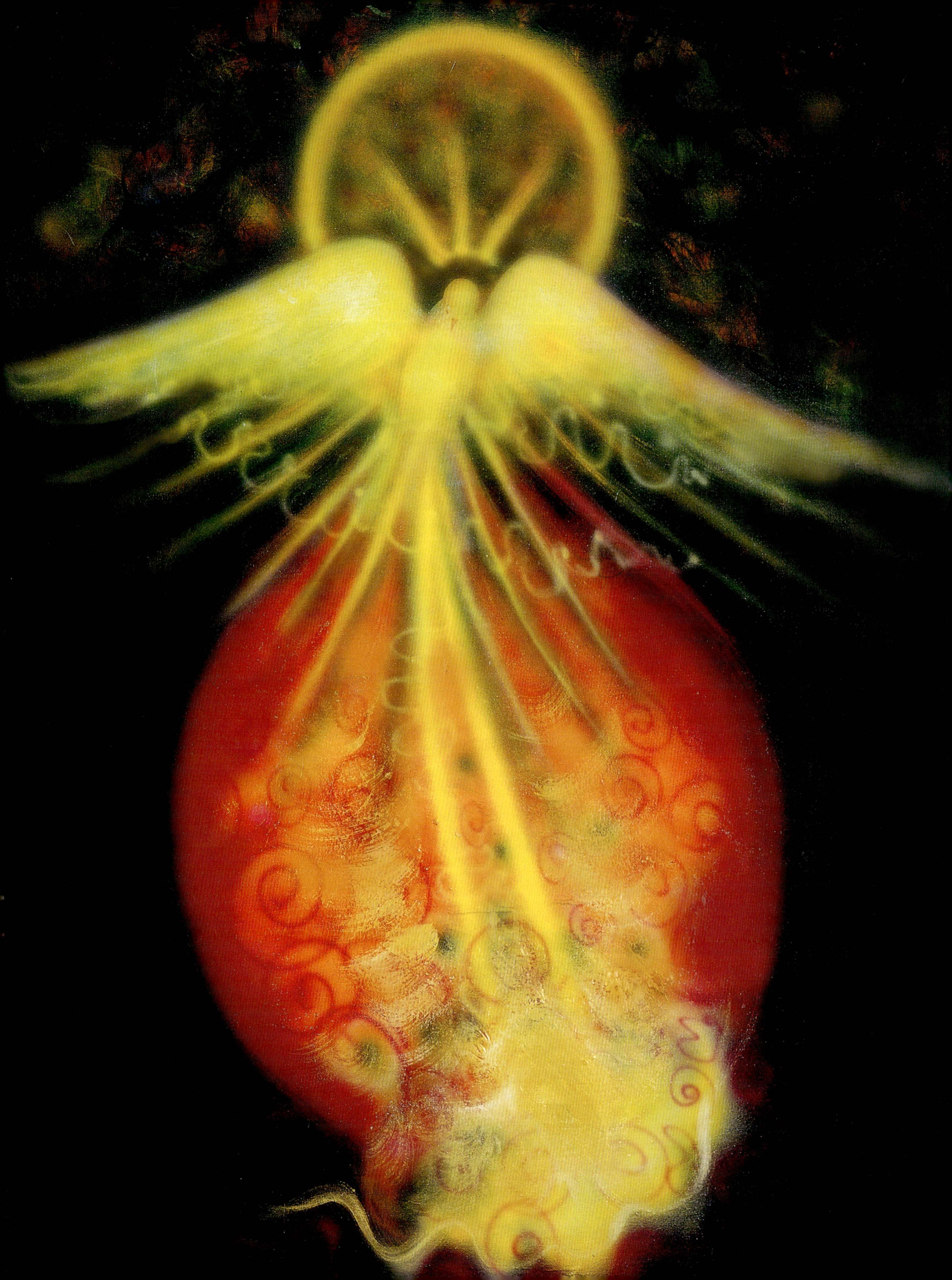

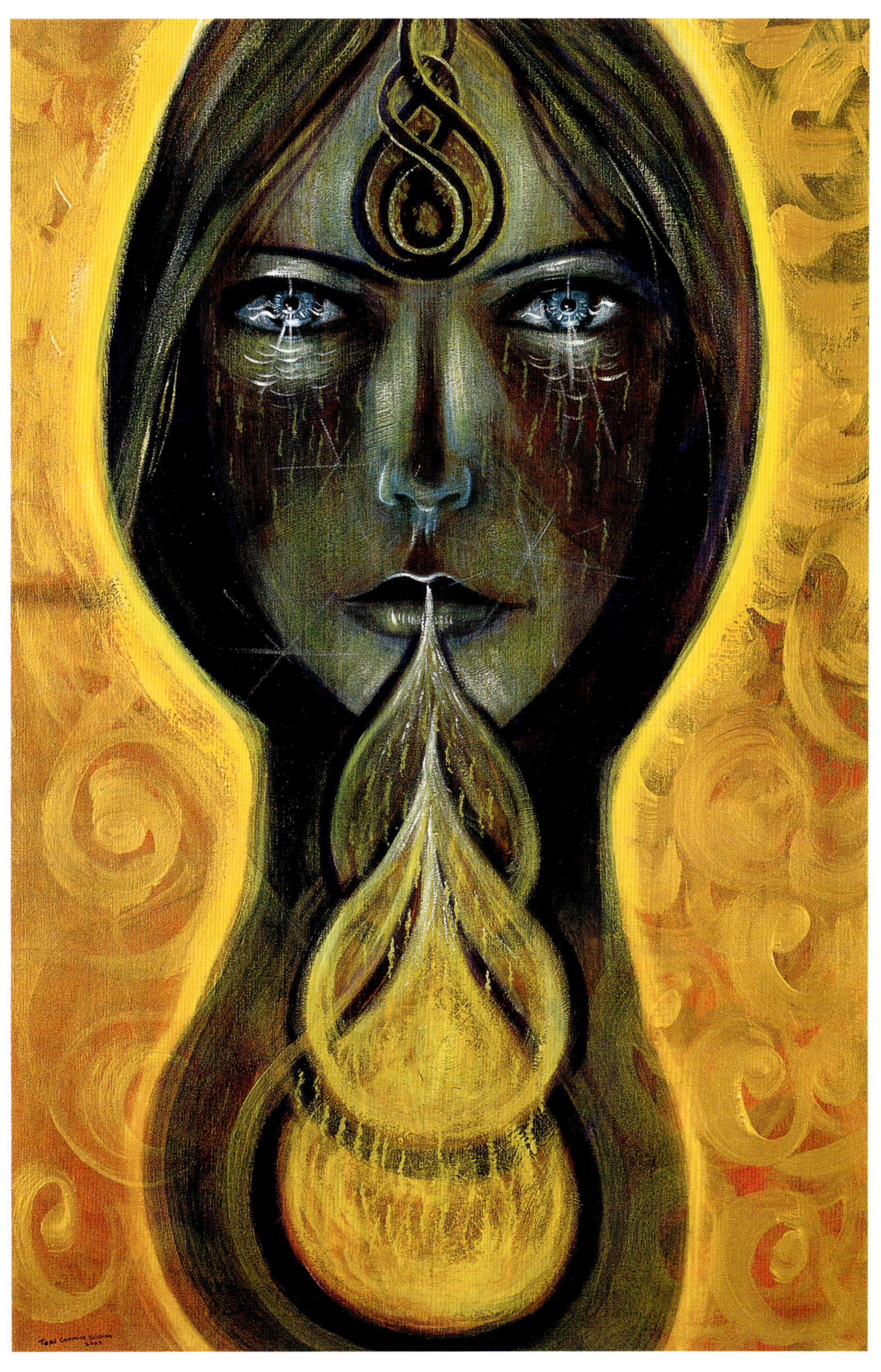

"Jewel" *Acrylic on canvas*
Previous page: *"Birth"* *Acrylic on canvas*

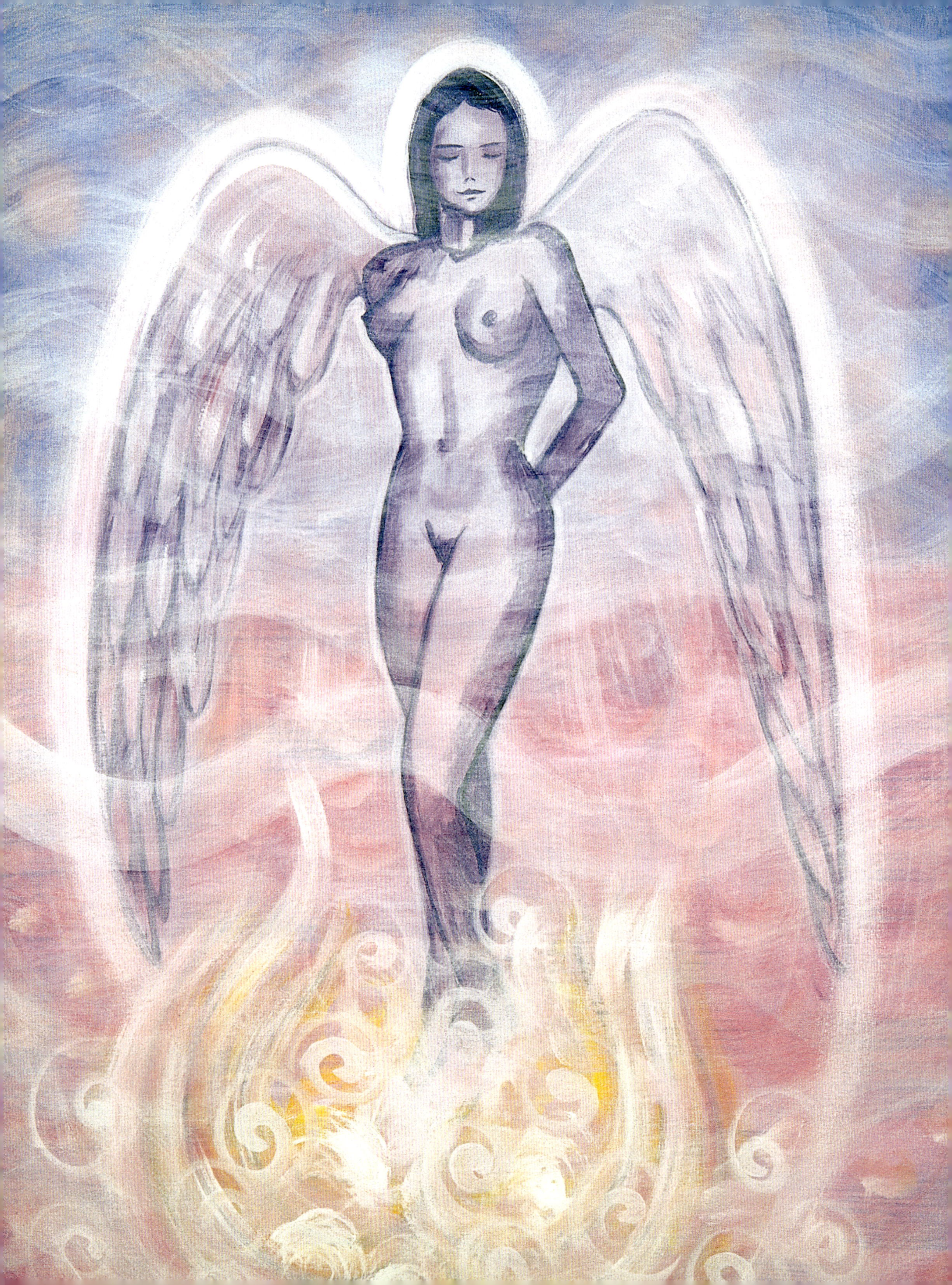

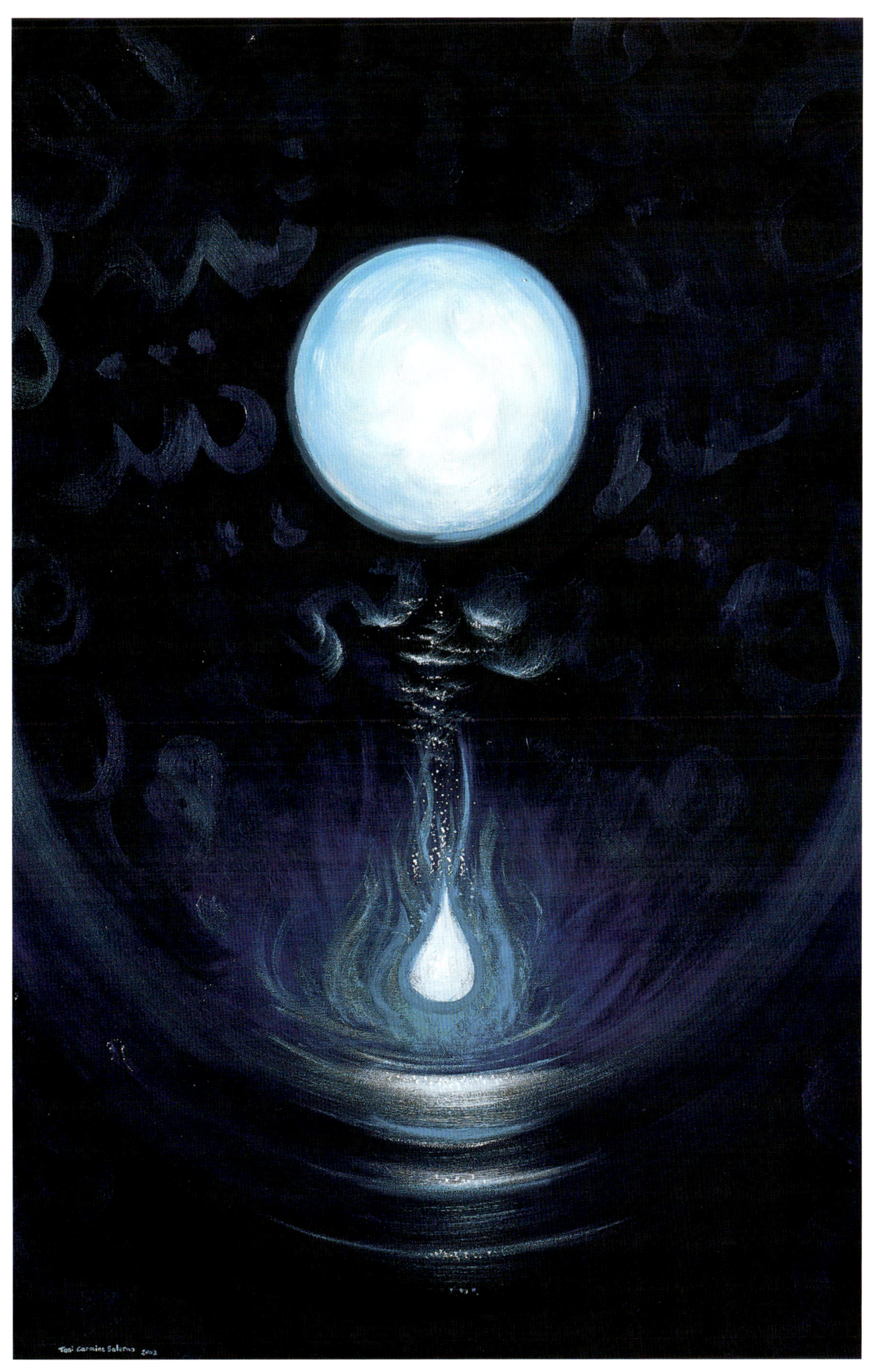

"In The Beginning" Acrylic on canvas
Previous page: "Tranquility" Acrylic on canvas

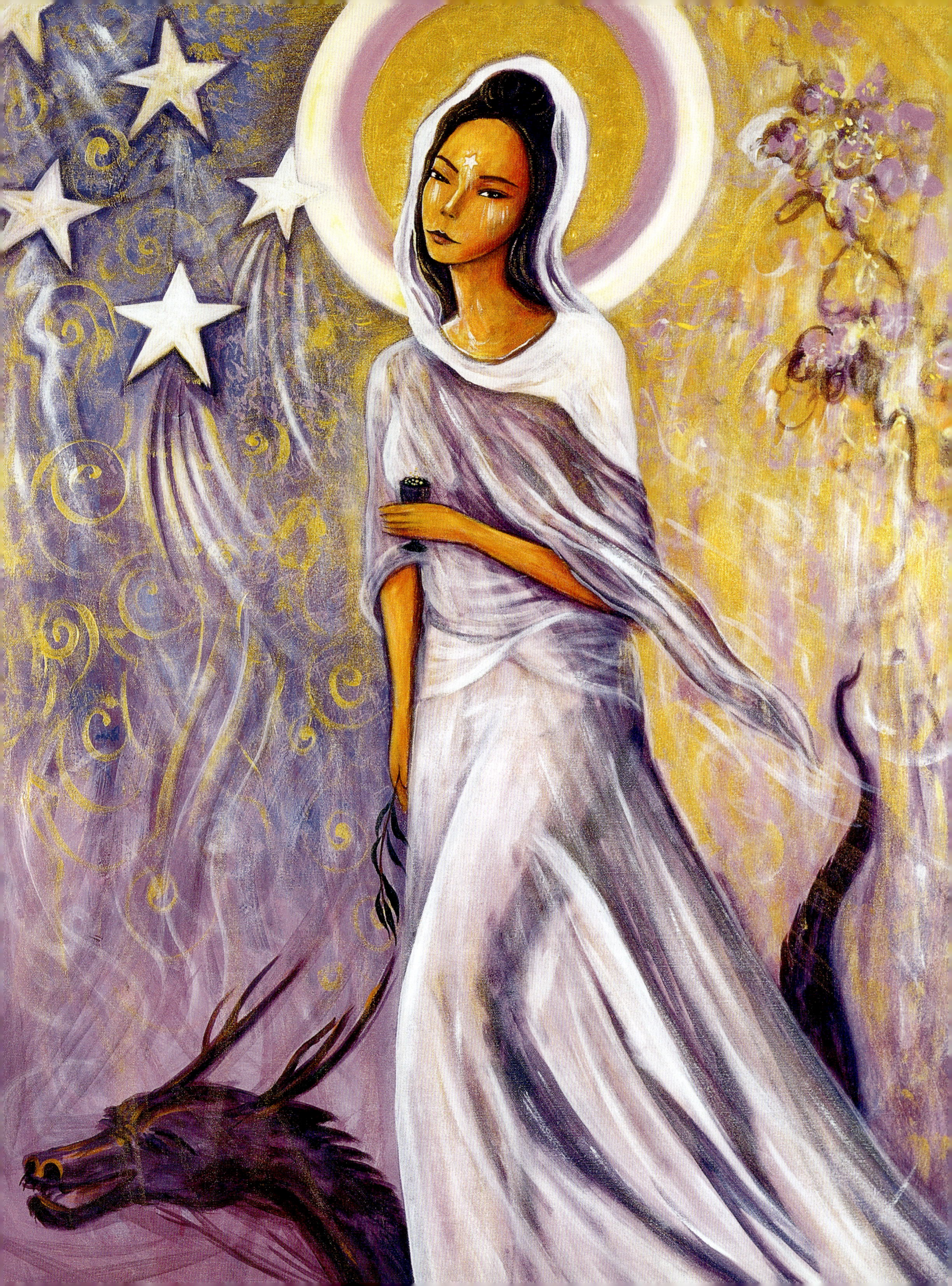

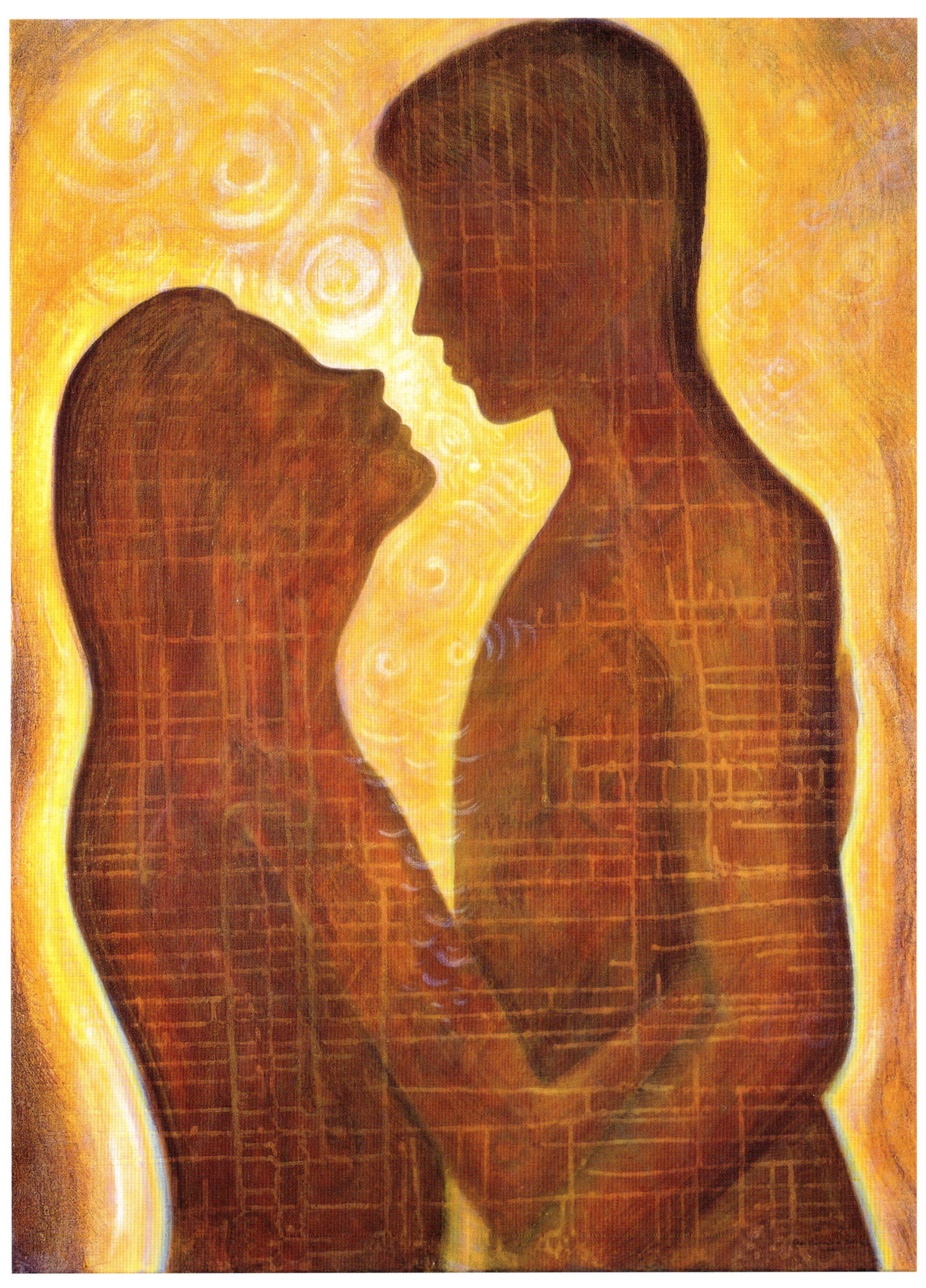

"Soul Mates" *Acrylic on canvas*
Previous page: *"Cherry Blossom"* *Acrylic on canvas*

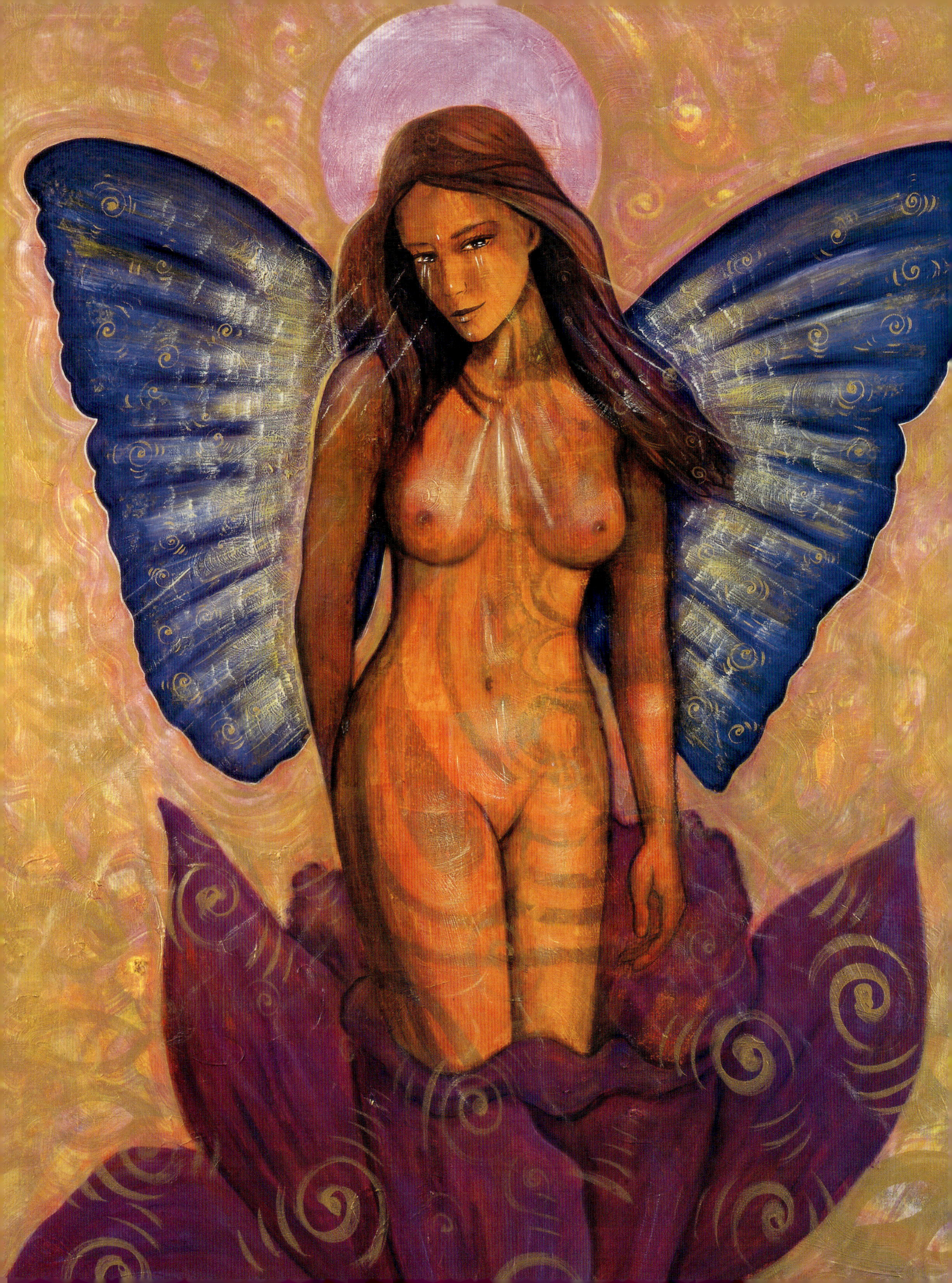

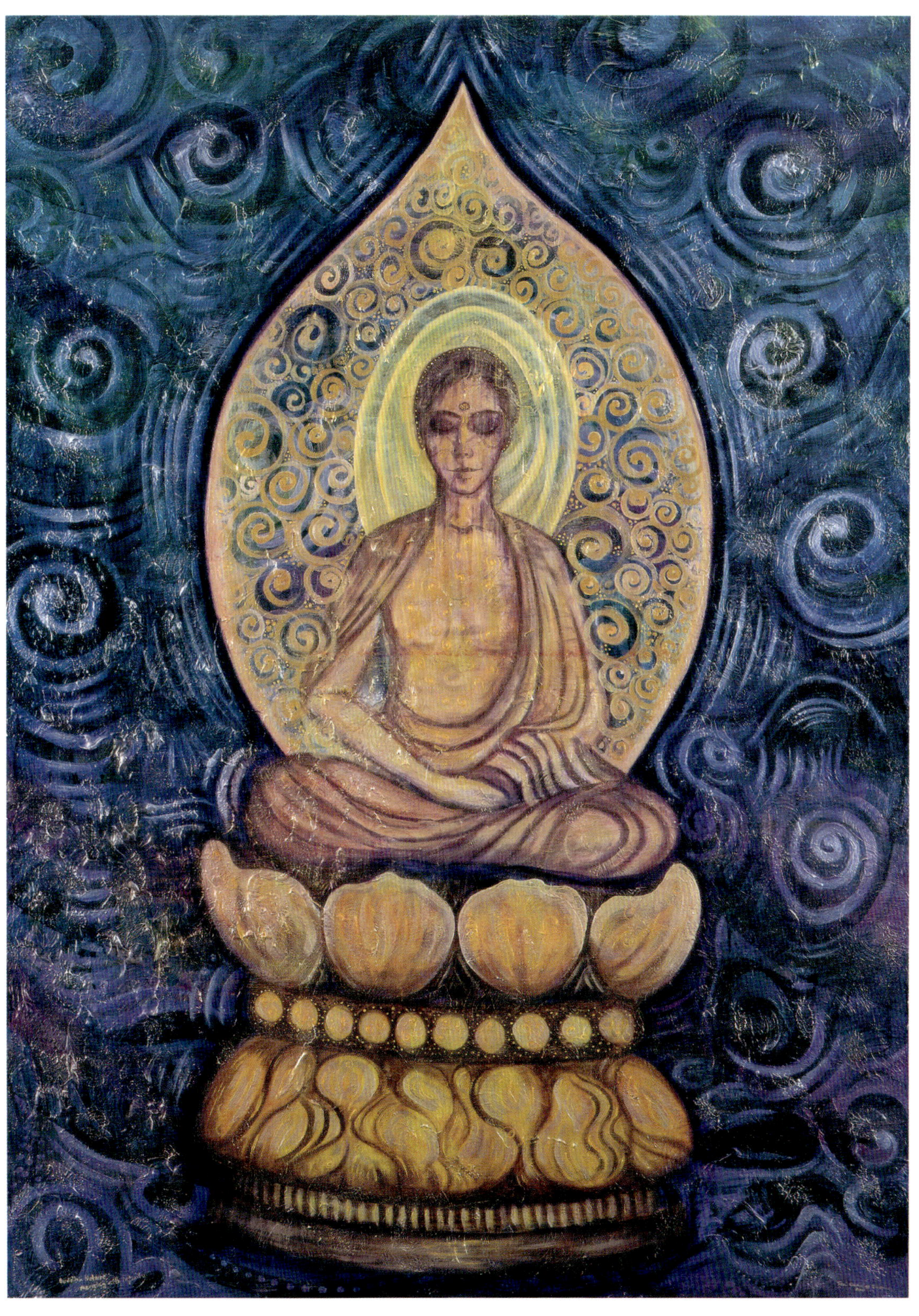

"Buddha Nature" *Acrylic on canvas*
Previous page: "Butterfly Wings" *Acrylic on canvas*

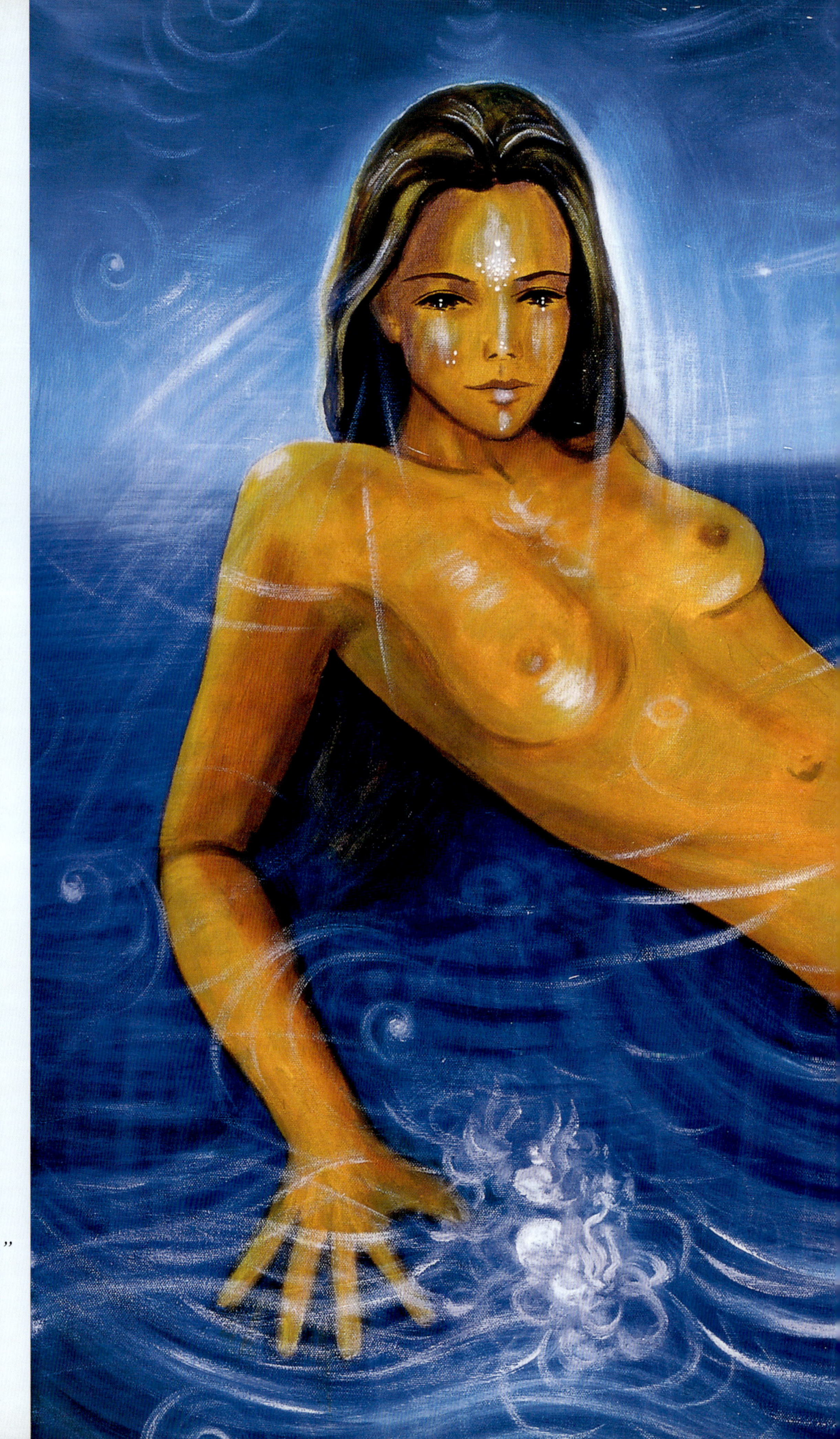

"Music Of The Spheres"
Acrylic on canvas

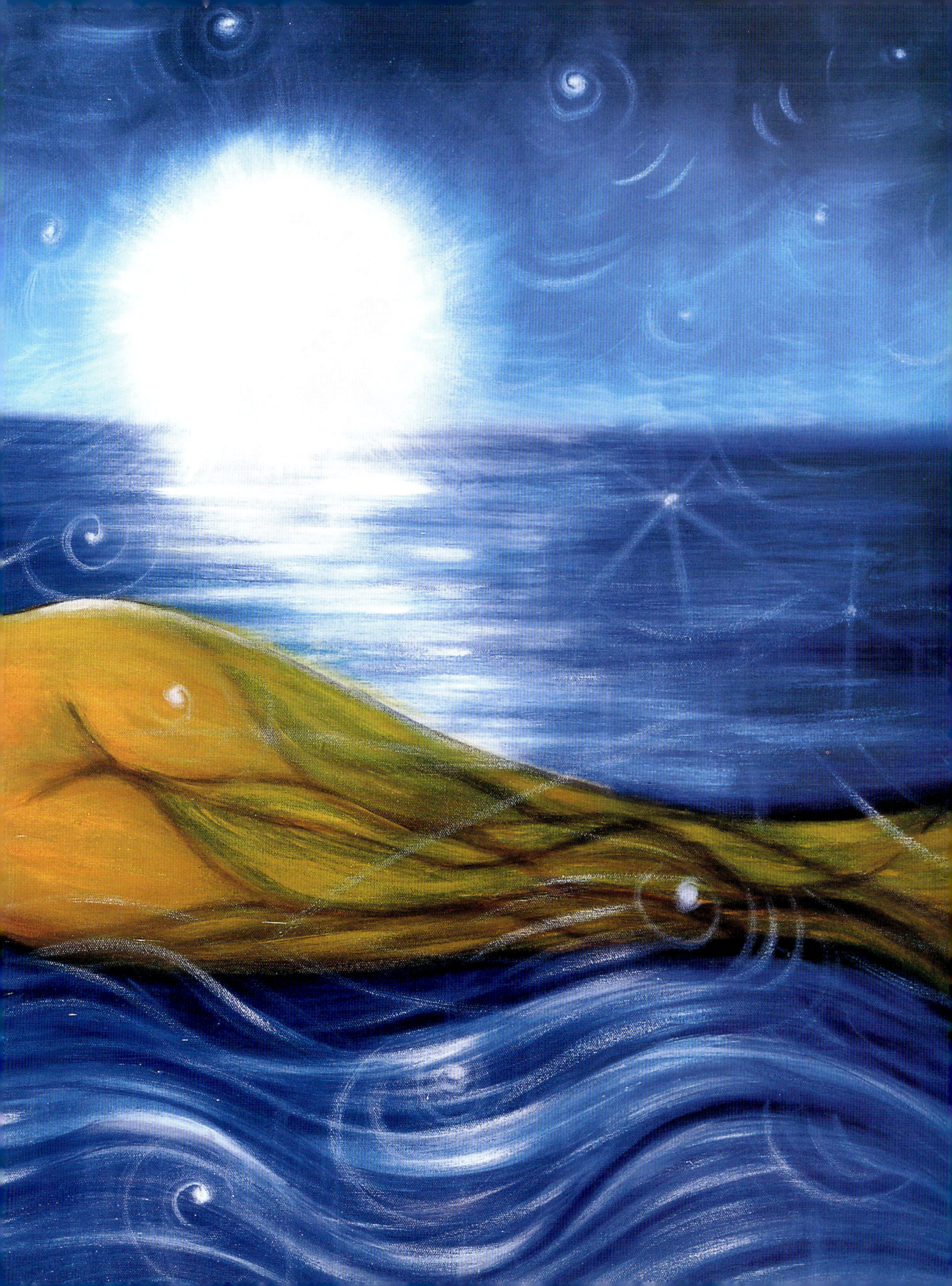

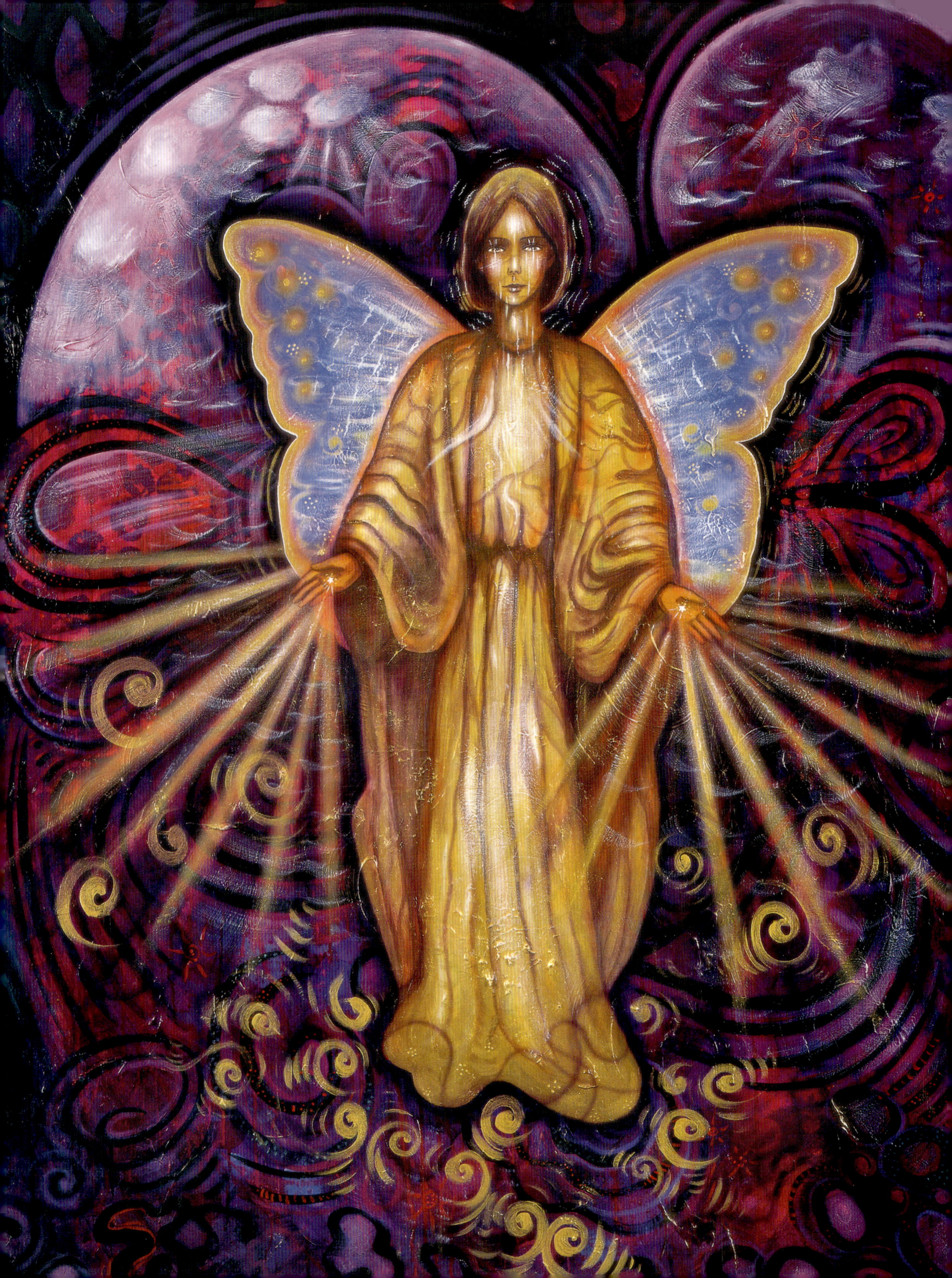

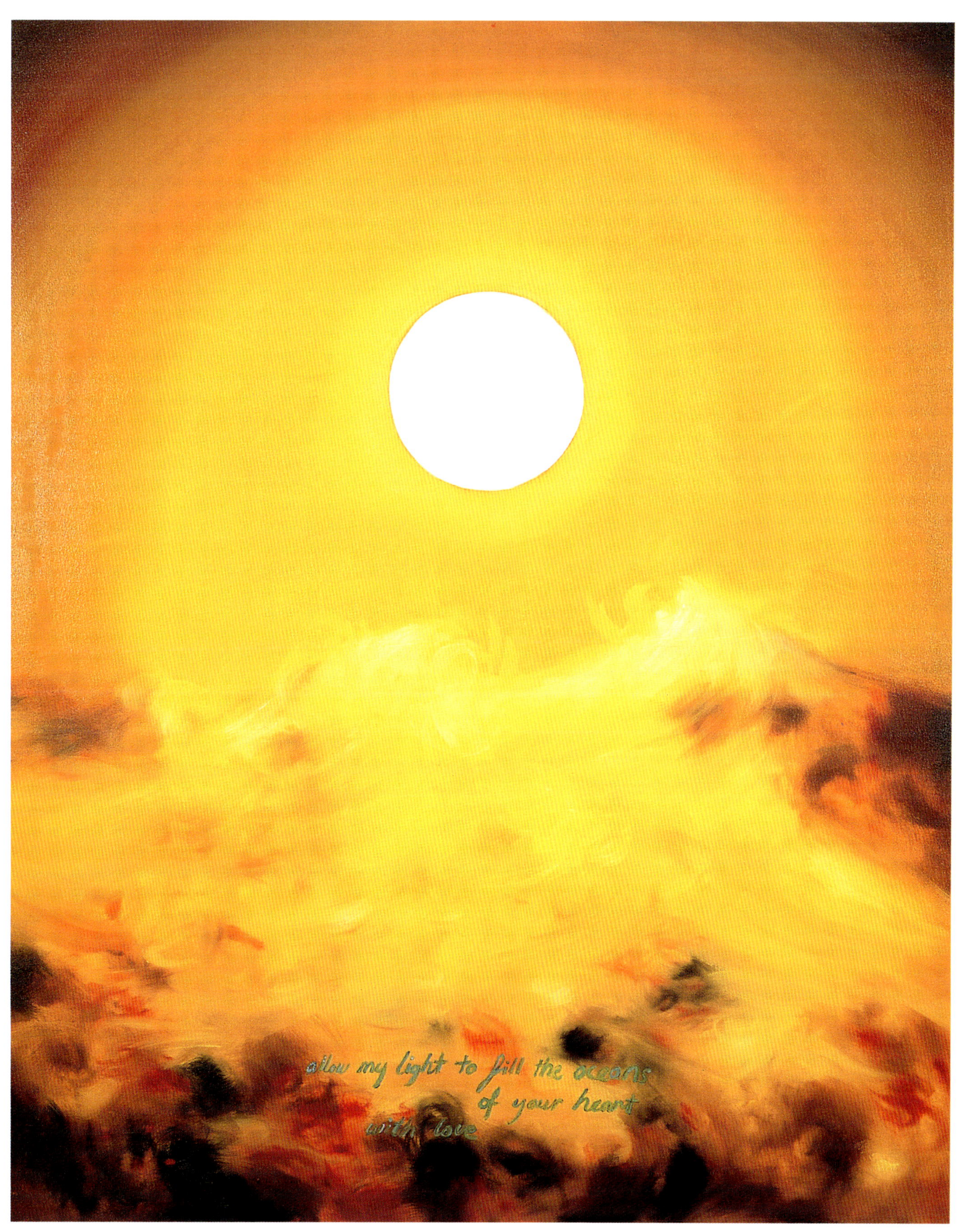

"Ocean Of Light" *Oil on canvas*
Previous page: *"Raphael"* *Acrylic on canvas*

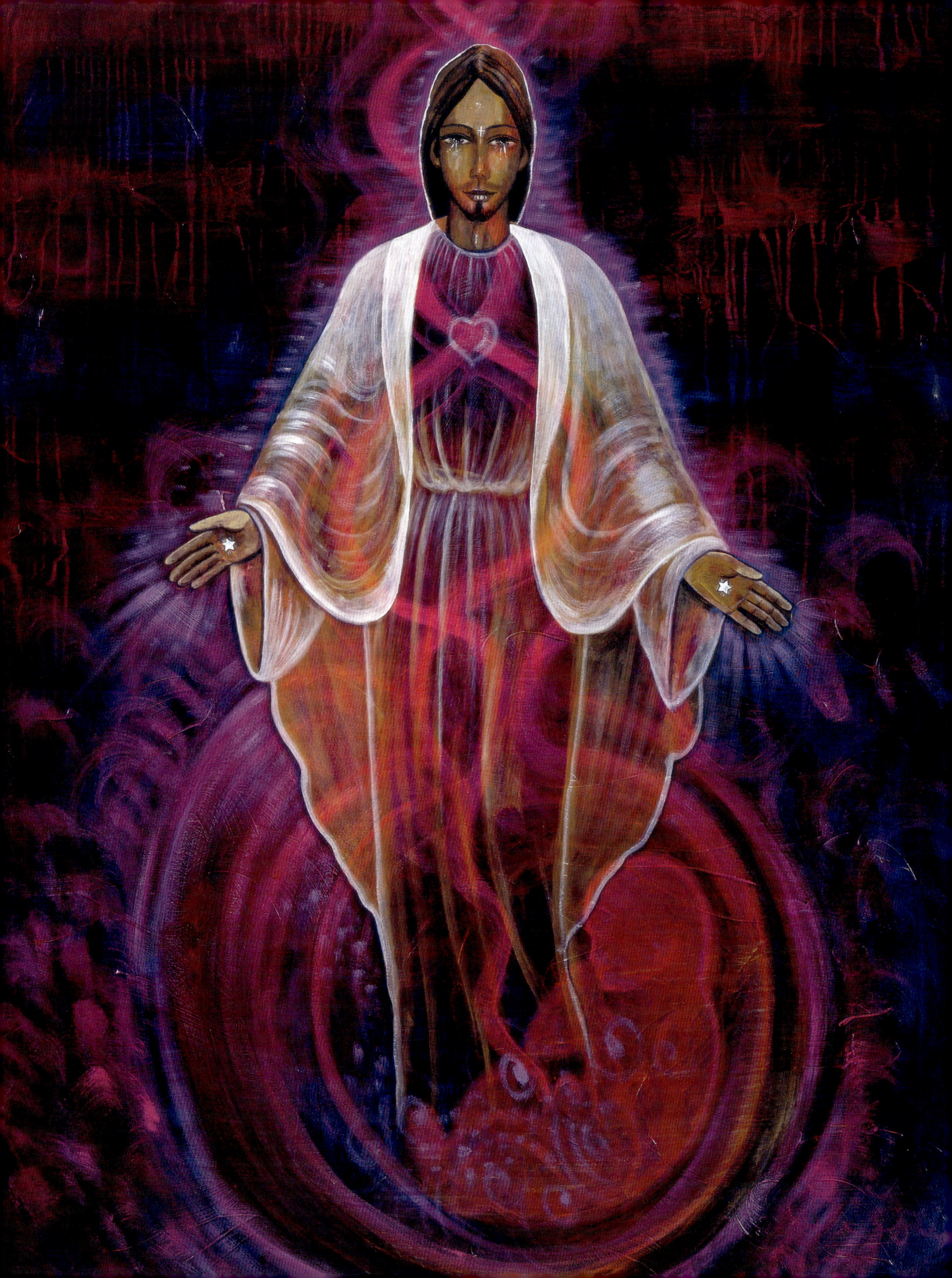

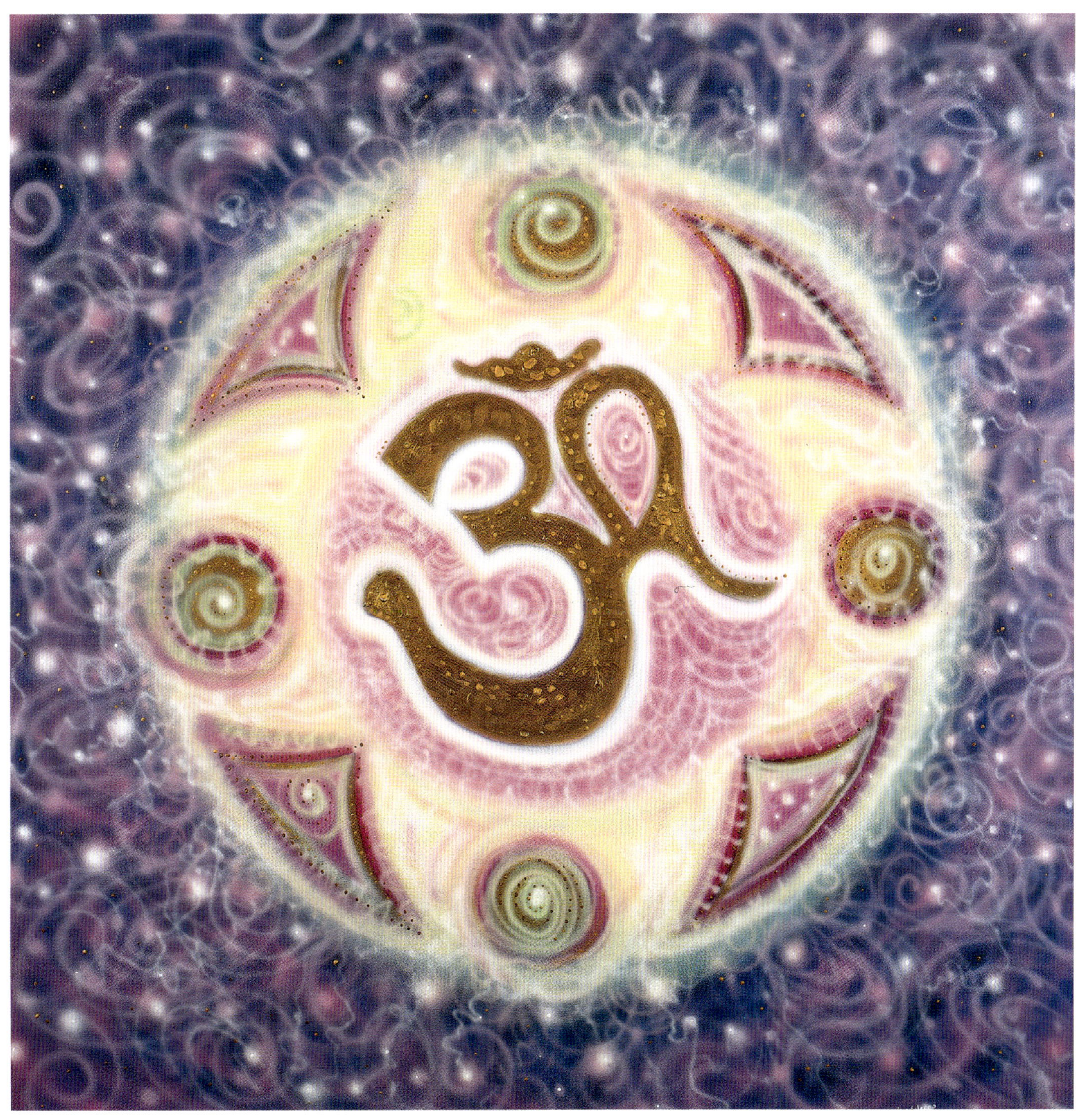

"Universal Om" *Acrylic on canvas*
Previous page: "No More Wounds" *Acrylic on canvas*

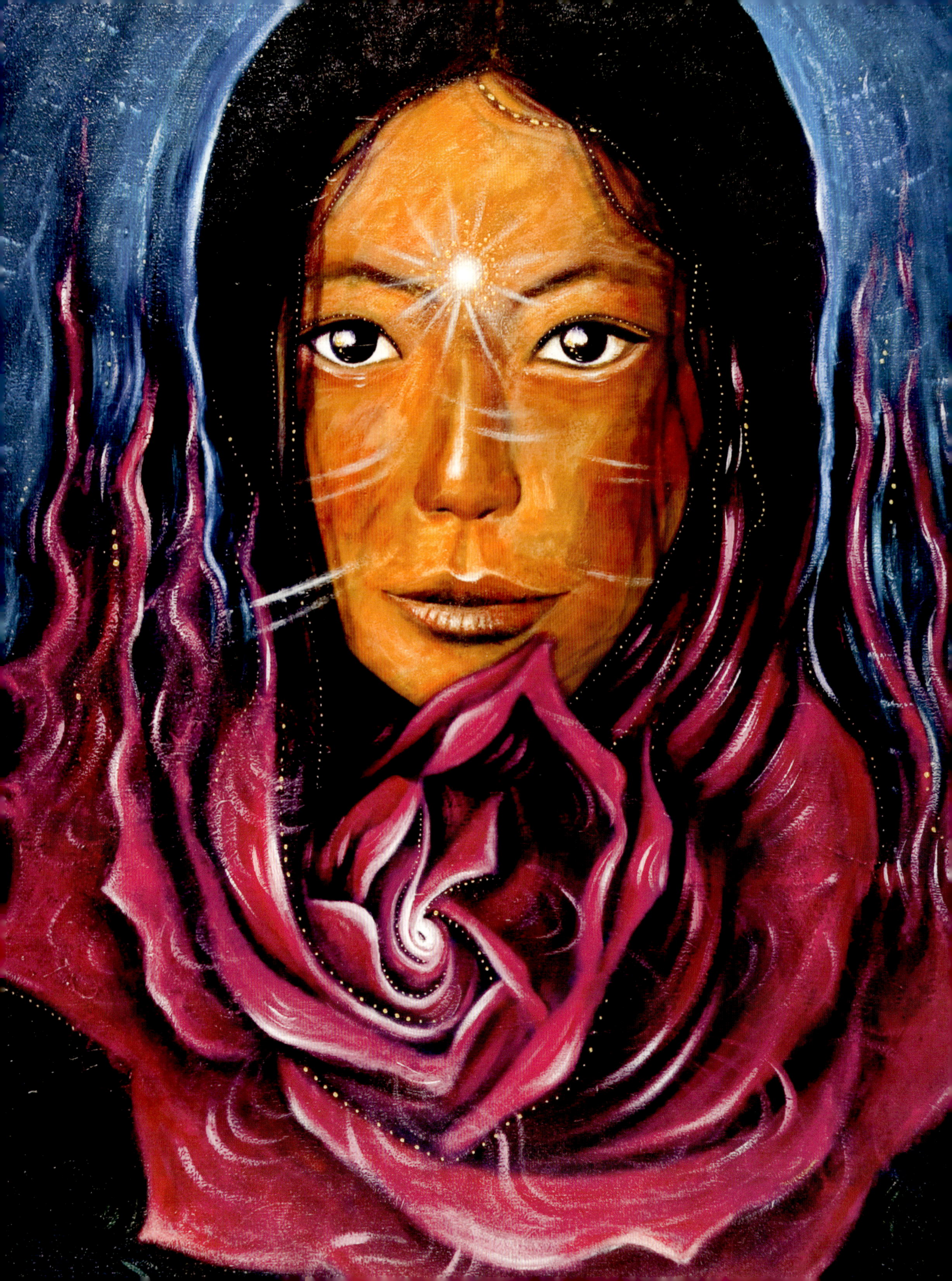

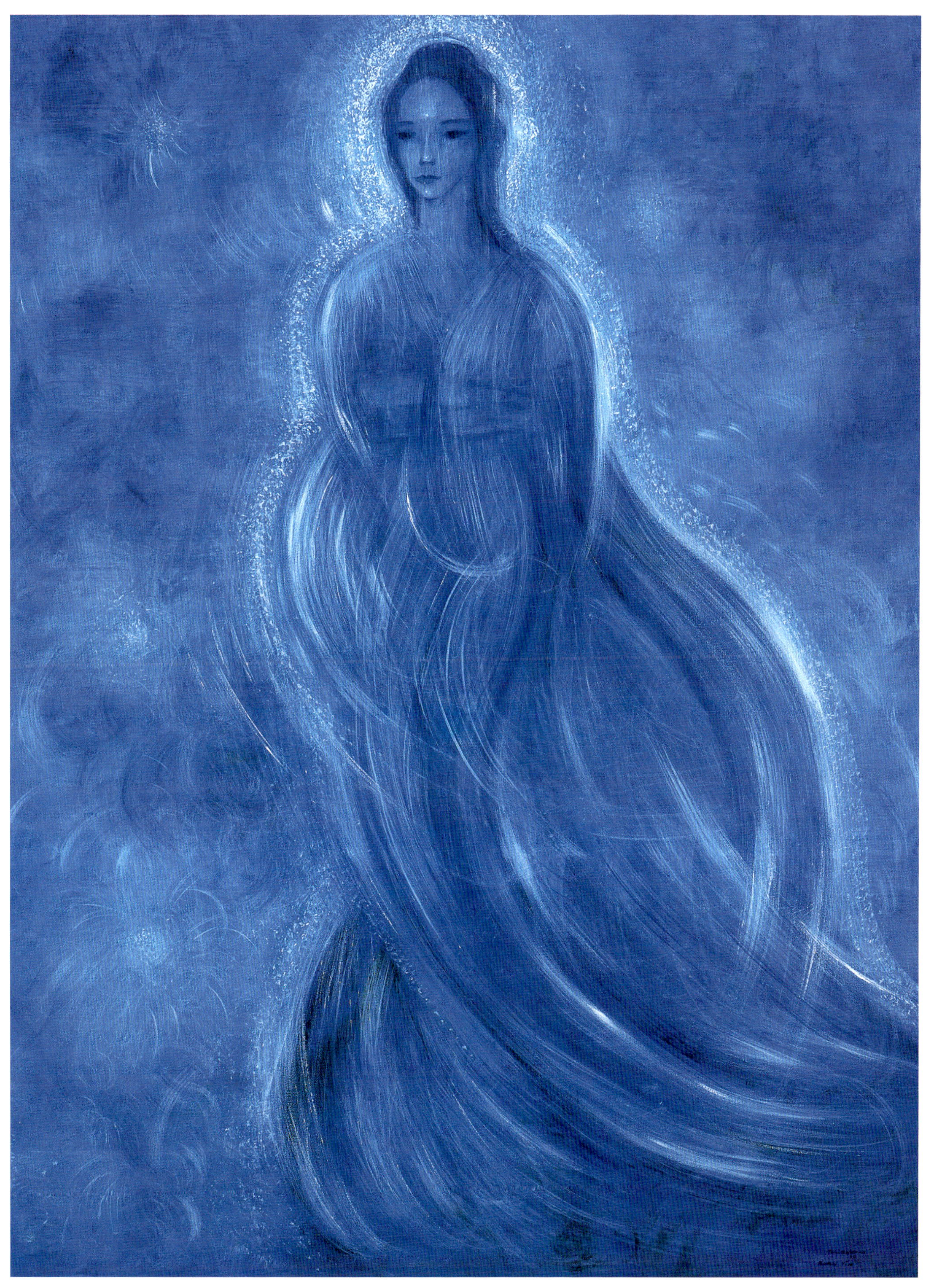

"Kuan Yin: Compassion" Acrylic on canvas
Previous page: *"Rose Heart"* Acrylic on canvas

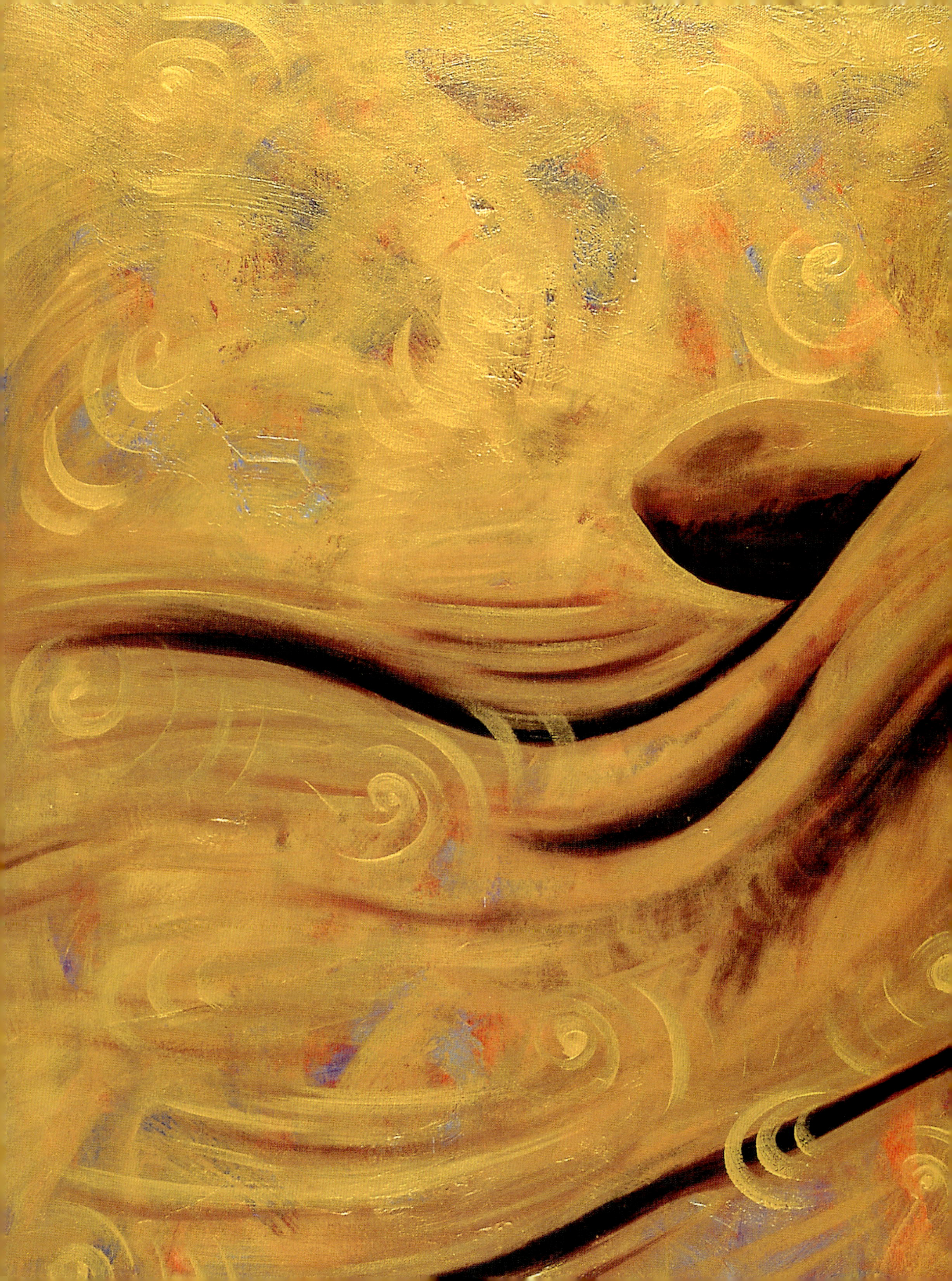

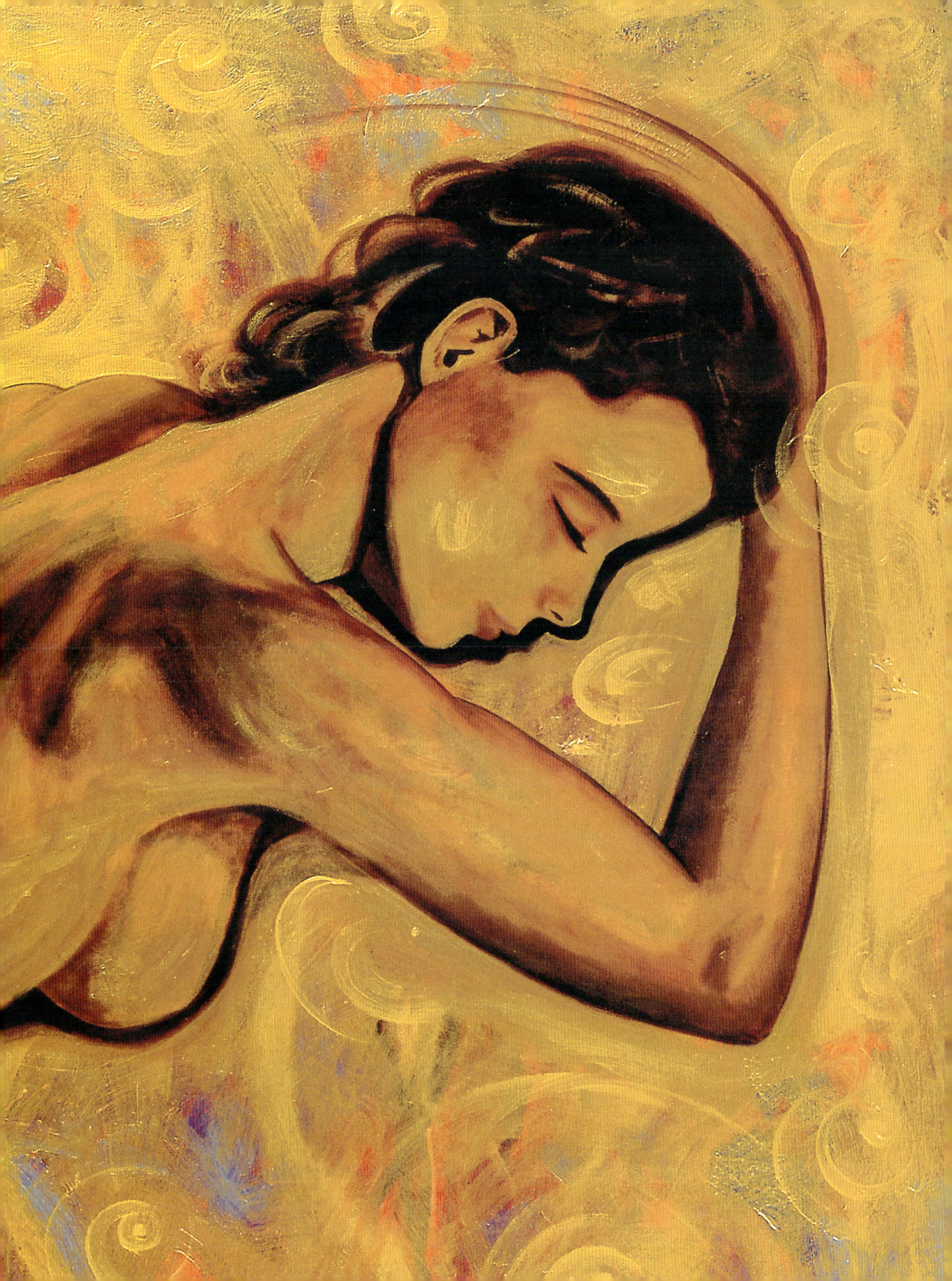

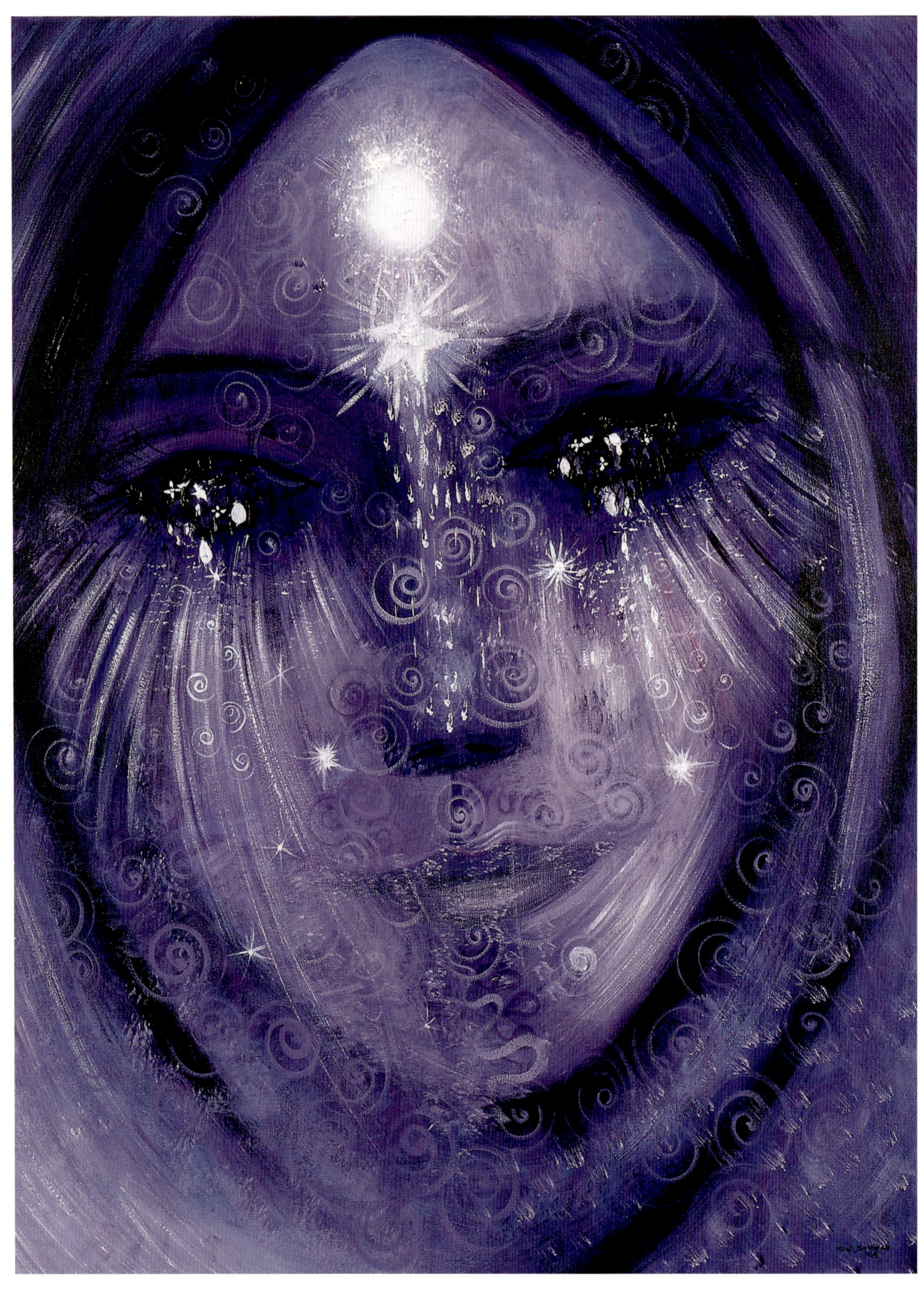

"Kuan Yin: Face" Acrylic on canvas

Previous page: "Metamorphosis" Acrylic on canvas
Next page: "Tree Of Life" Acrylic on canvas

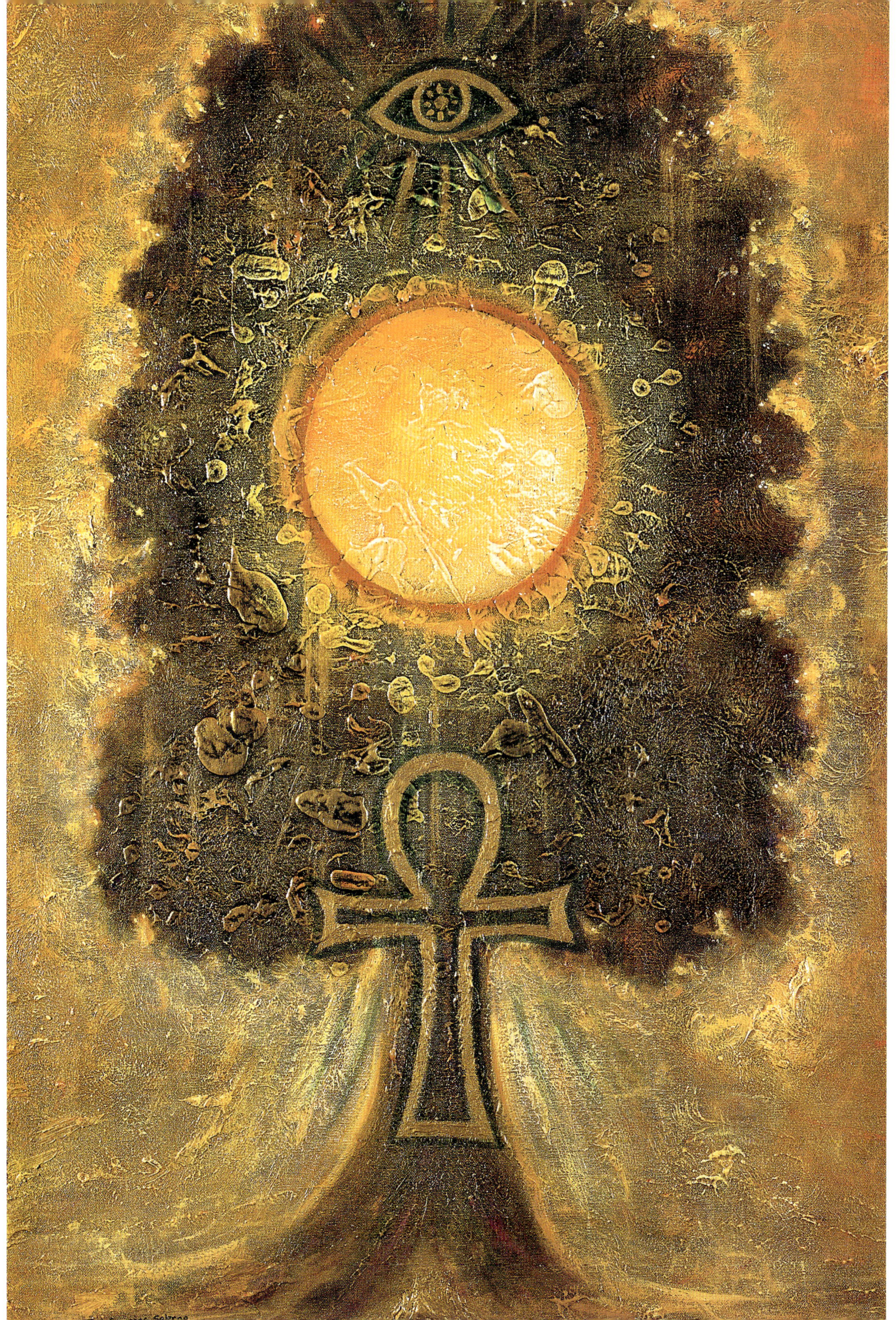

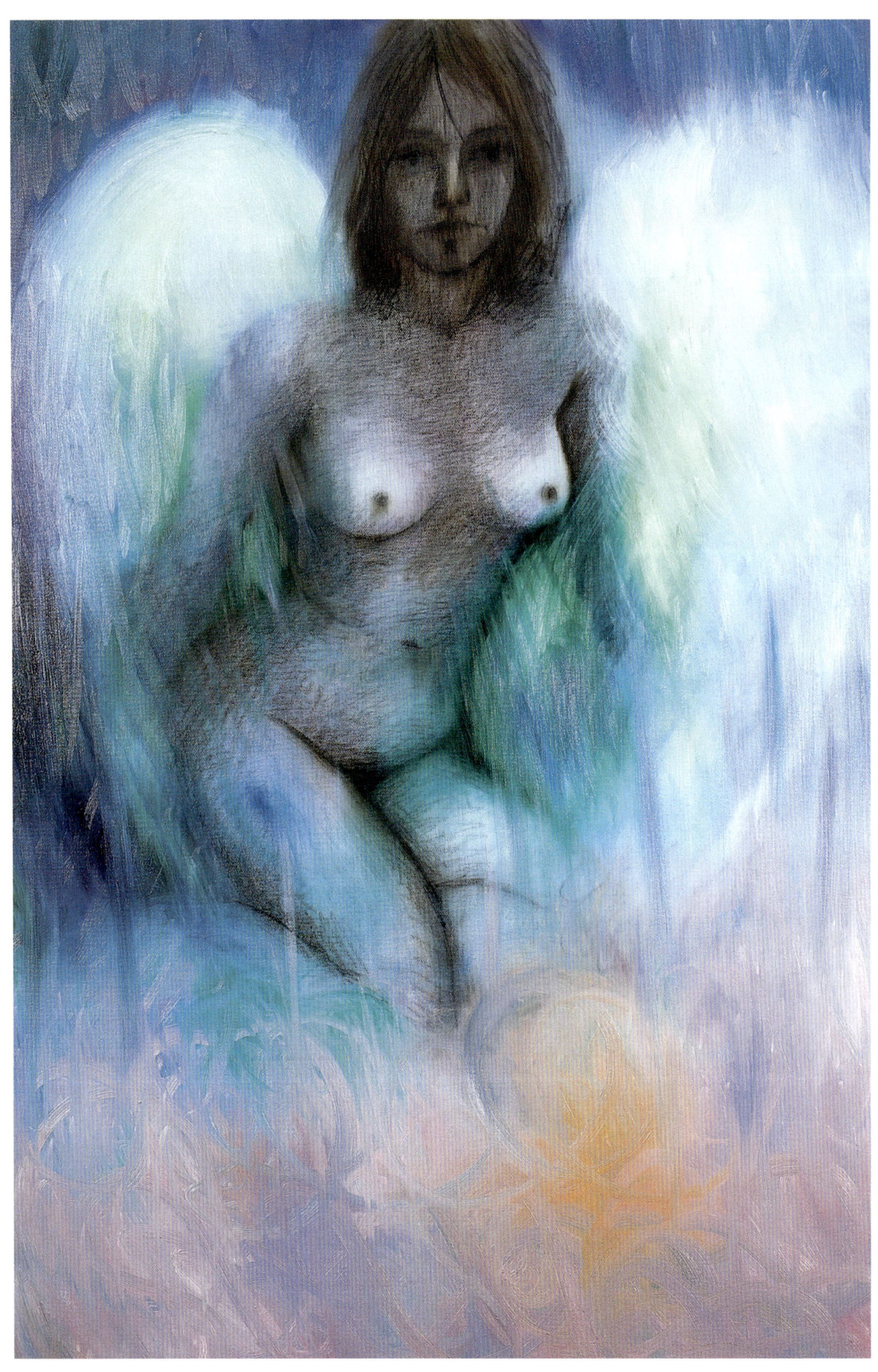

"Upon A Cloud" *Oil and pencil on canvas*

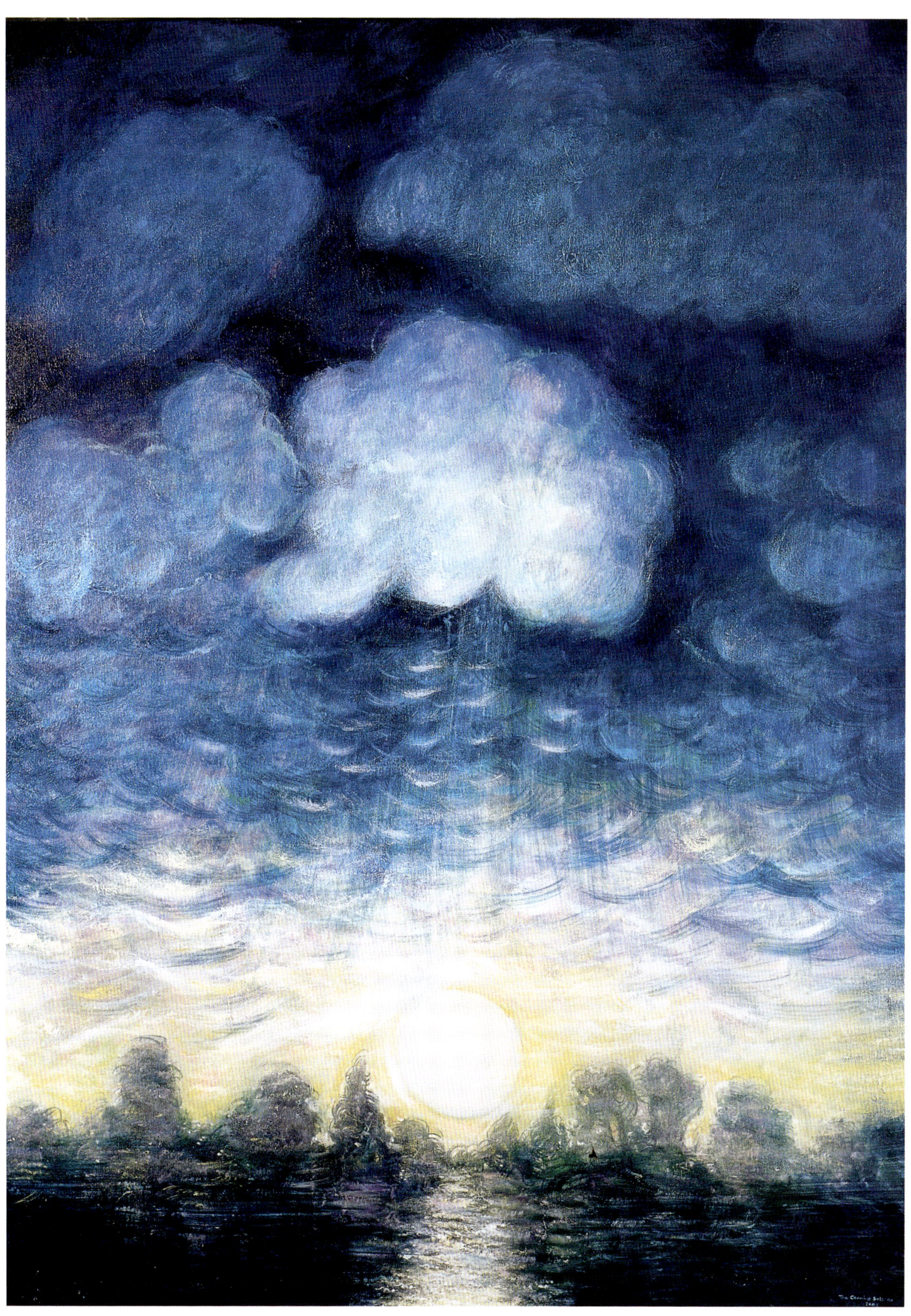

"Guidance" *Acrylic on canvas*

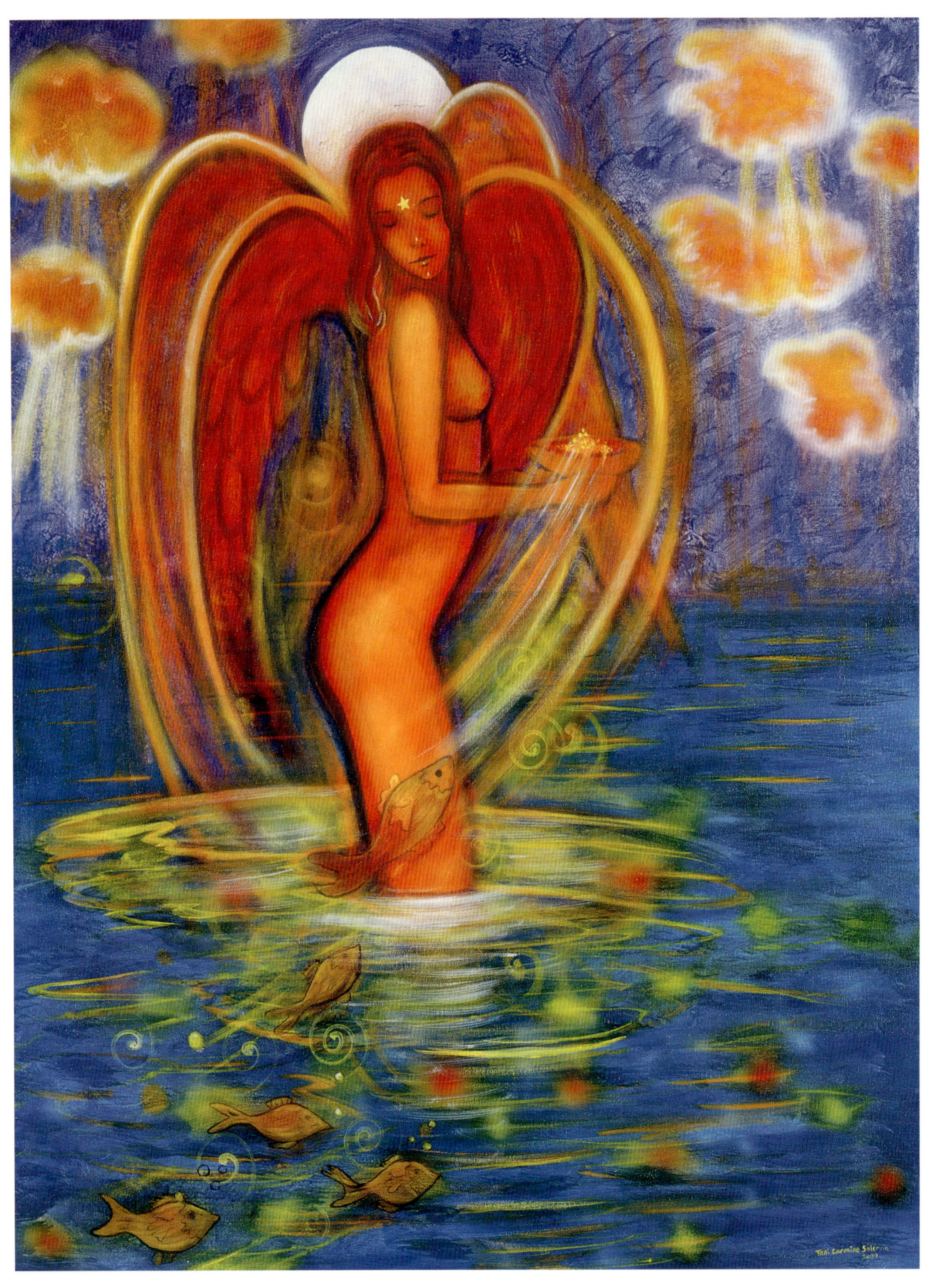

"Playfulness" *Acrylic on canvas*

Next page: "Rebirth" Acrylic on canvas

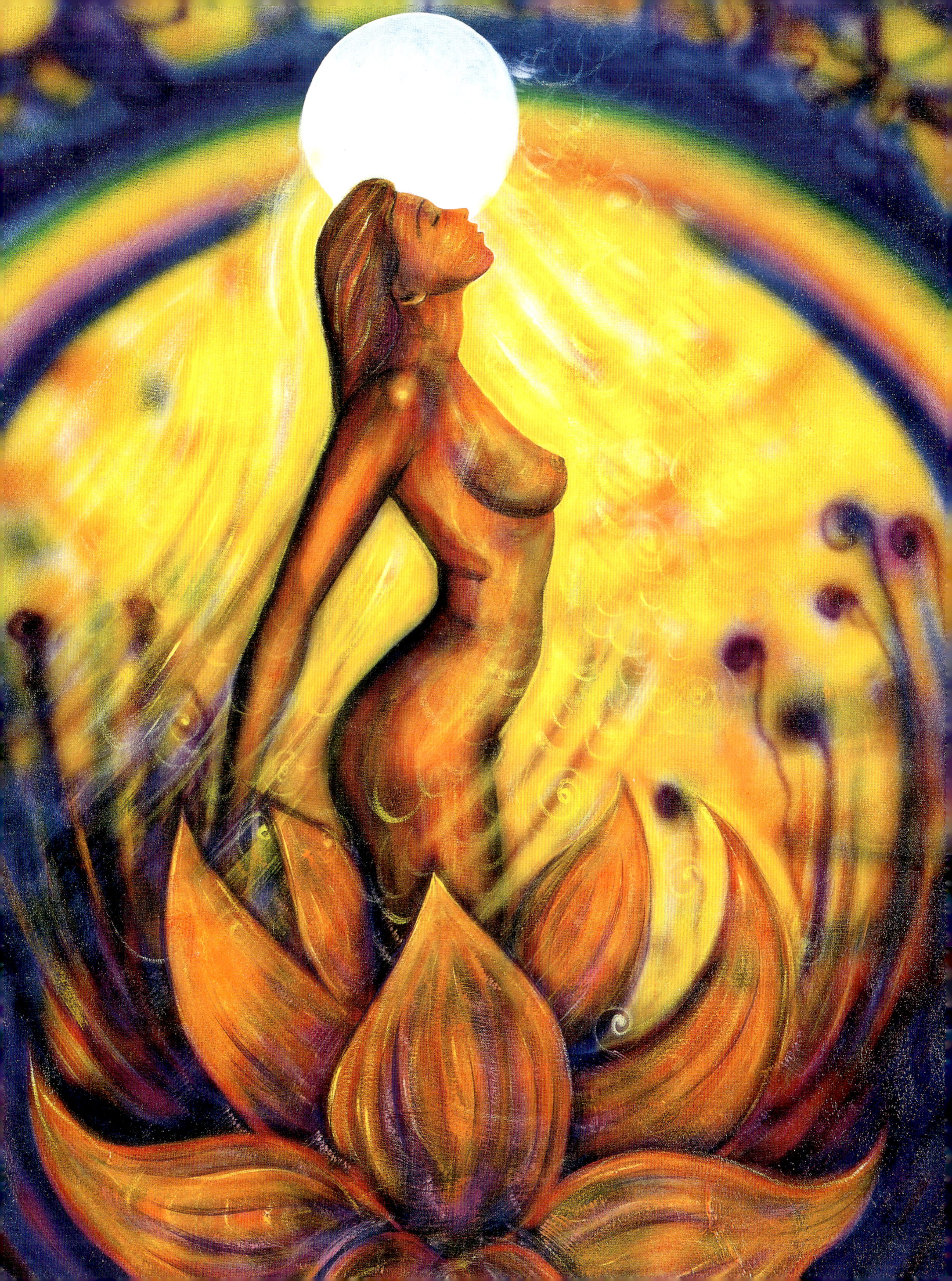

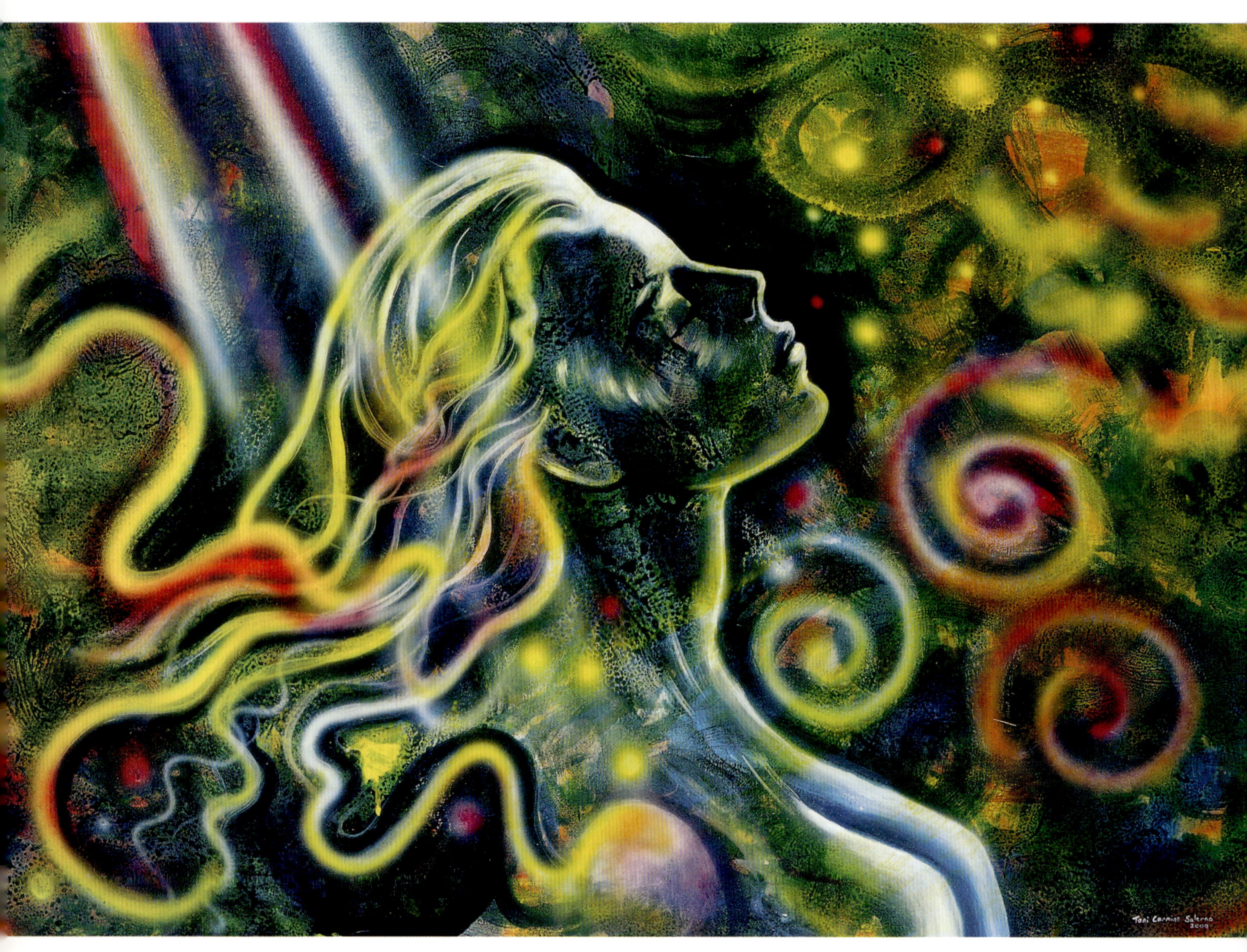

"Enchantment" *Acrylic on canvas*
Next page: "Viola" Acrylic on canvas

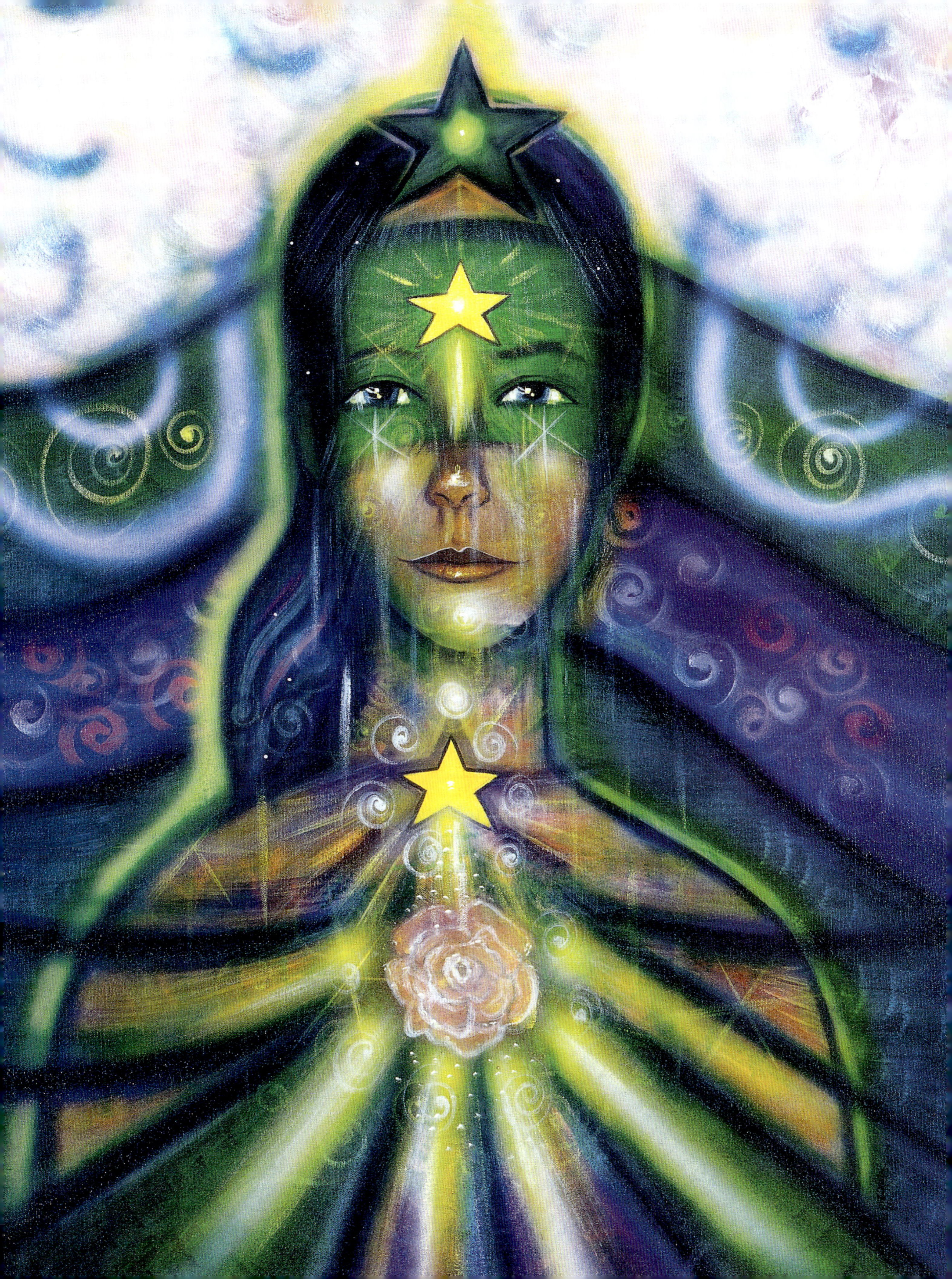

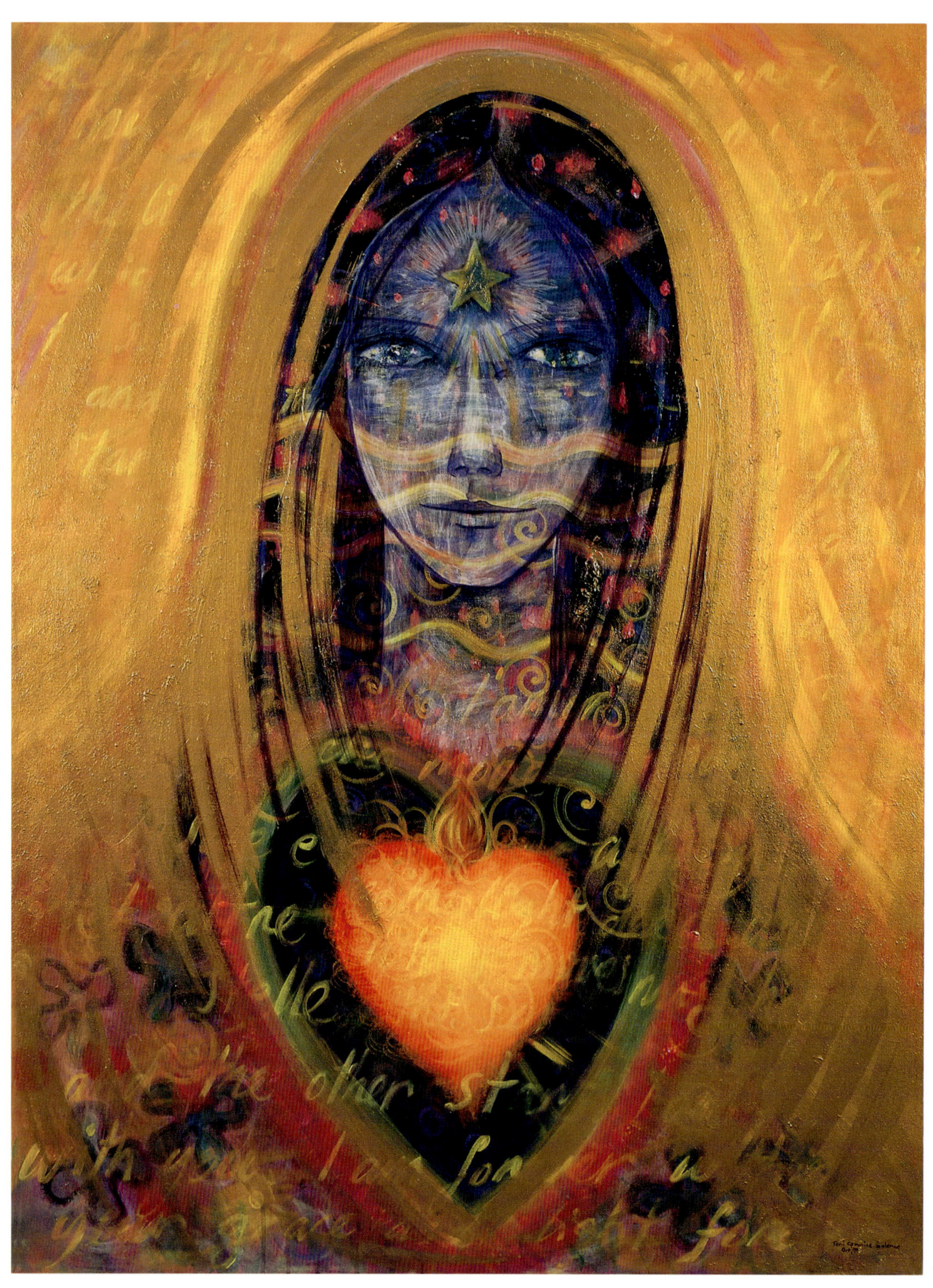

"Sacred Heart" Acrylic on canvas
Next page: *"Golden Path"* Oil on canvas

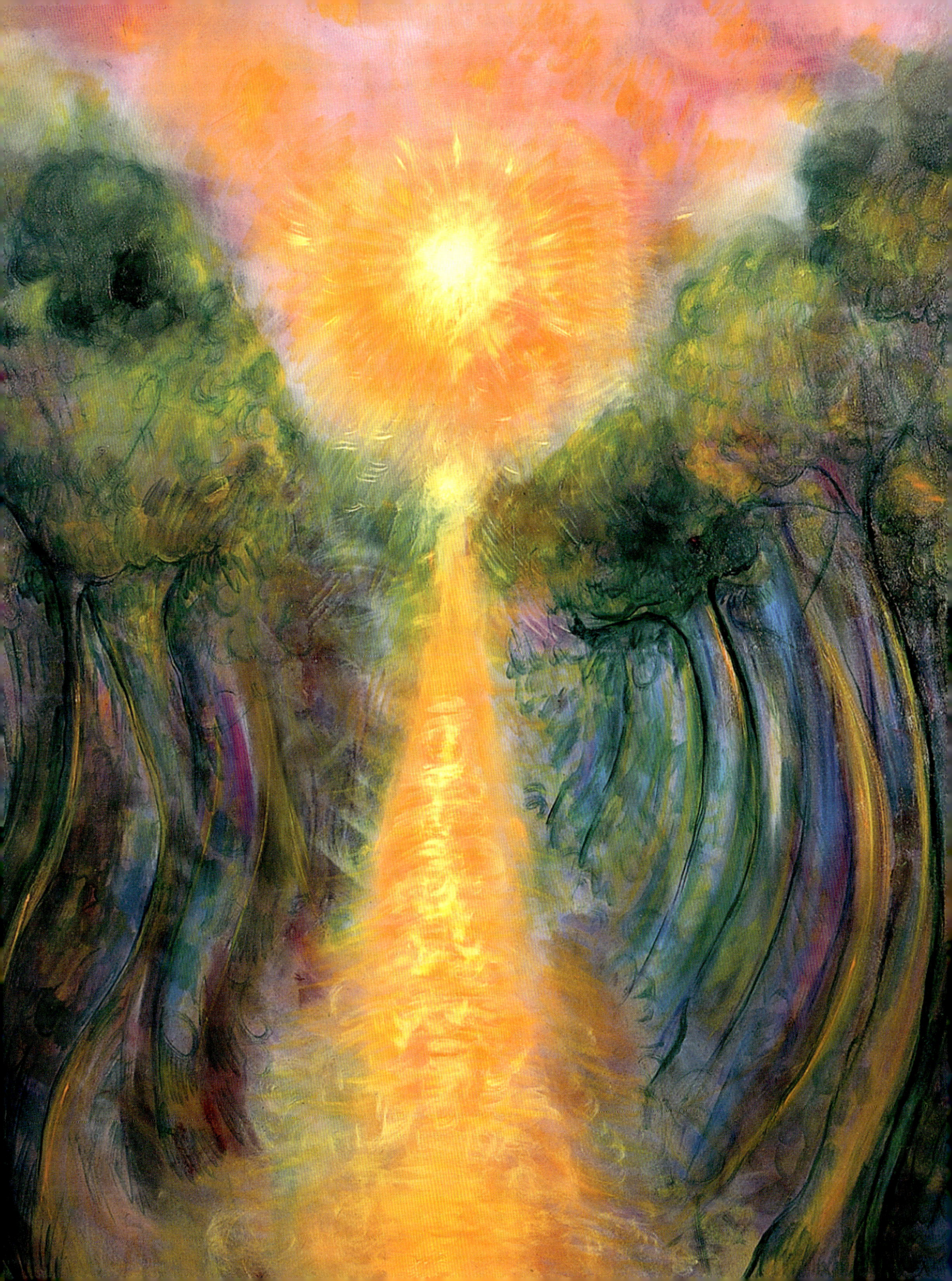

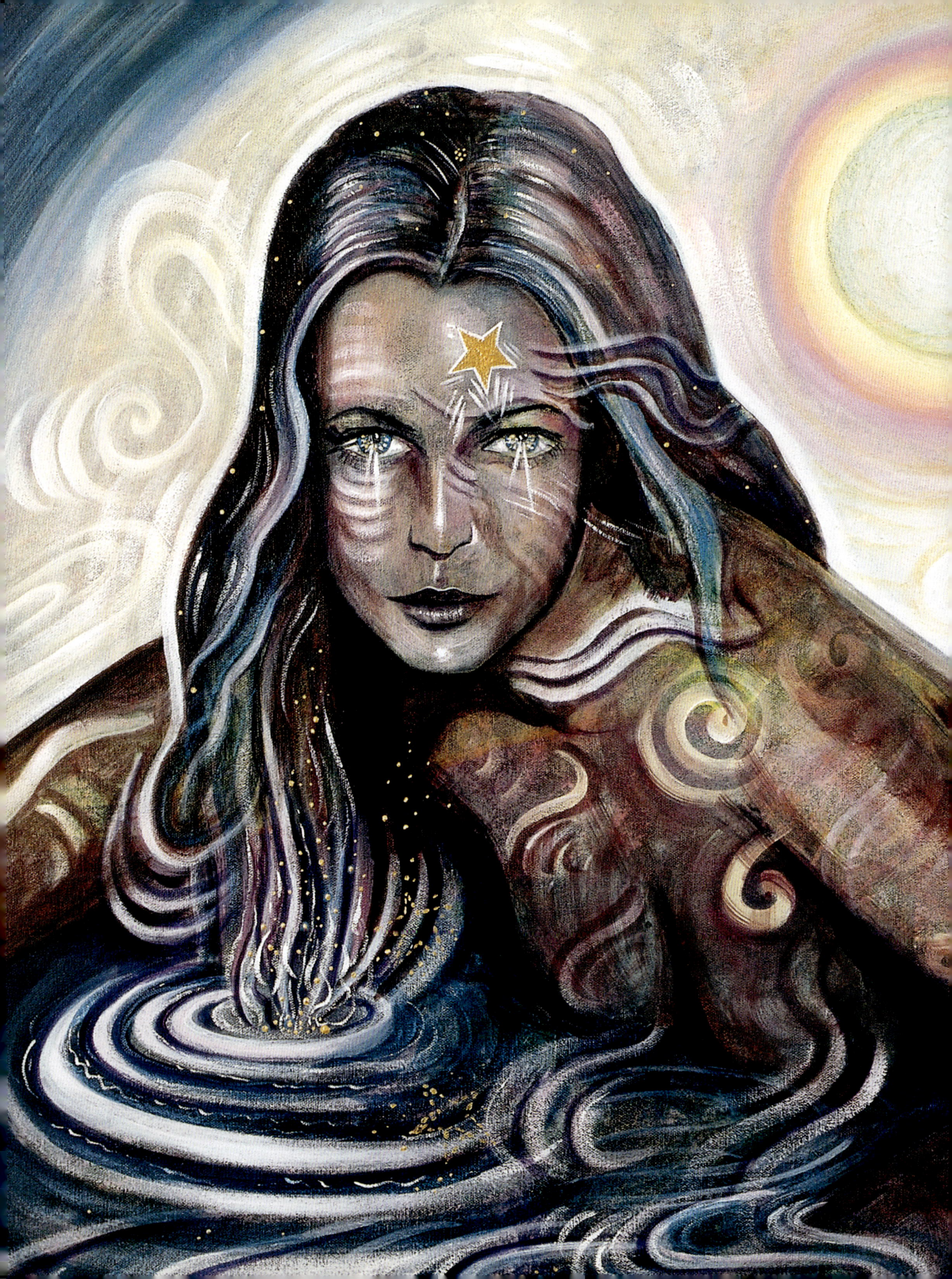

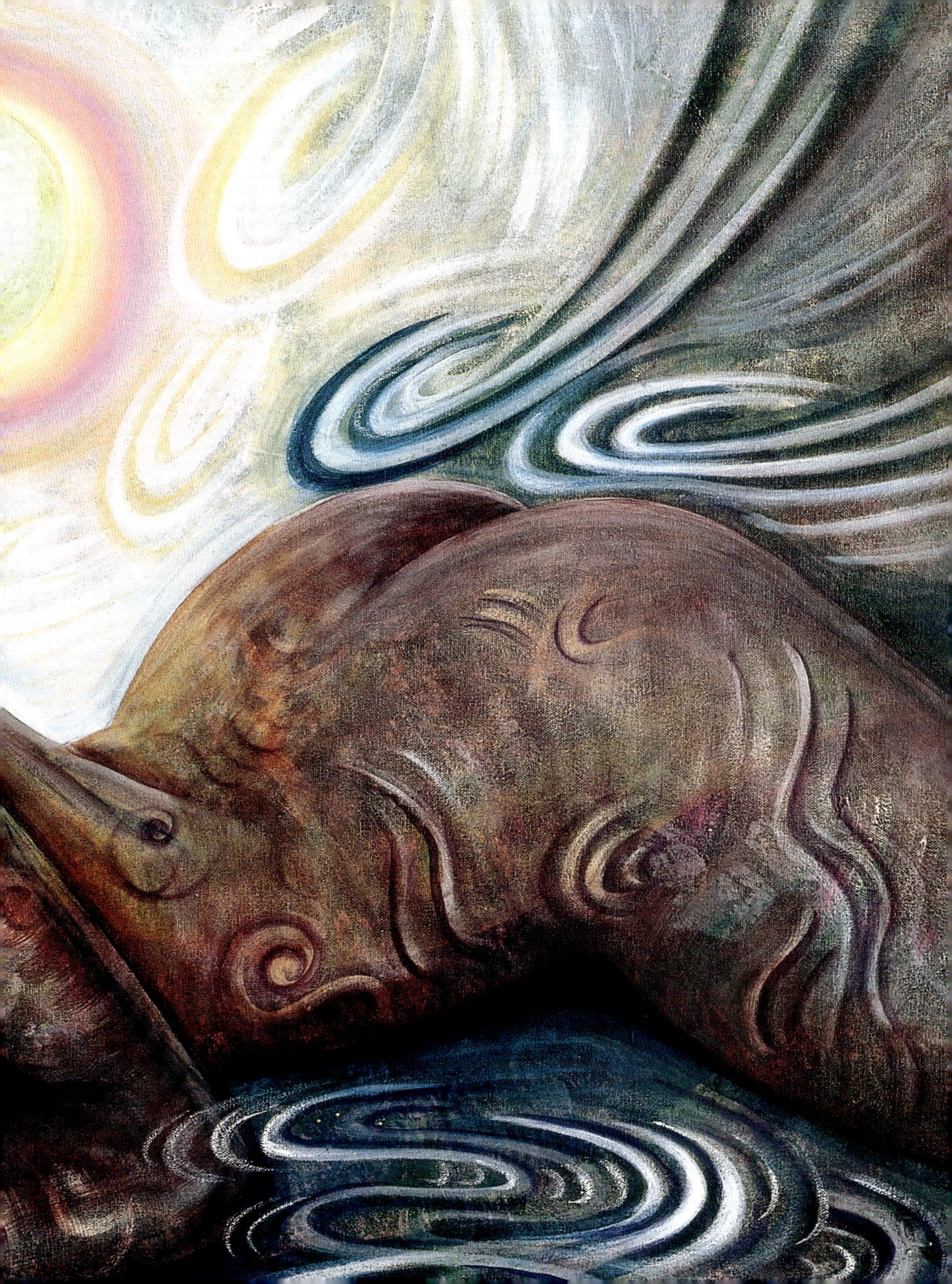

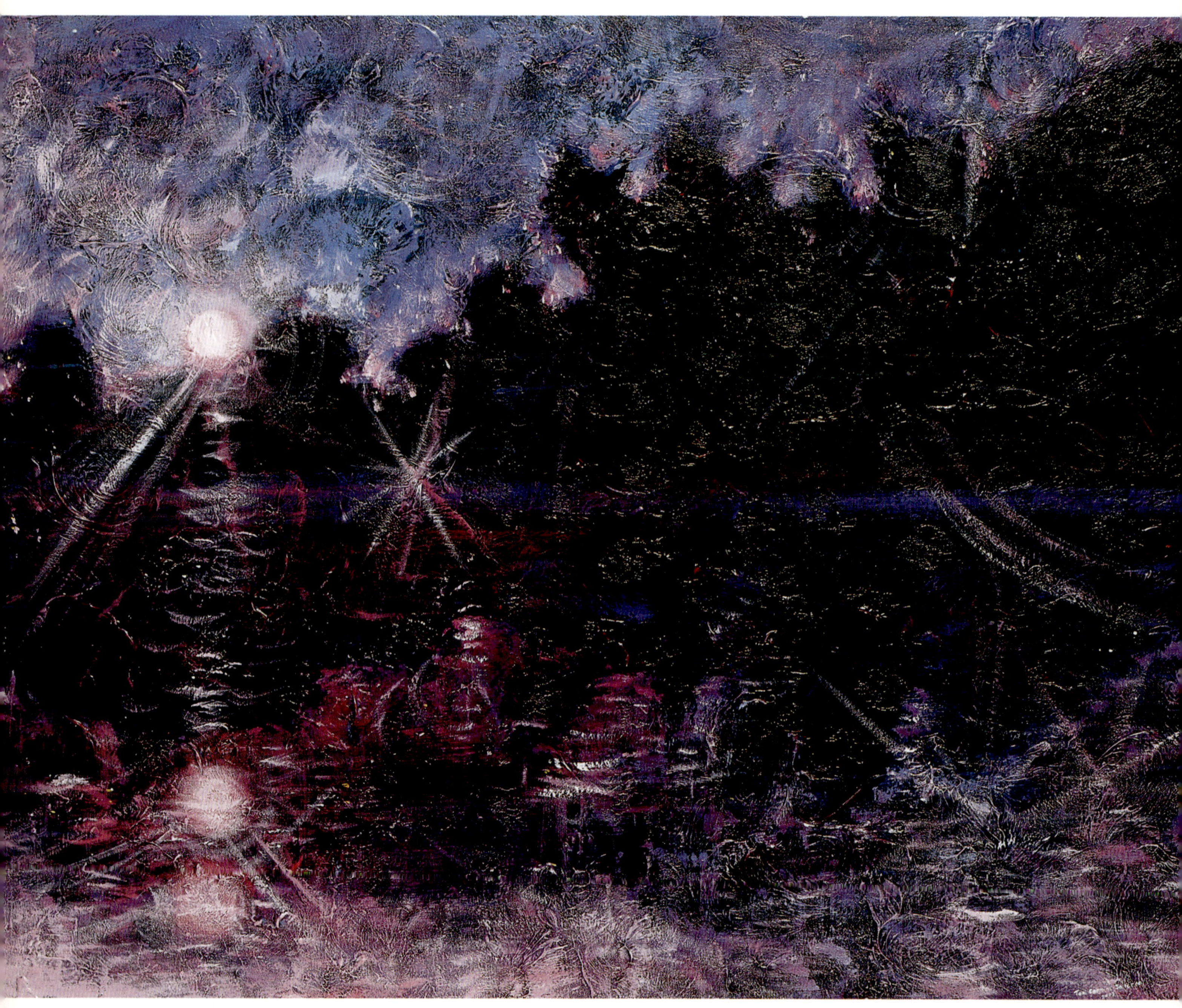

"Emotional Breakthrough" *Acrylic on canvas*
Previous page: *"Water Spirit"* *Acrylic on canvas*
Next page: *"Magdalene"* *Acrylic on canvas*

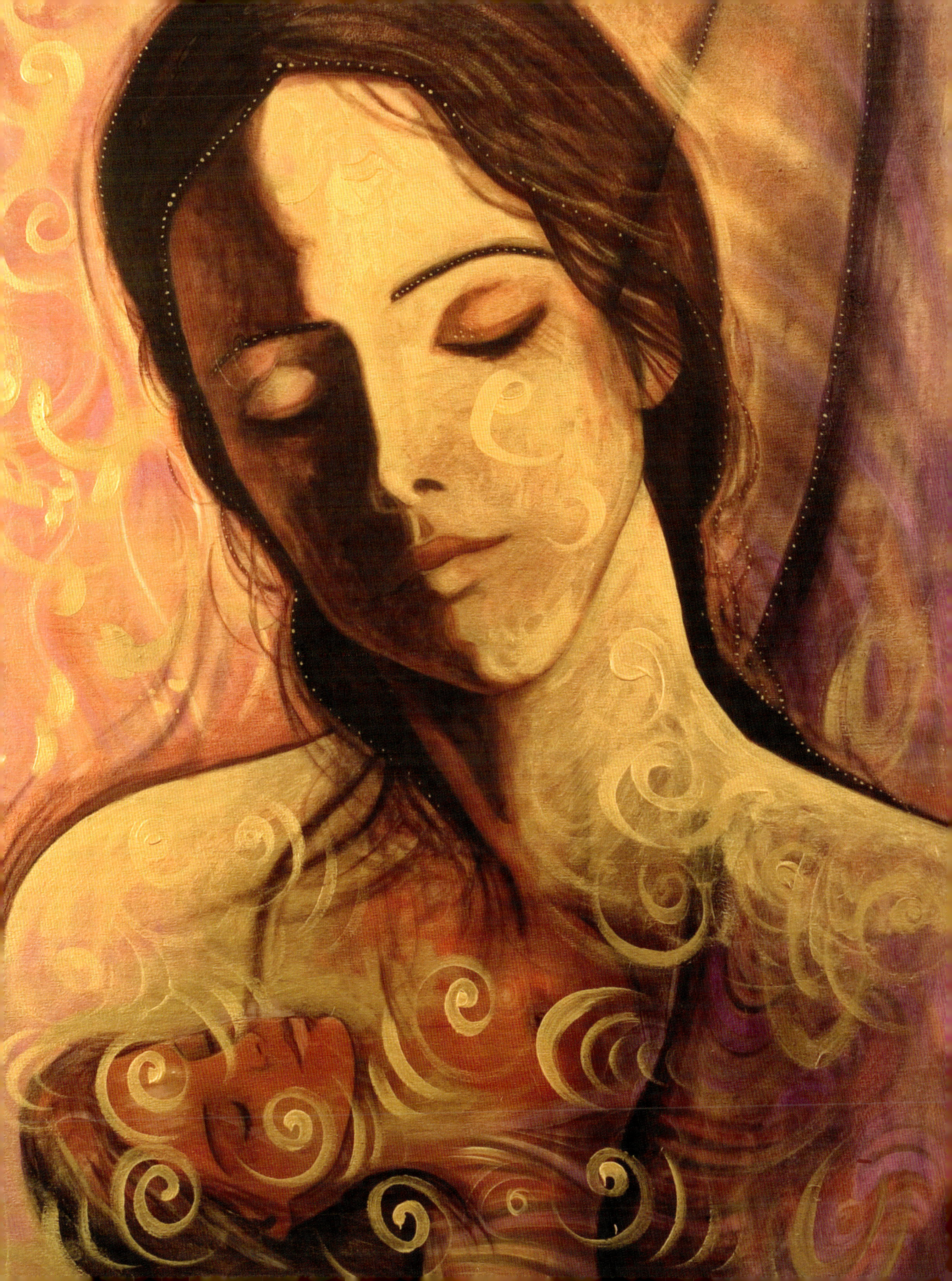

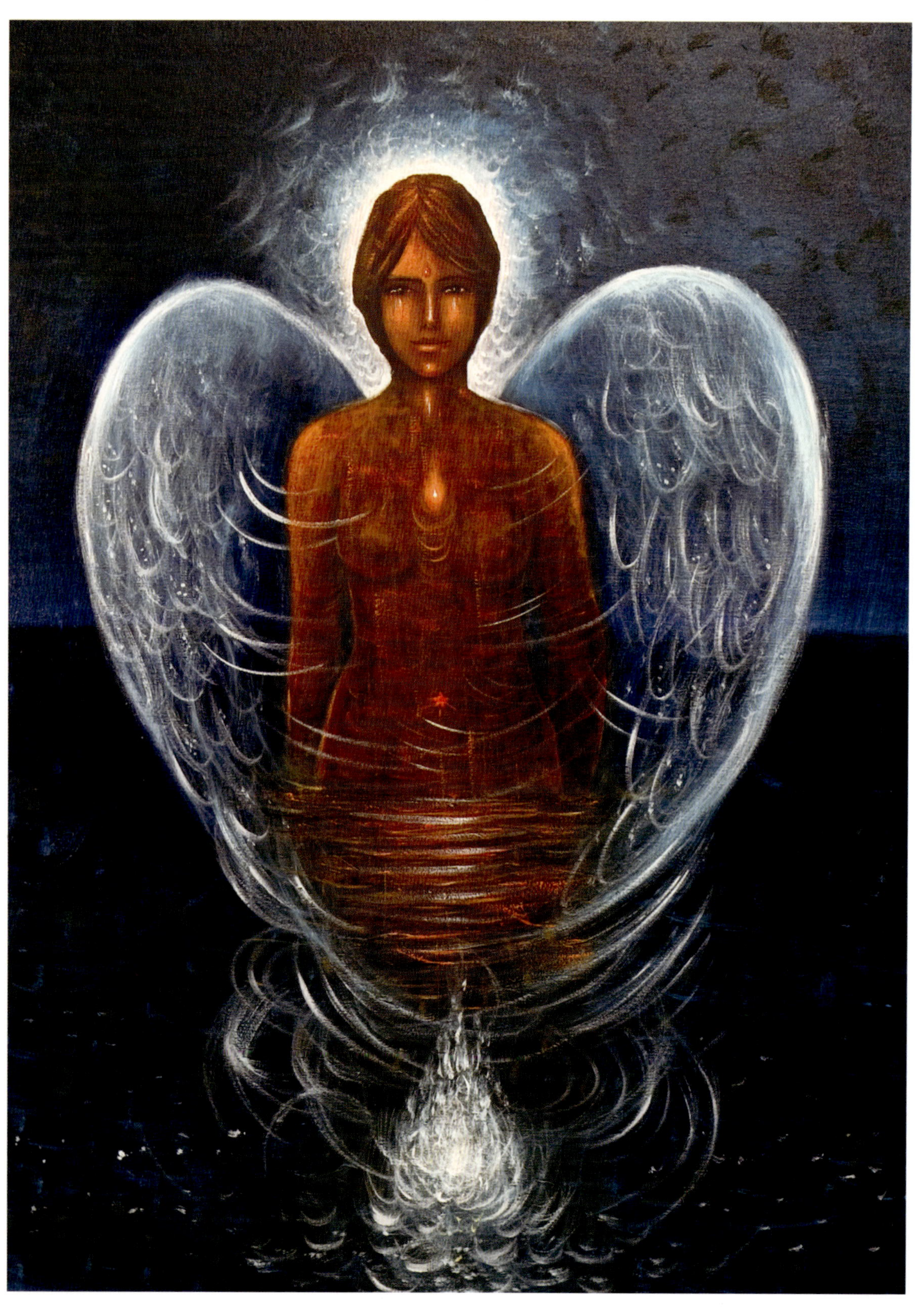

"The Messenger" Acrylic on canvas
Next page: "Eternity" Acrylic on canvas

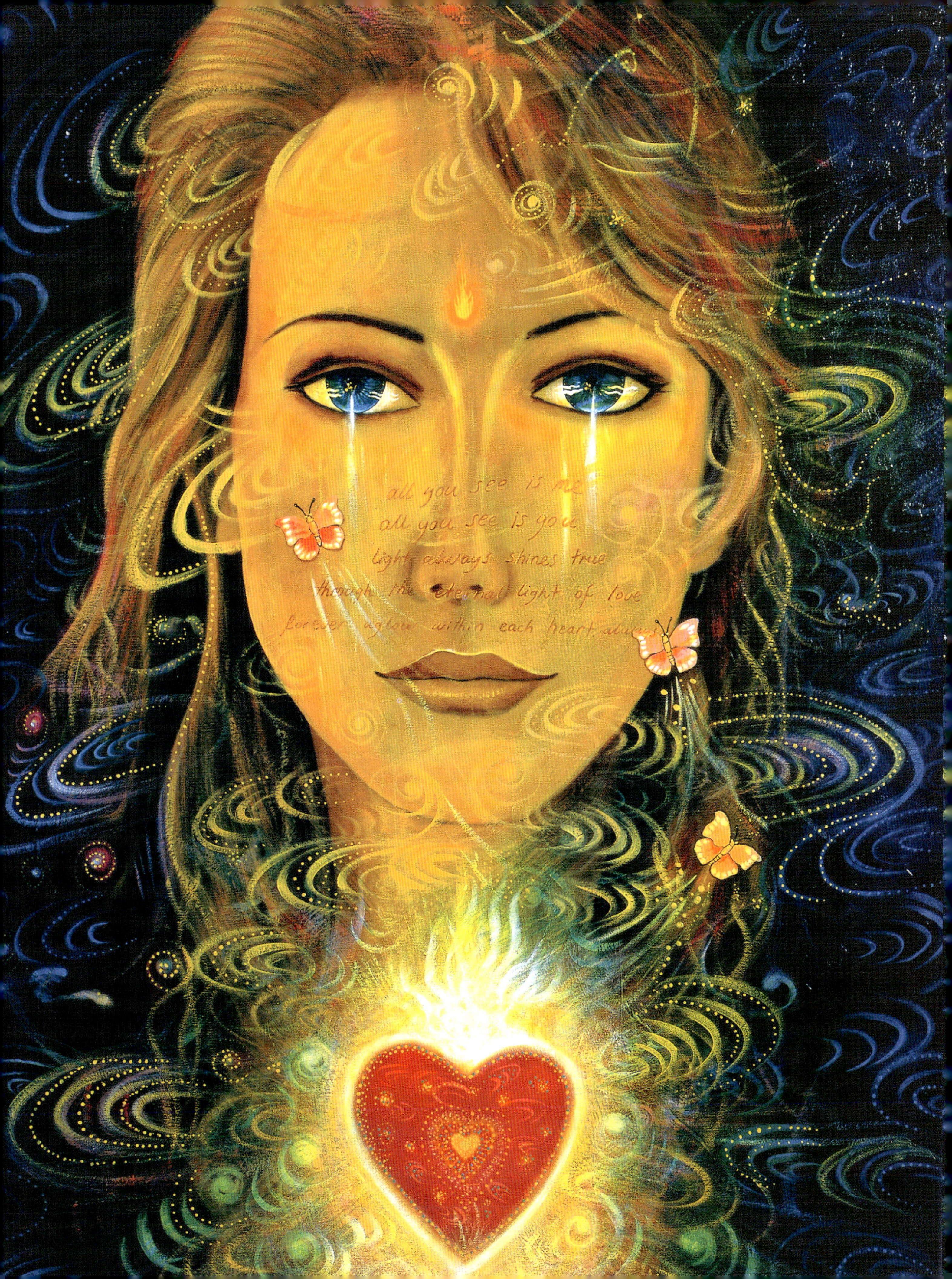
all you see is me
all you see is you
light always shines true
through the eternal light of love
forever aglow within each heart

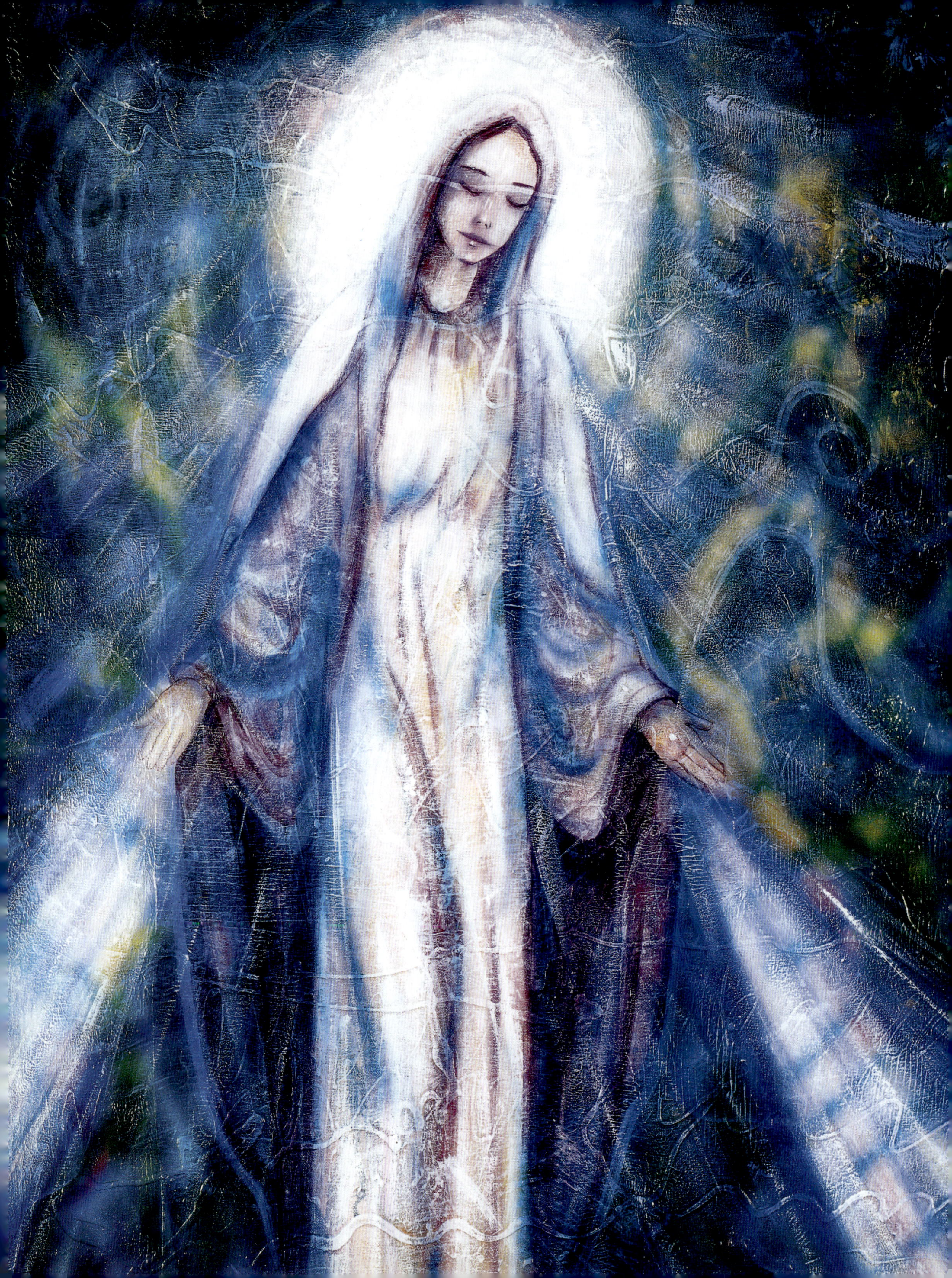

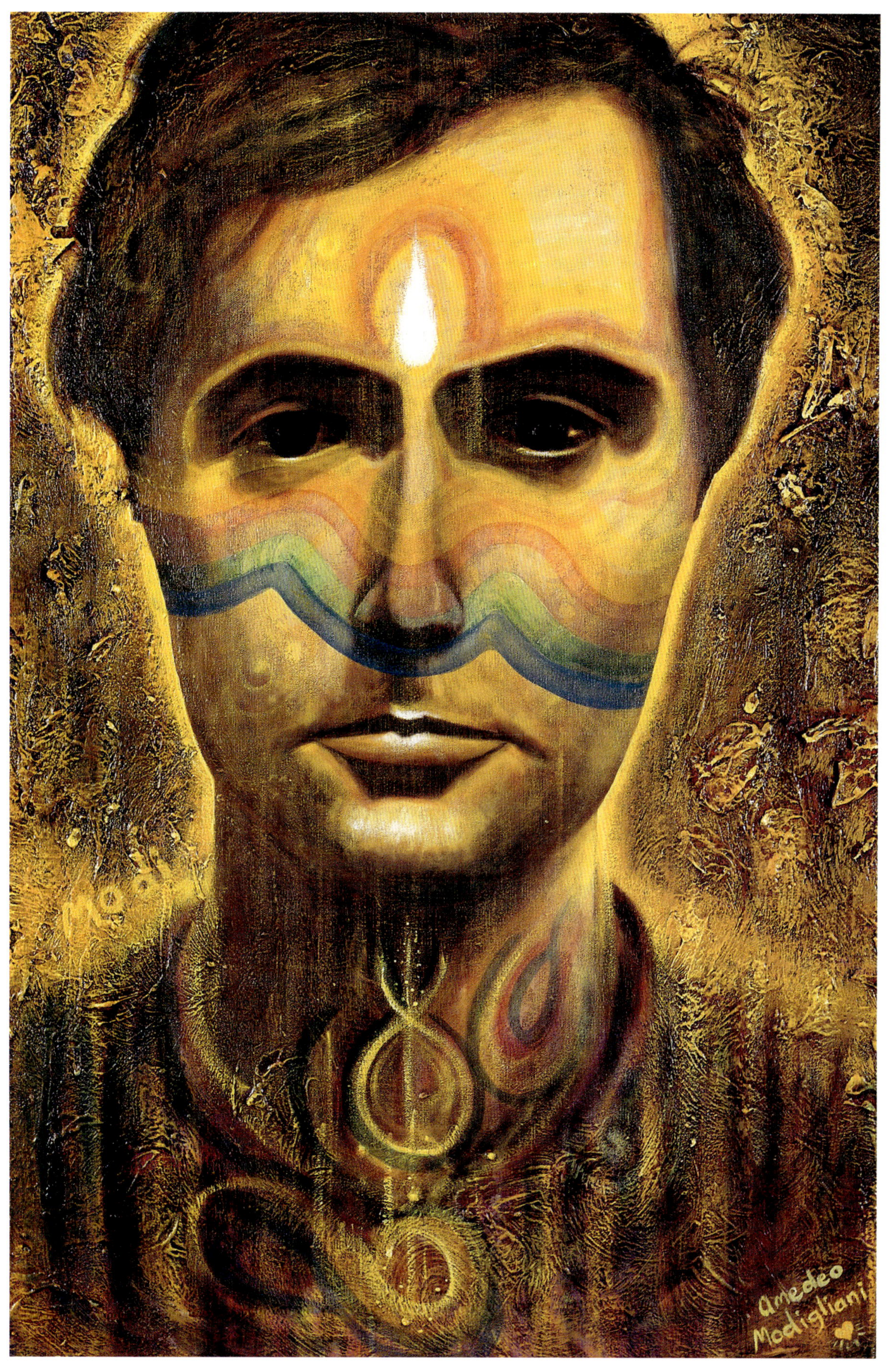

"Modi" Acrylic on canvas

Previous page: "Mother Of The Sacred Heart" Acrylic on canvas

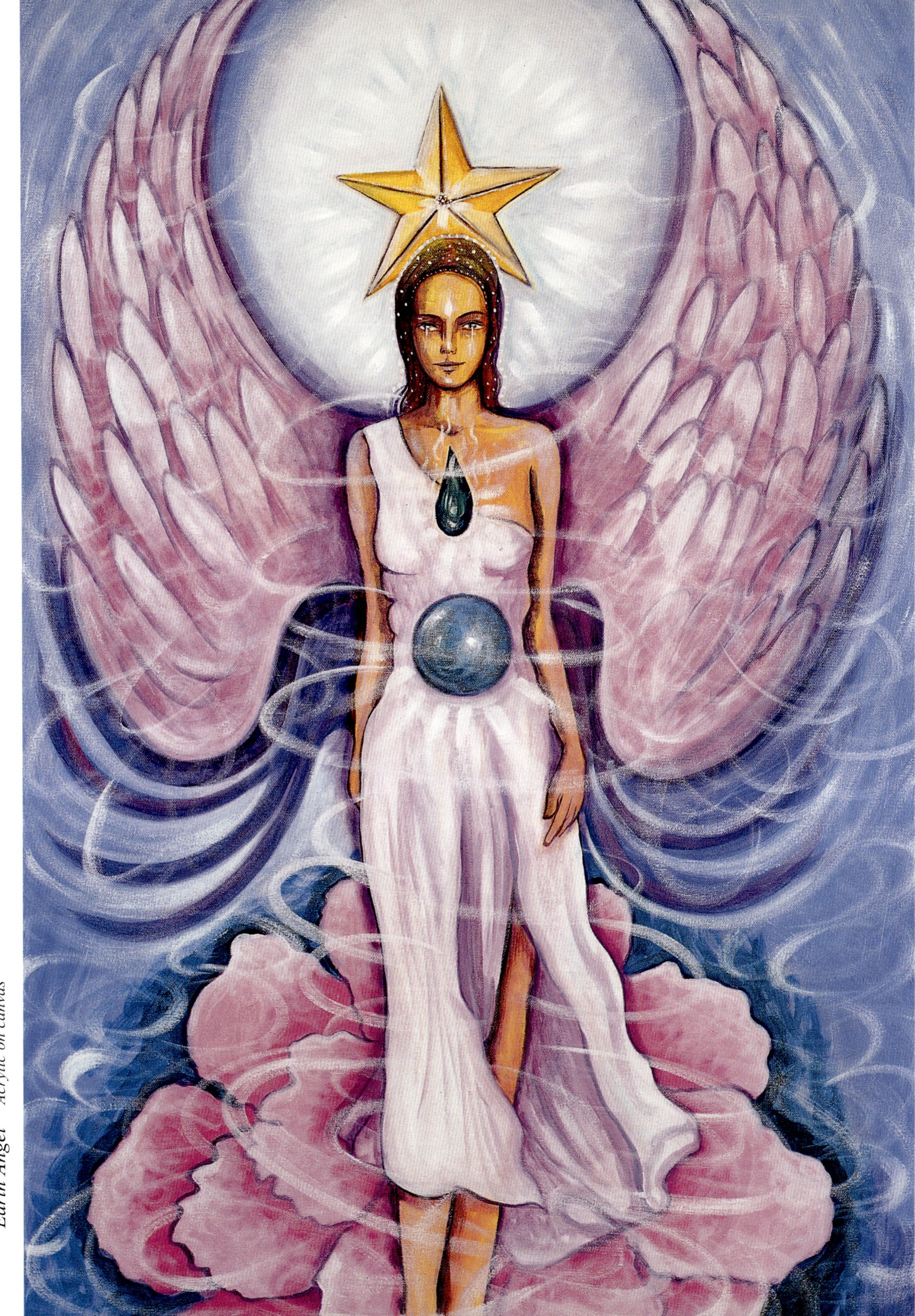

"Earth Angel" *Acrylic on canvas*

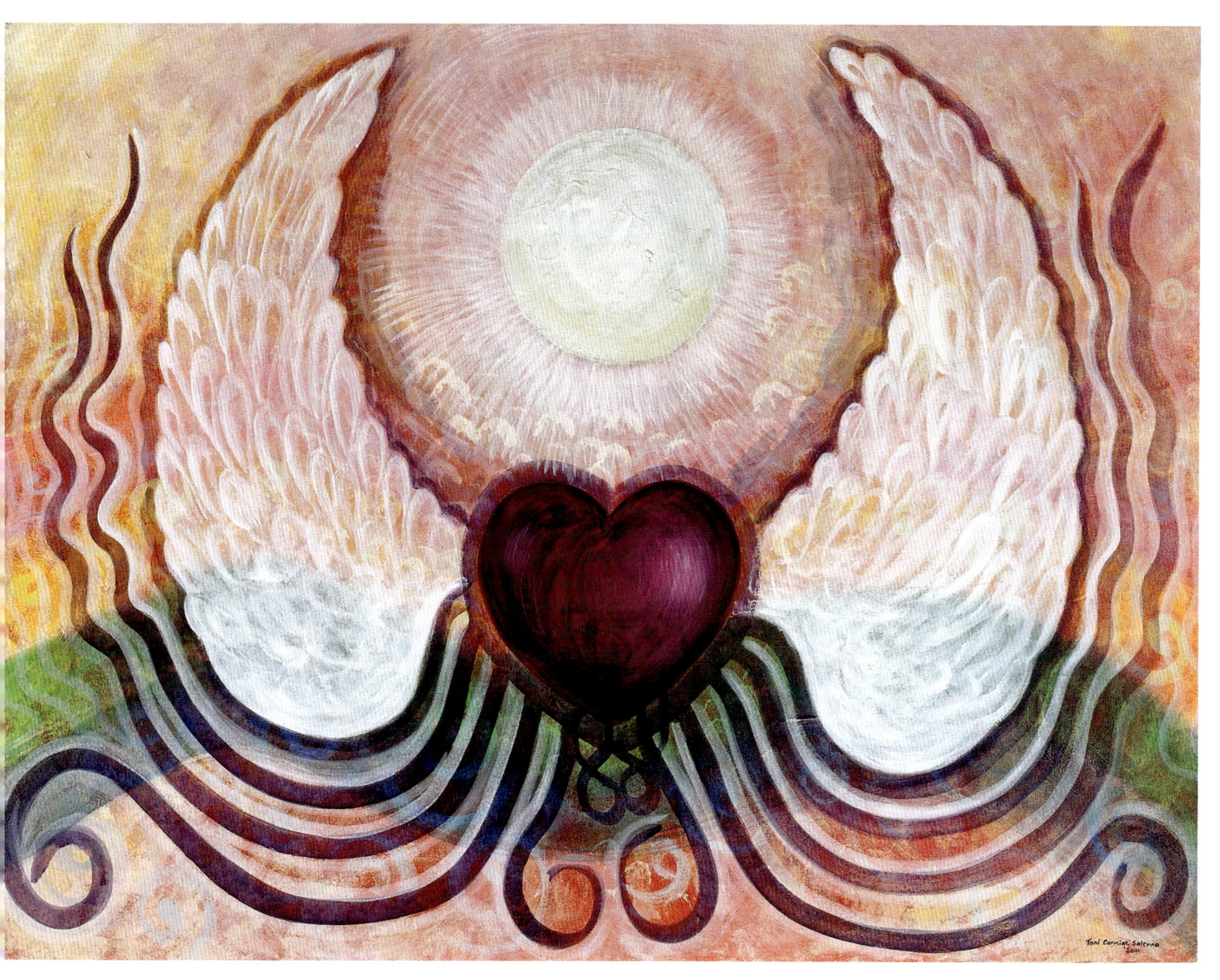

"Rainbow Wings" *Acrylic on canvas*
Next page: "Memory Of You" *Acrylic on canvas*

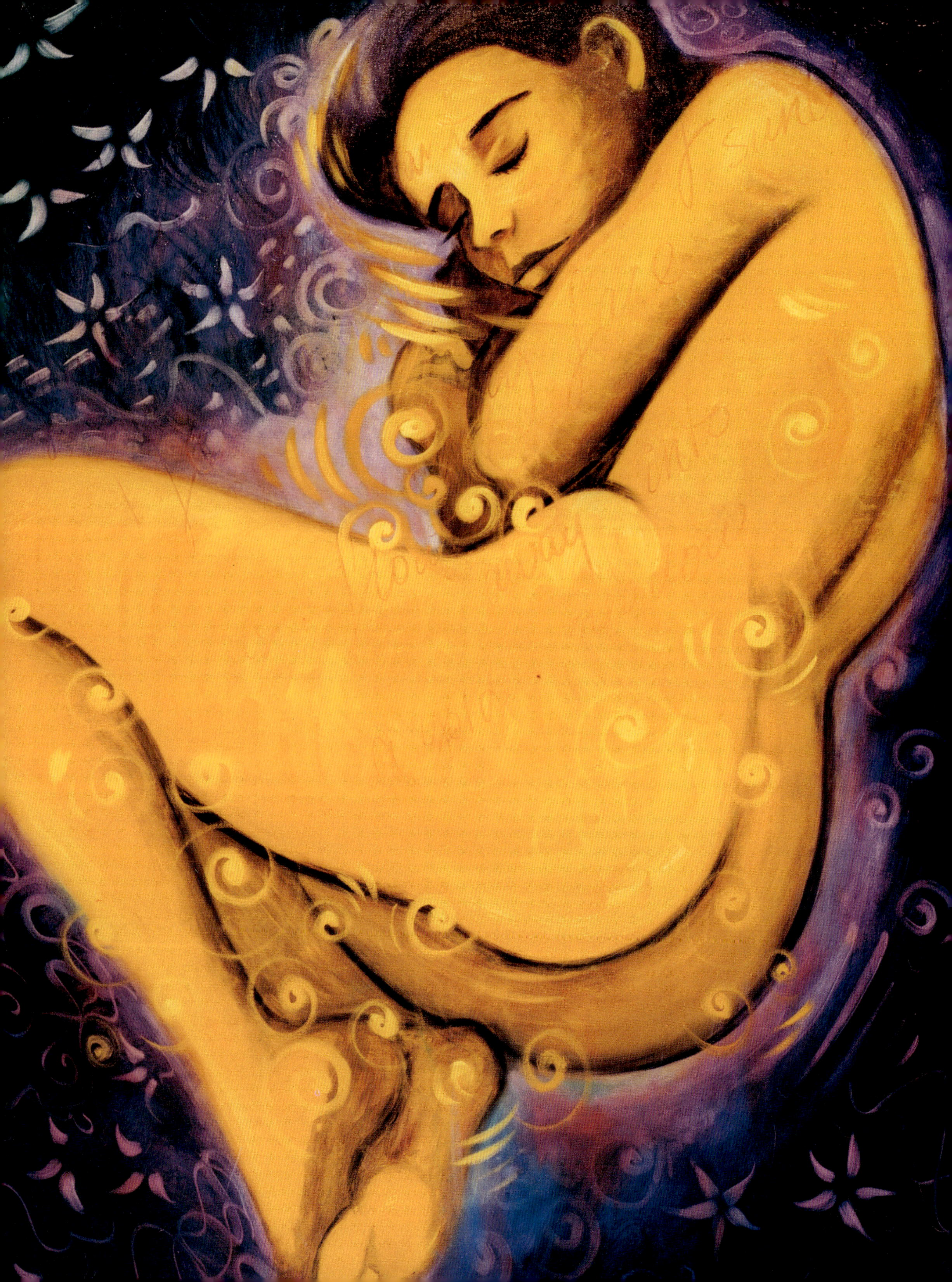

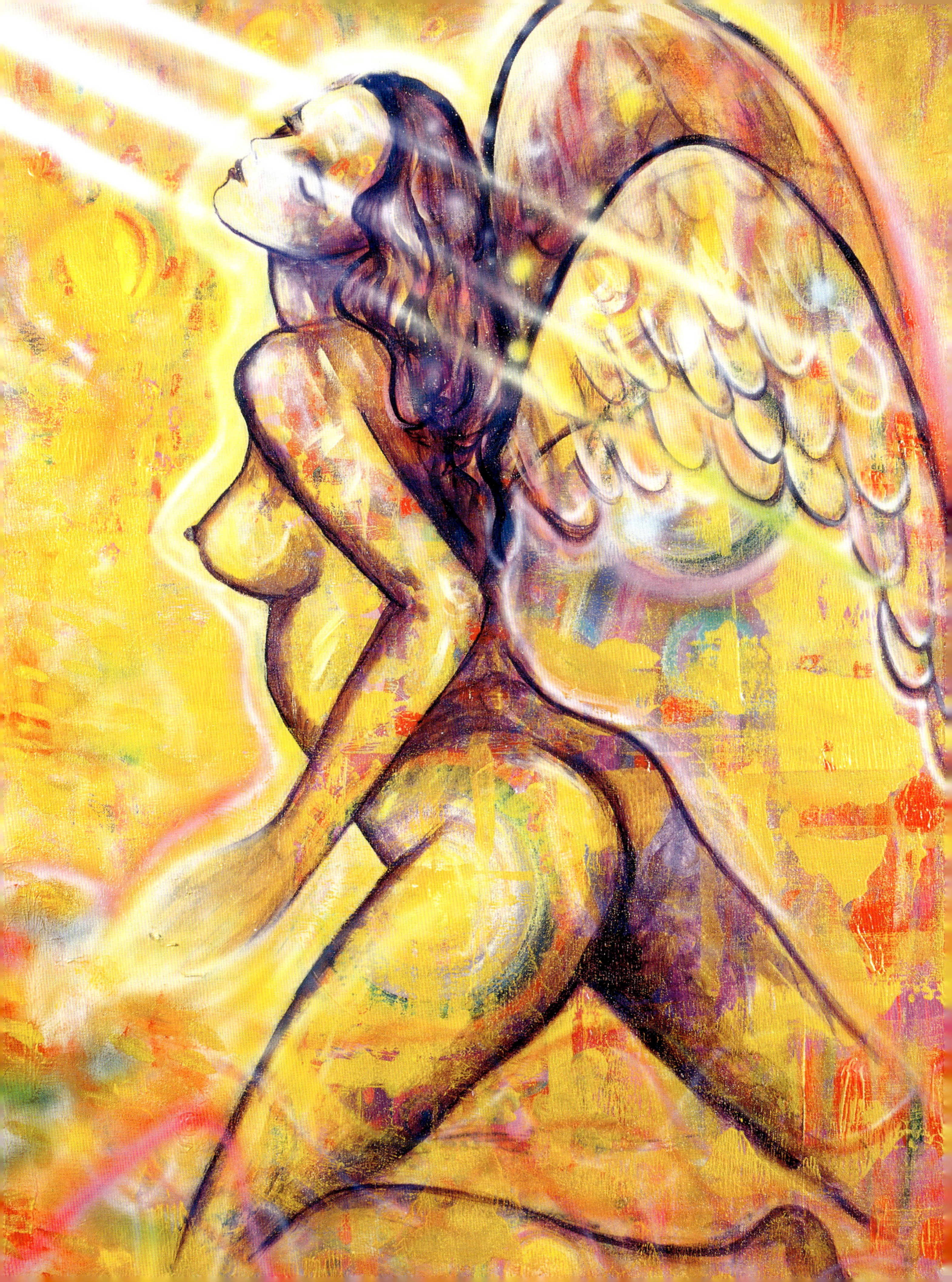

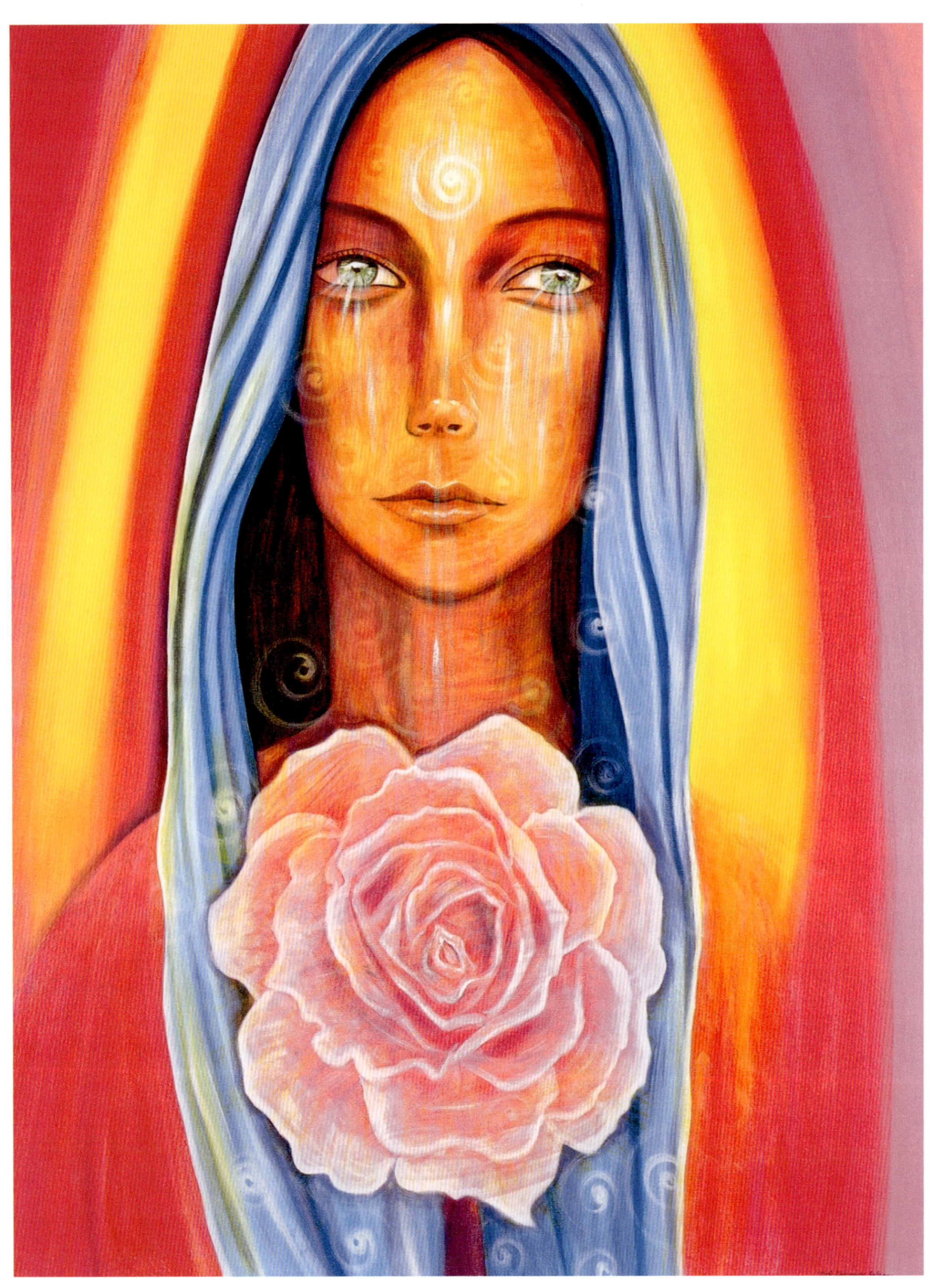

"Mary" Acrylic on canvas
Previous page: "From The Golden Ray" Acrylic on canvas
Next page: "I Am" Oil on canvas

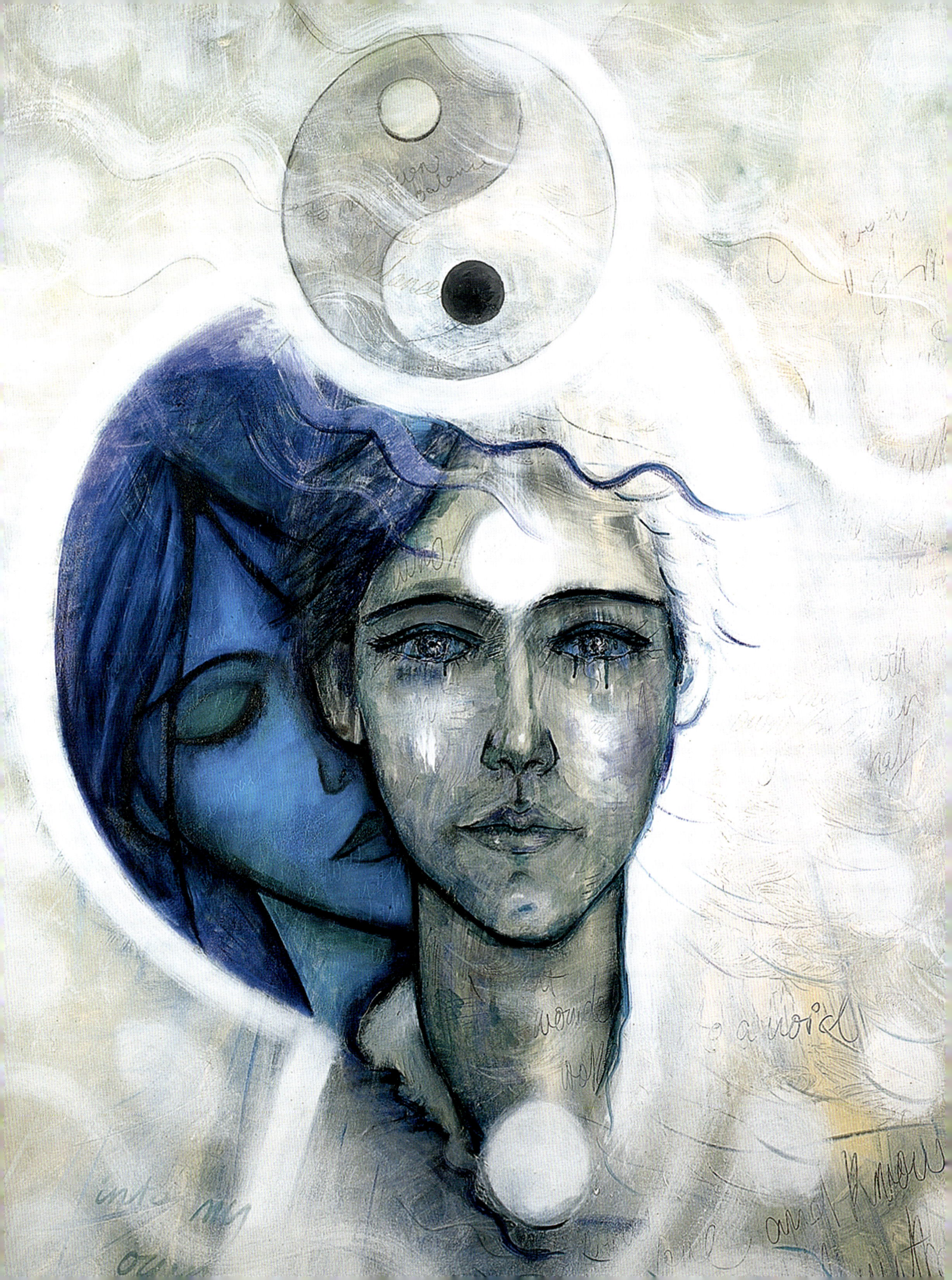
a void
and know

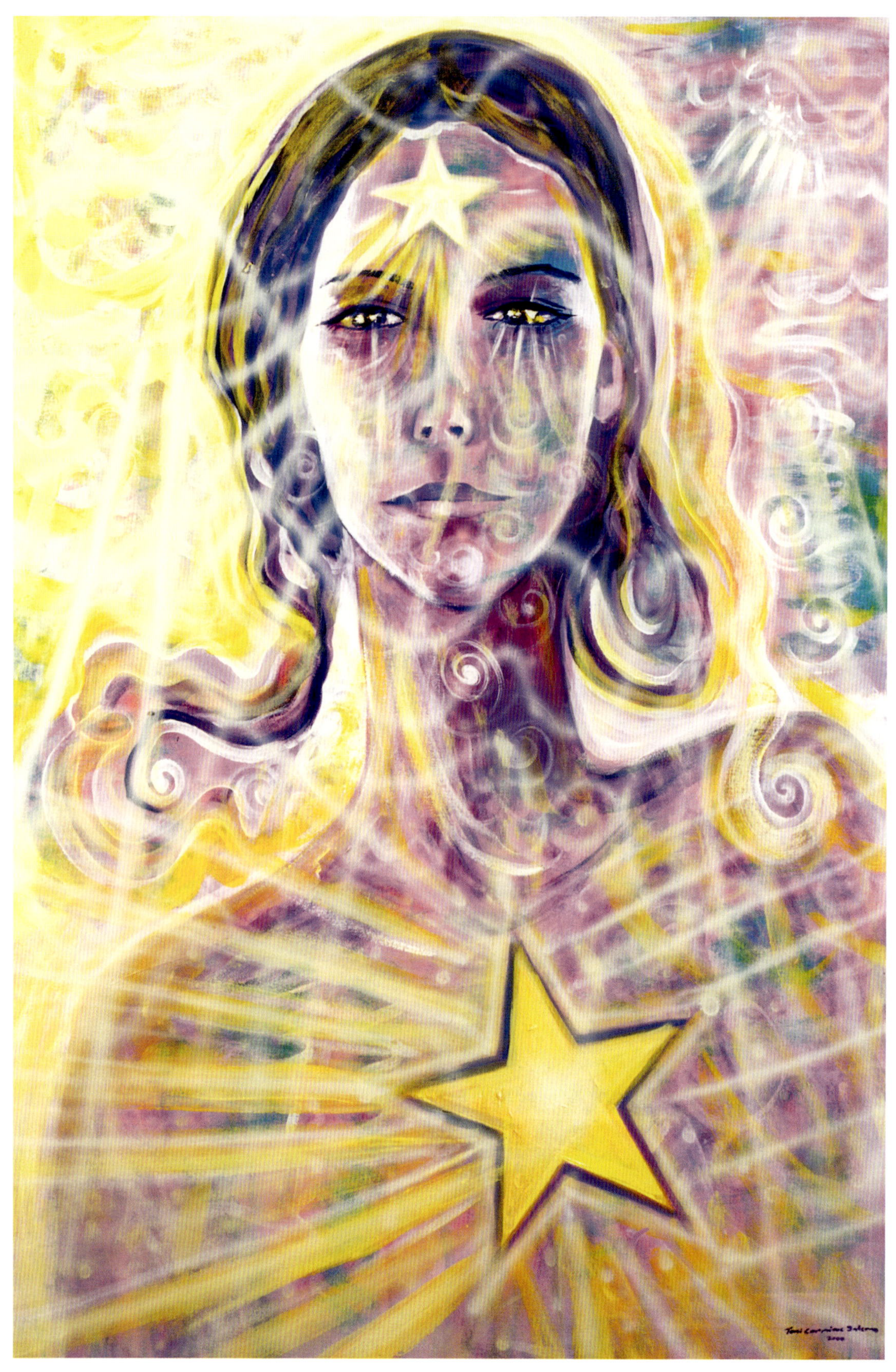

"Healing" *Acrylic on canvas*
Next page: "Just Imagine" *Acrylic on canvas*

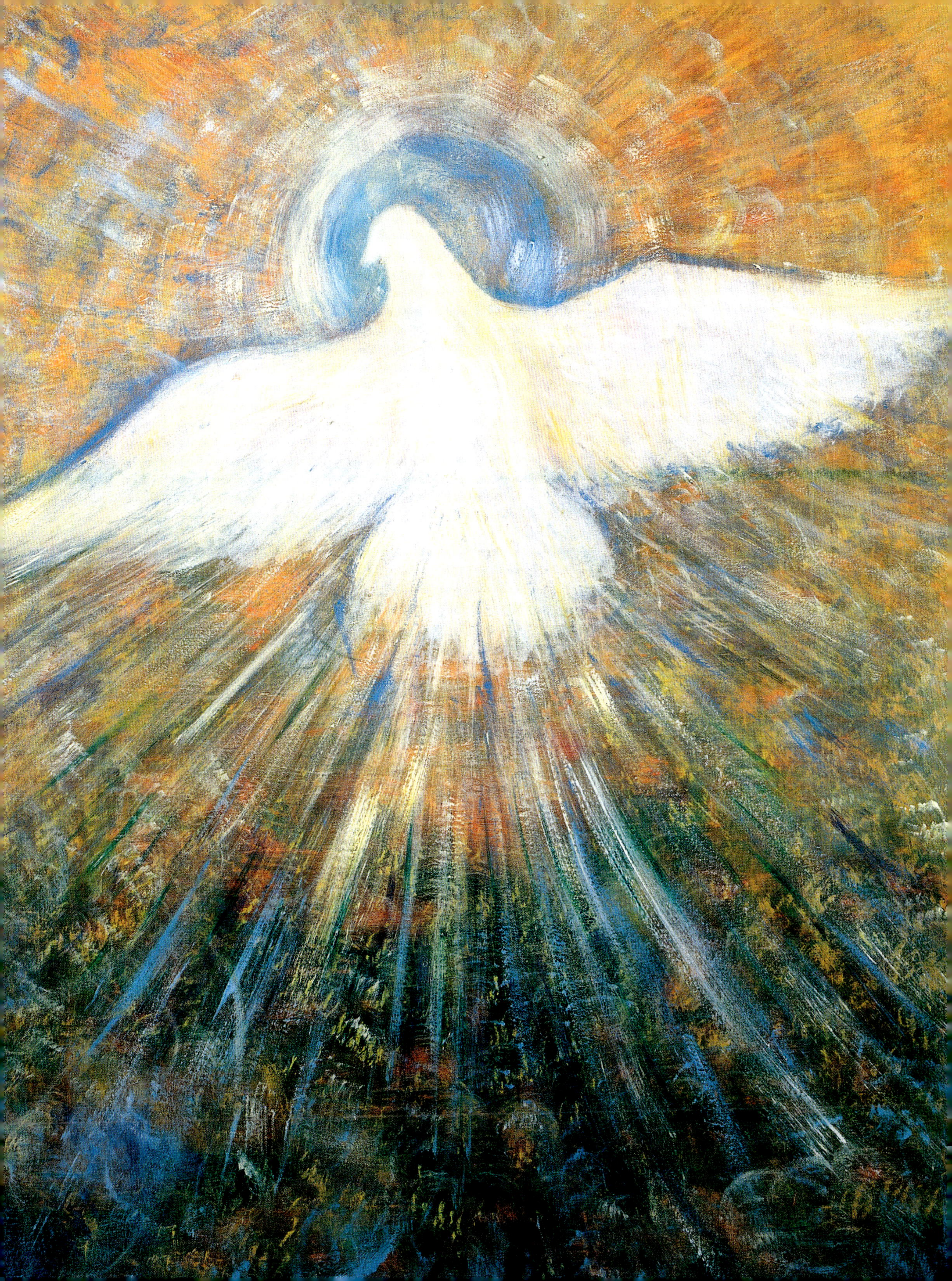

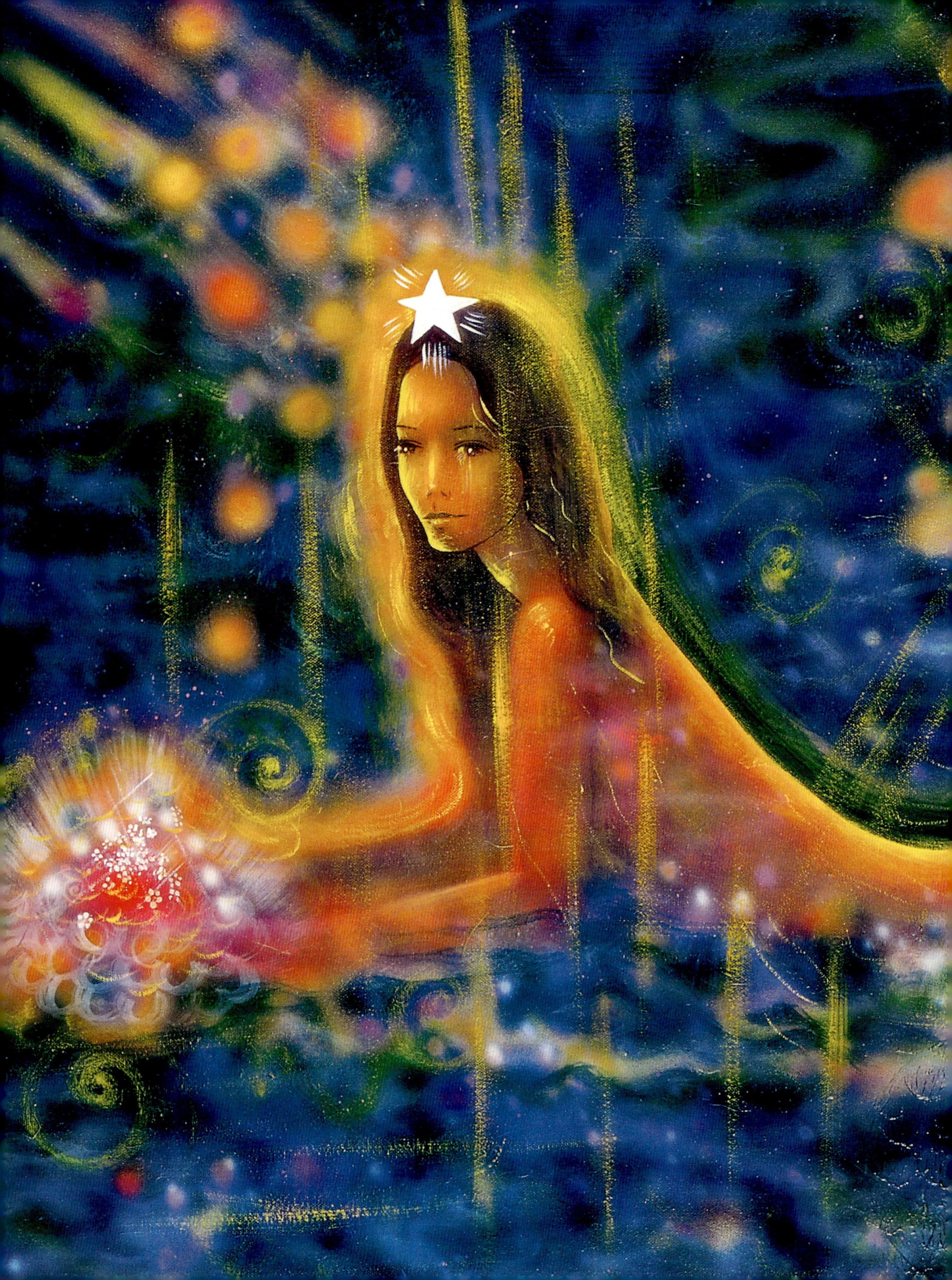

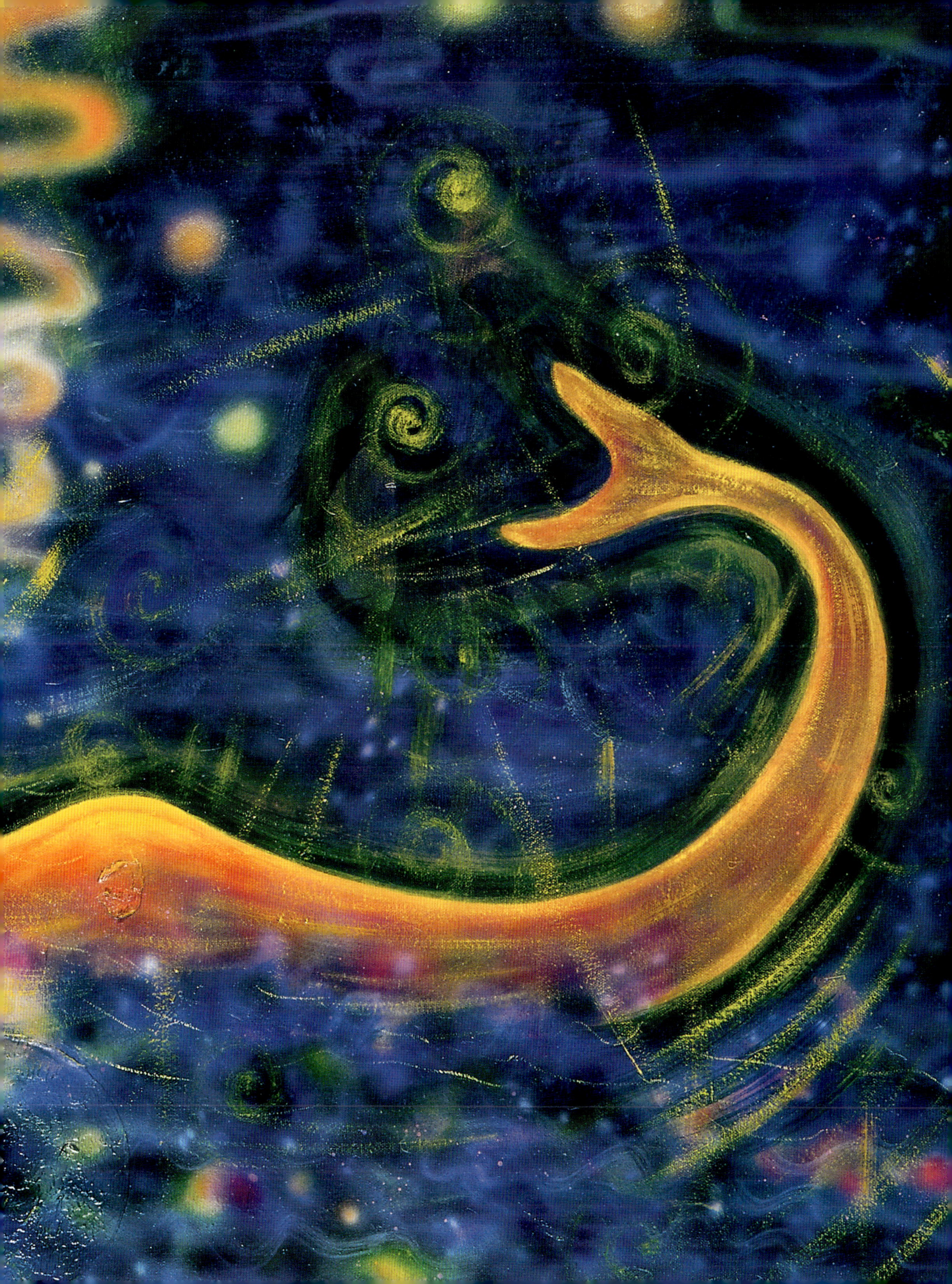

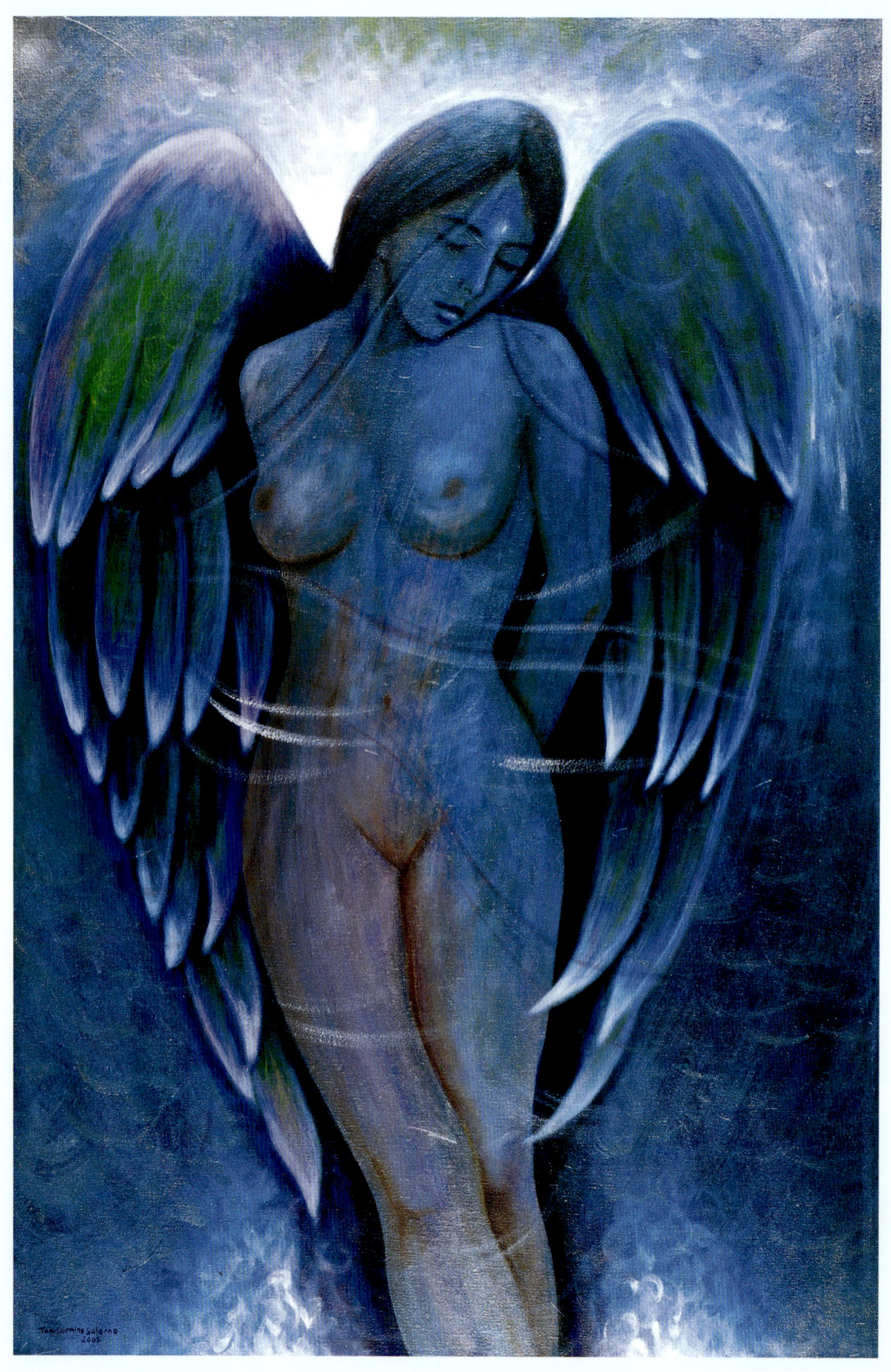

"Italia" Acrylic on canvas
Previous page: "Oceana" Acrylic on canvas

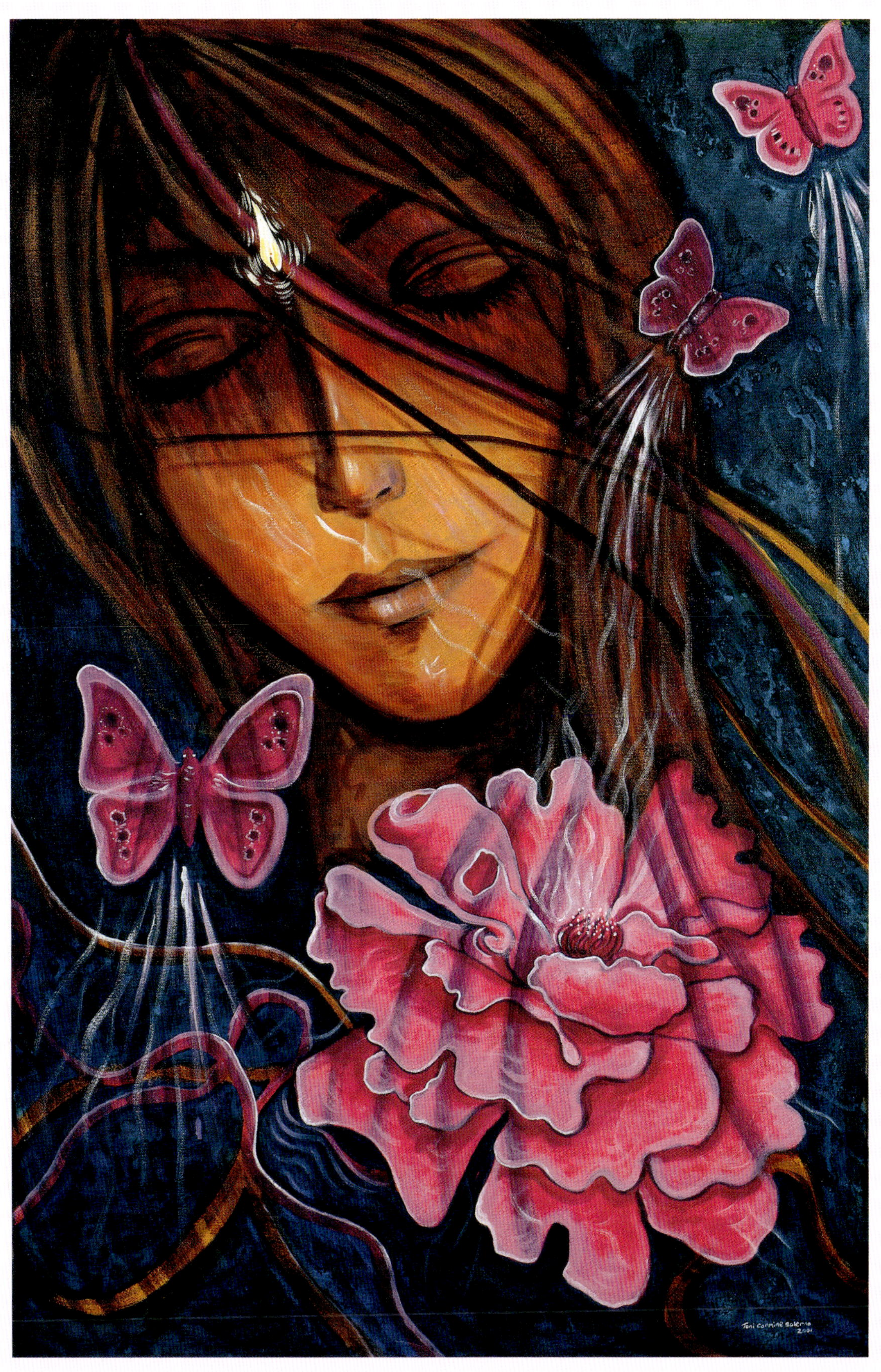

"Love" *Acrylic on canvas*
Next page: "Mother Earth" Acrylic on canvas

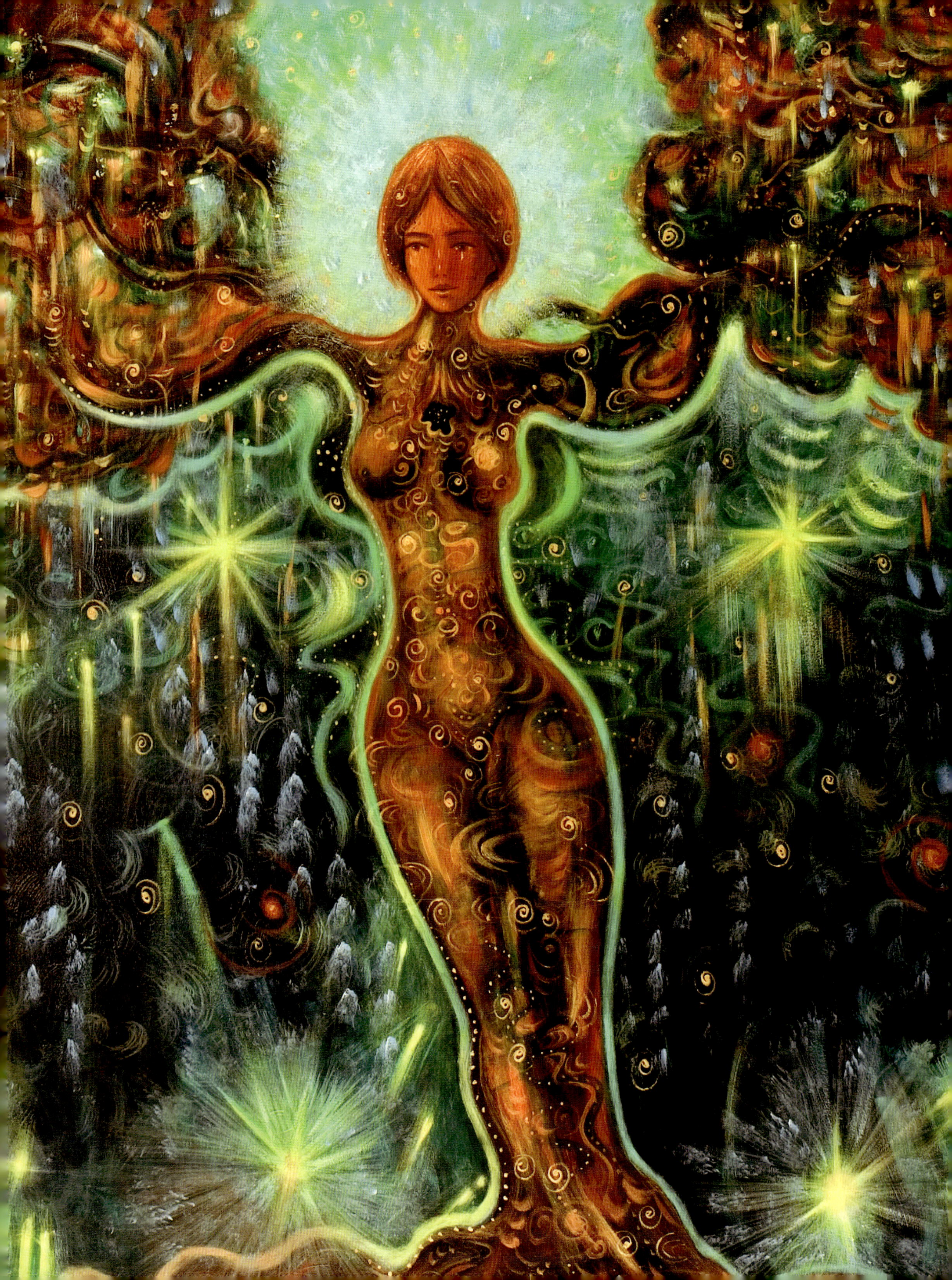

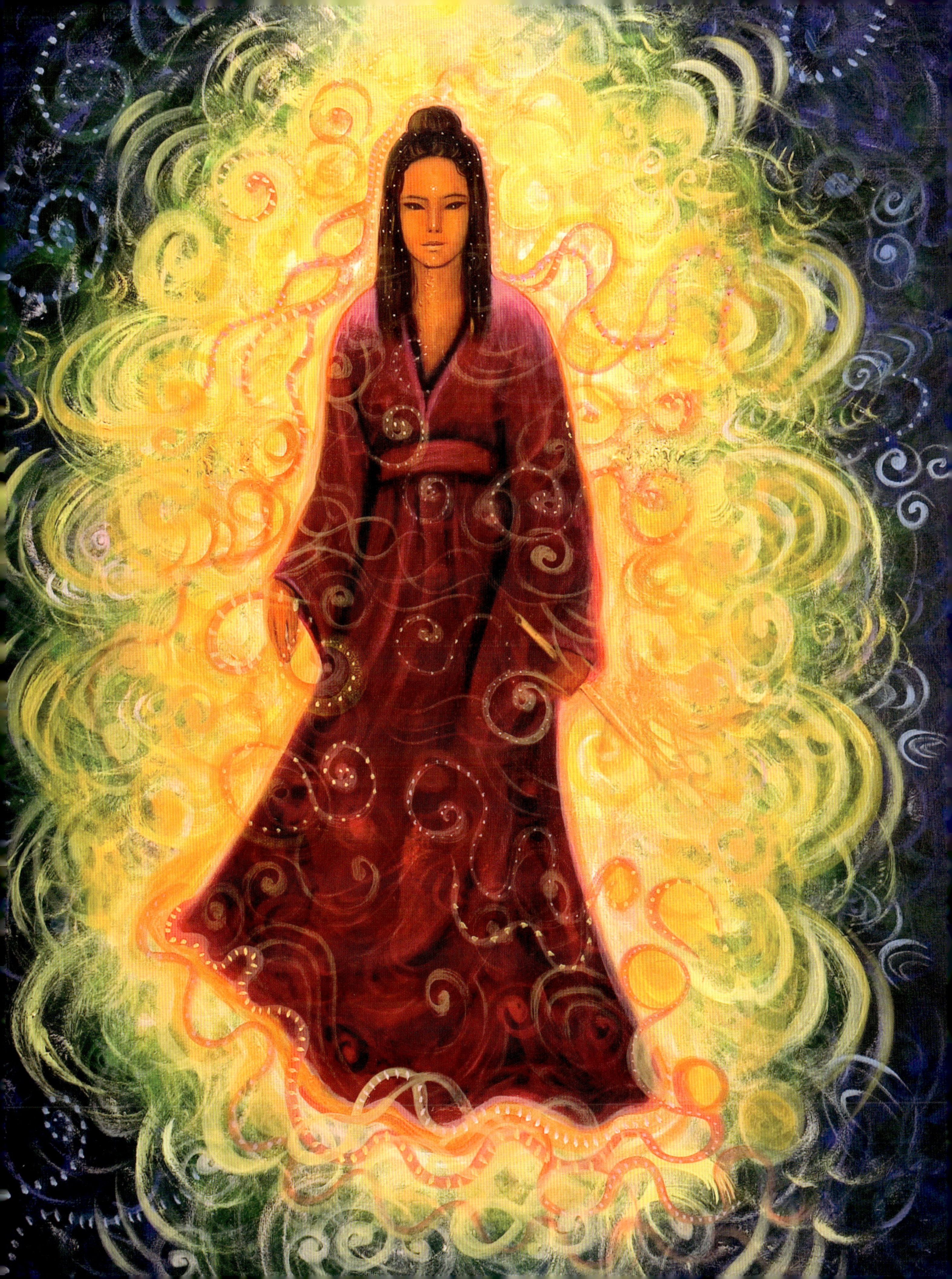

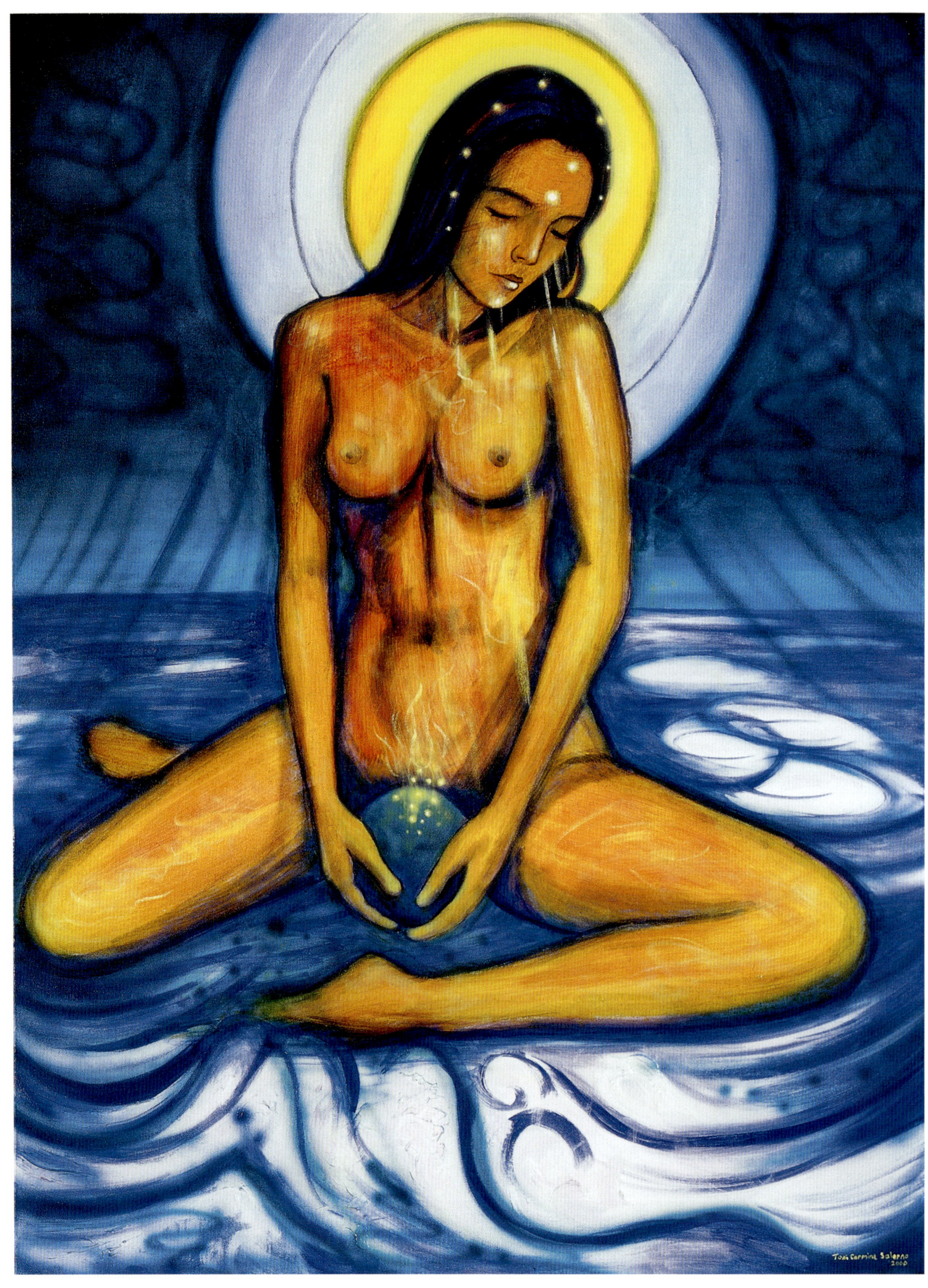

"Healing Sounds" *Acrylic on canvas*
Previous page: *"Kuan Yin: Protection"* *Acrylic on canvas*

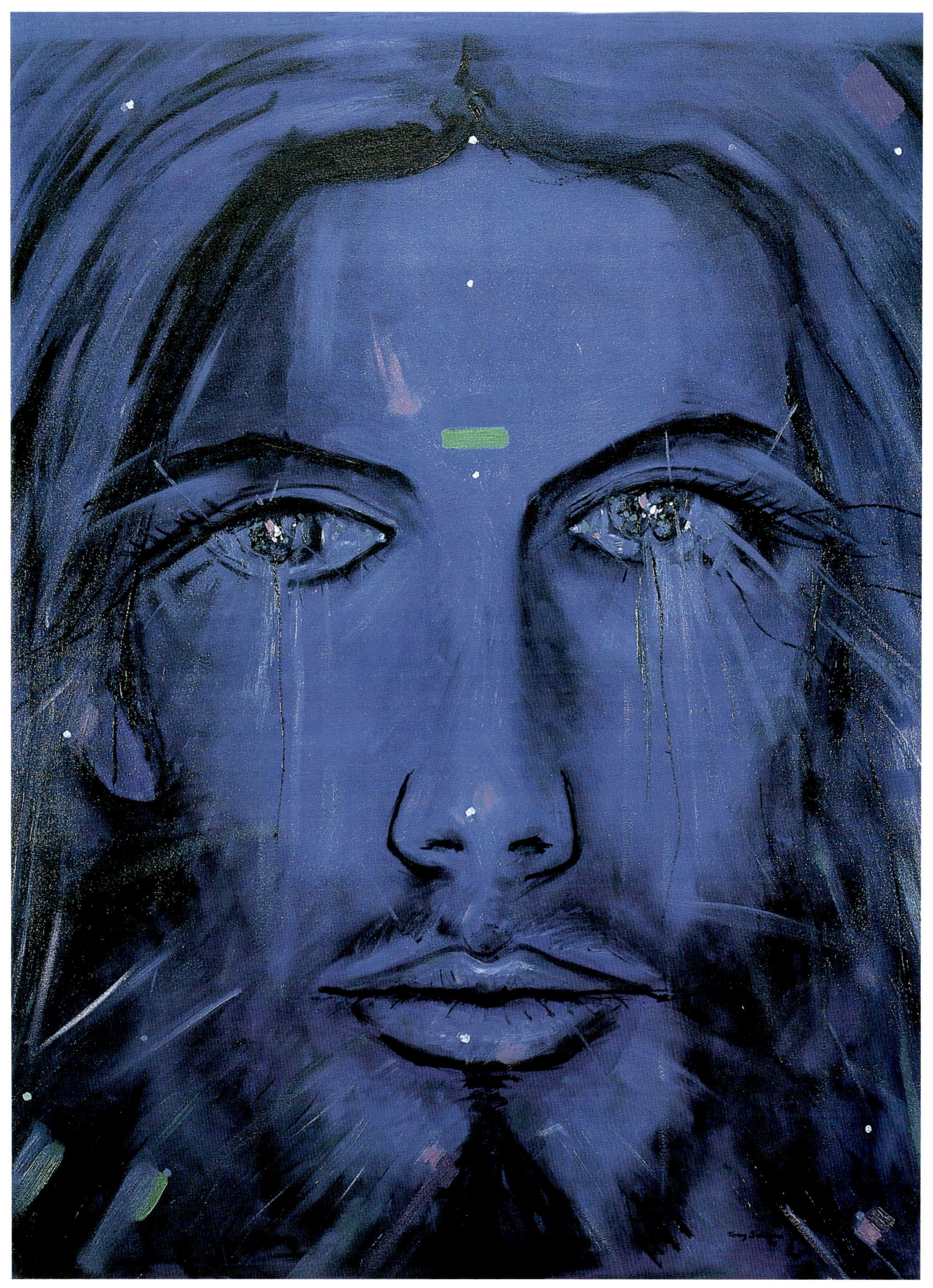

"Universal Christ" Oil on canvas

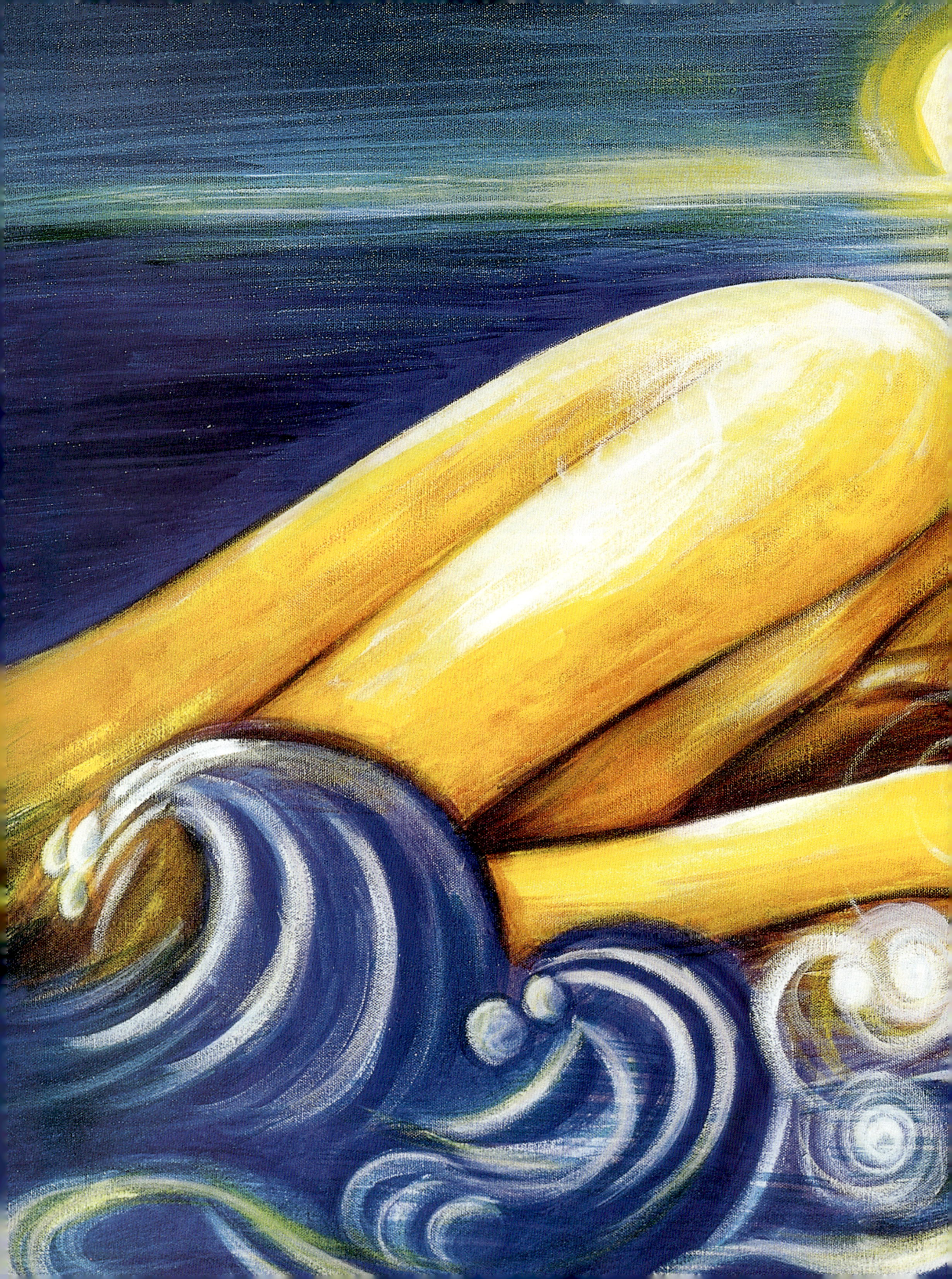

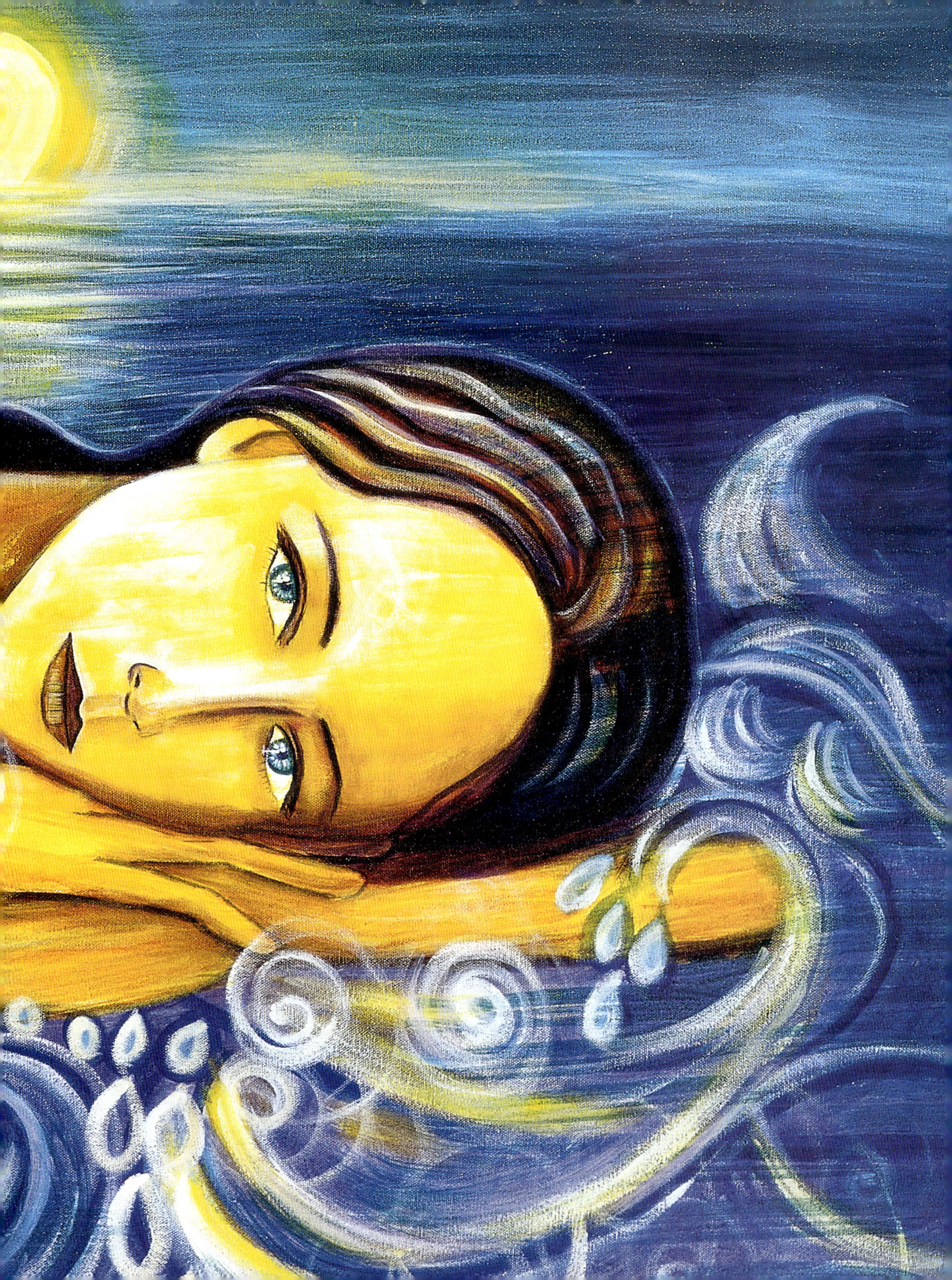

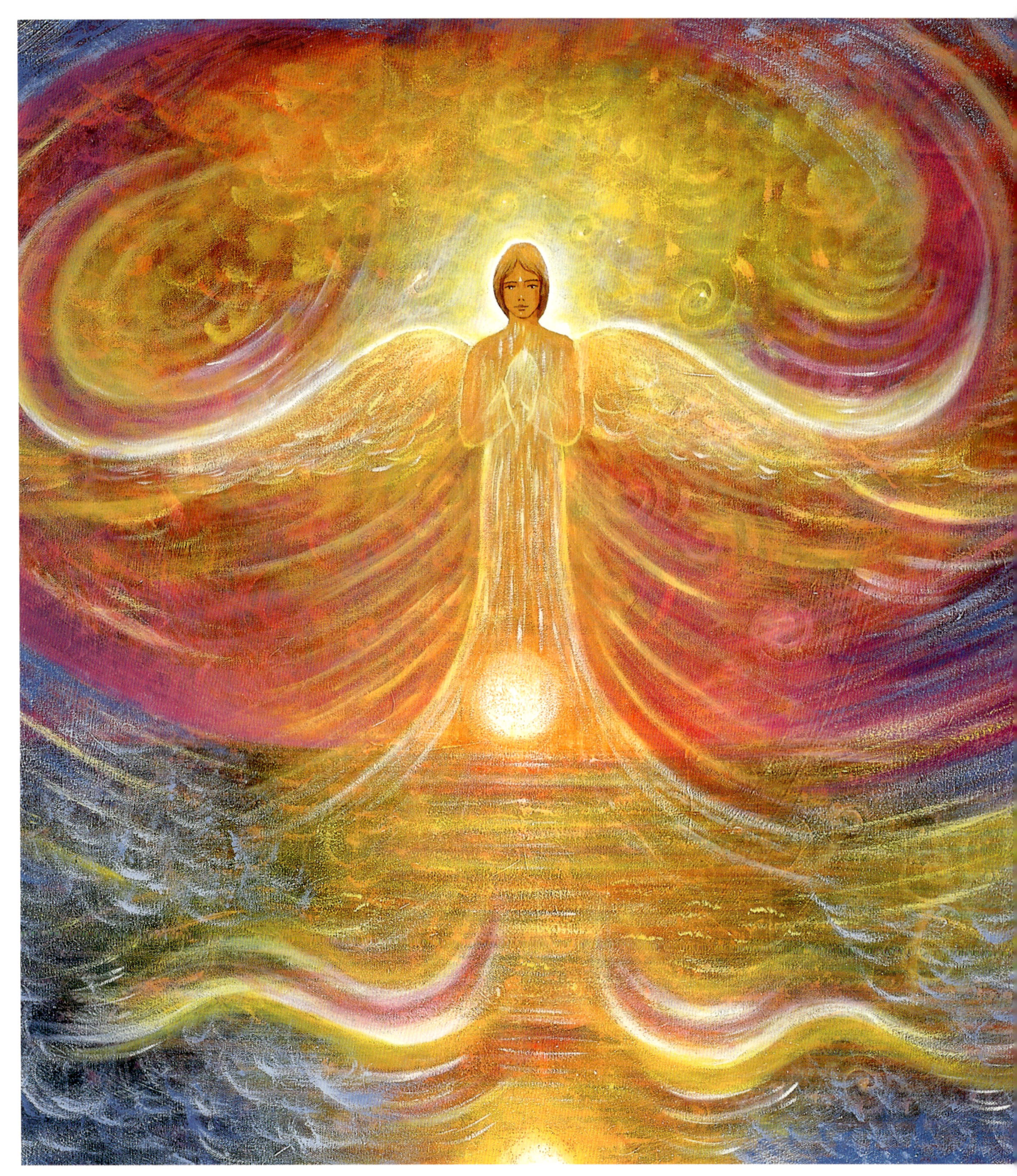

"Guardian Angel" *Acrylic on canvas*
Previous page: "Lumerian Dream" *Acrylic on canvas*

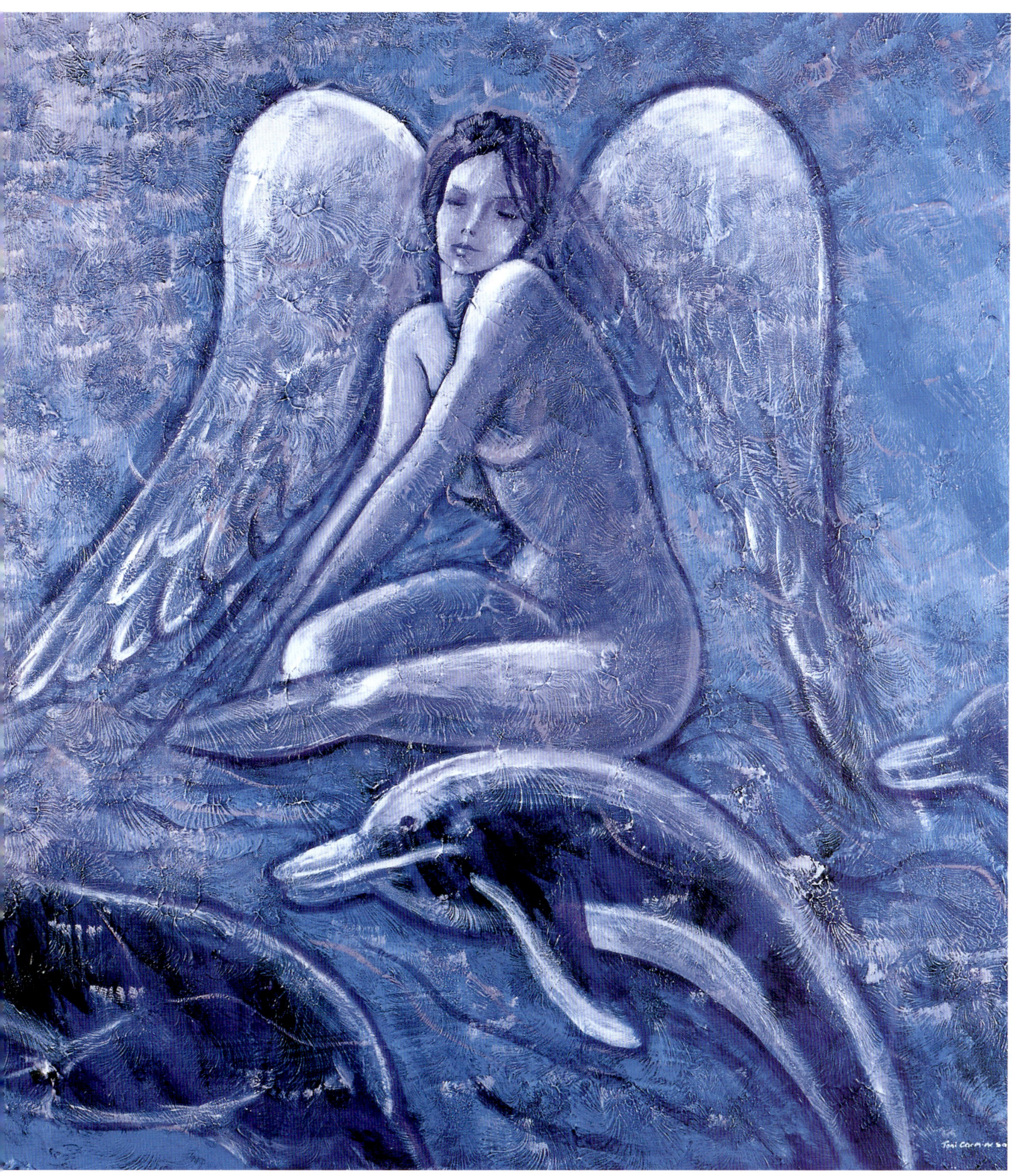

"Upon The Ocean Breeze" *Acrylic on canvas*

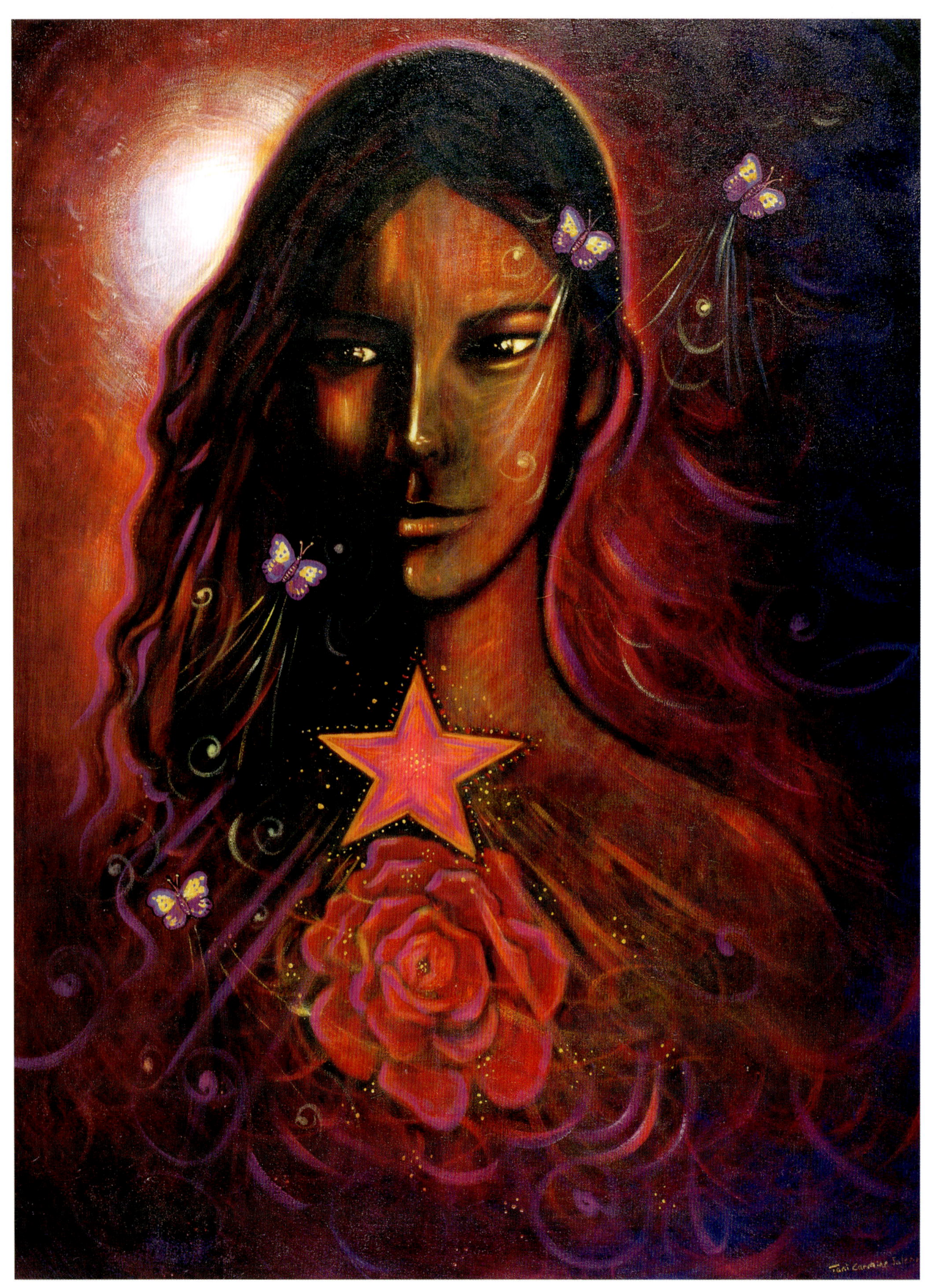

"Crimson Glow" Acrylic on canvas
Next page: "Tantric Union 2" Acrylic on canvas

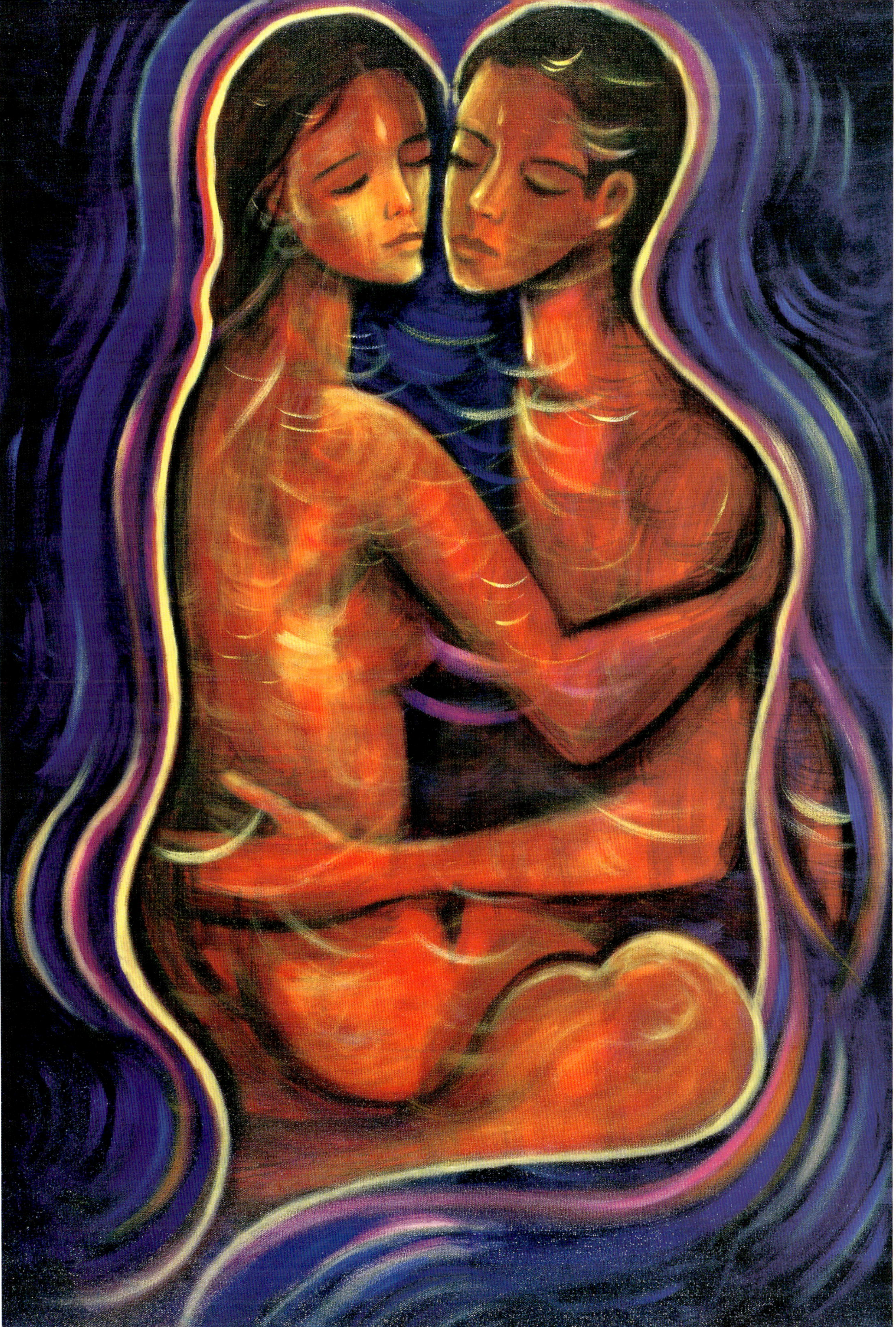

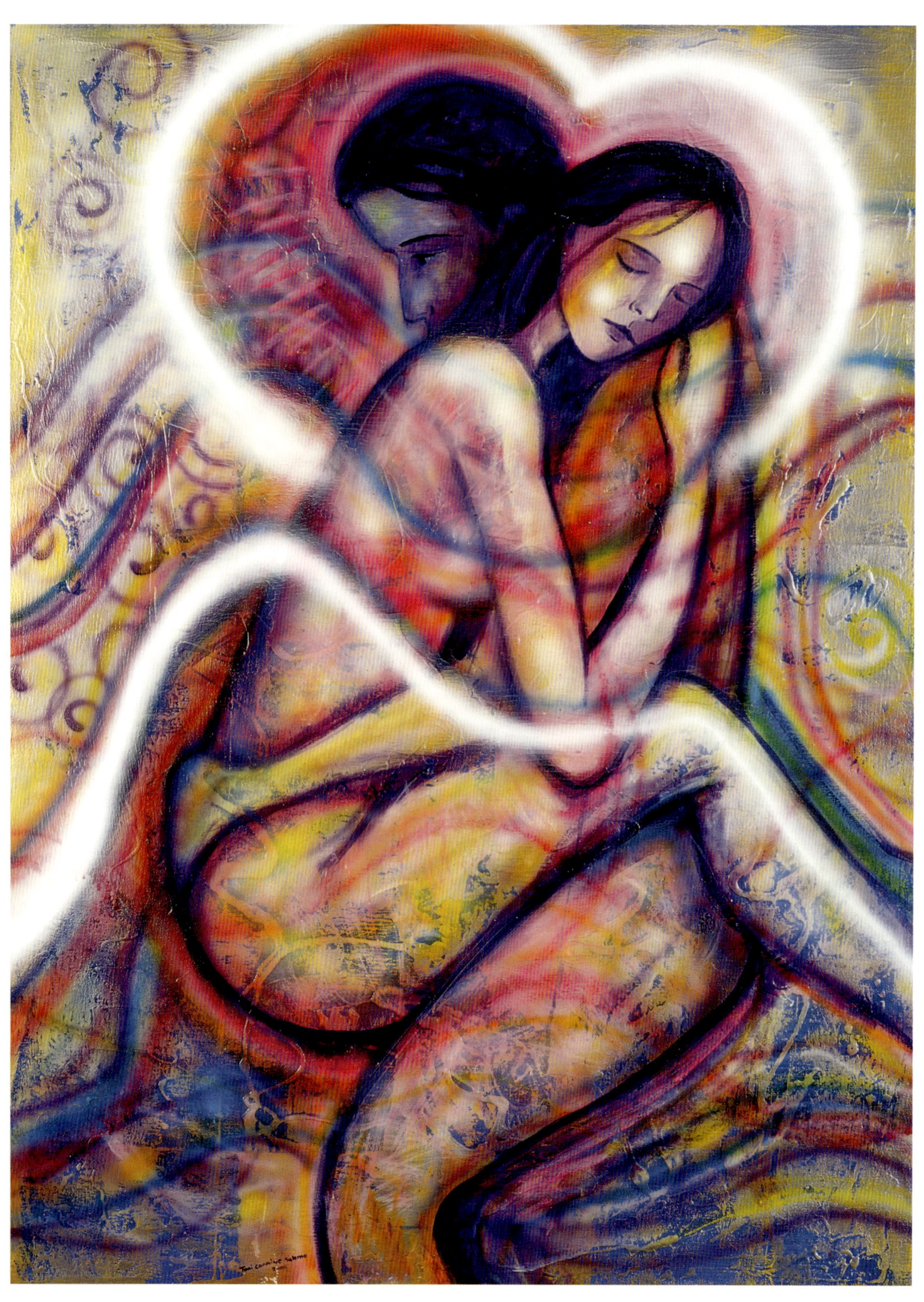

"Twin Flame" *Acrylic on canvas*
Next page: "Transience" Acrylic on canvas

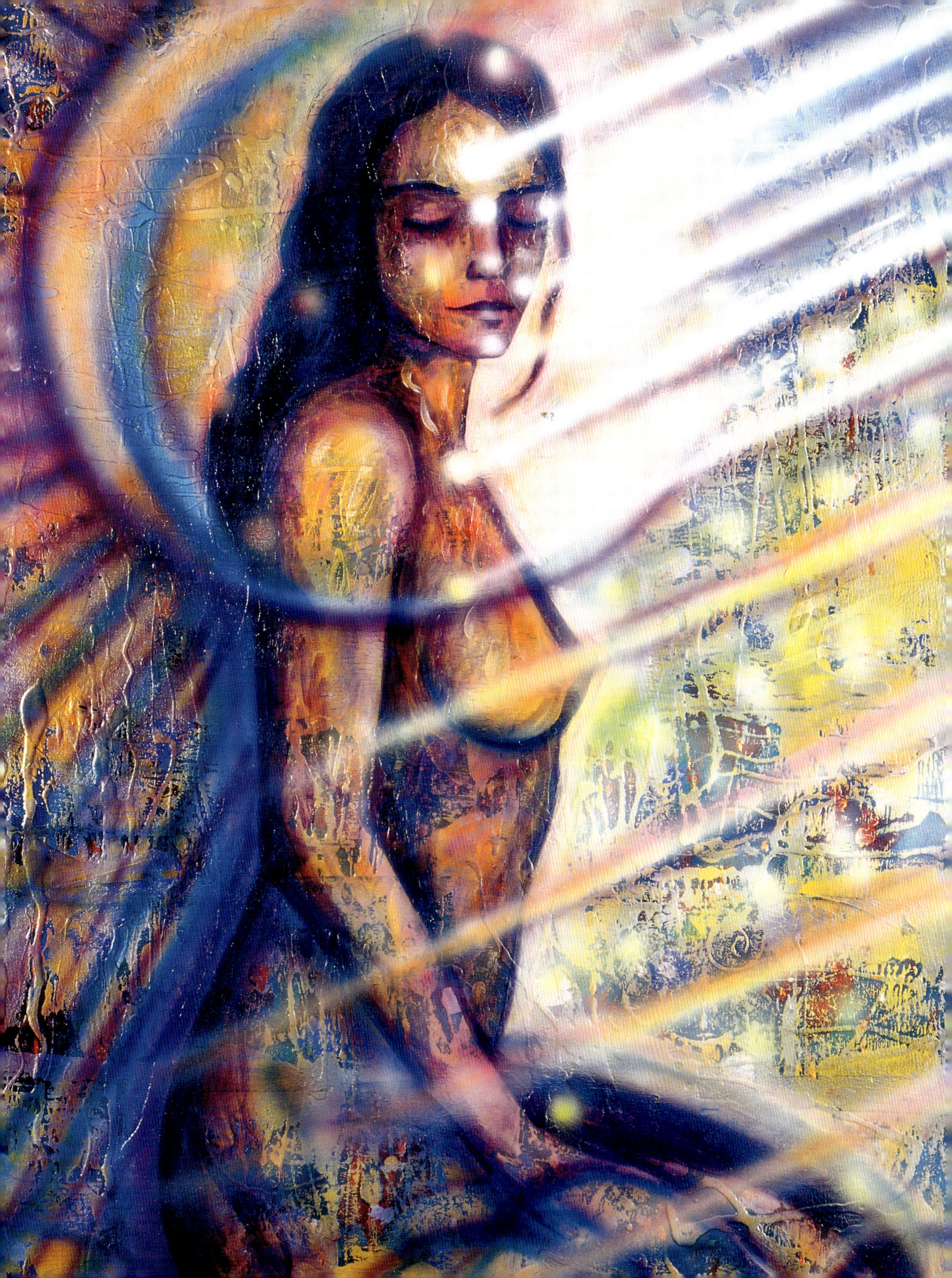

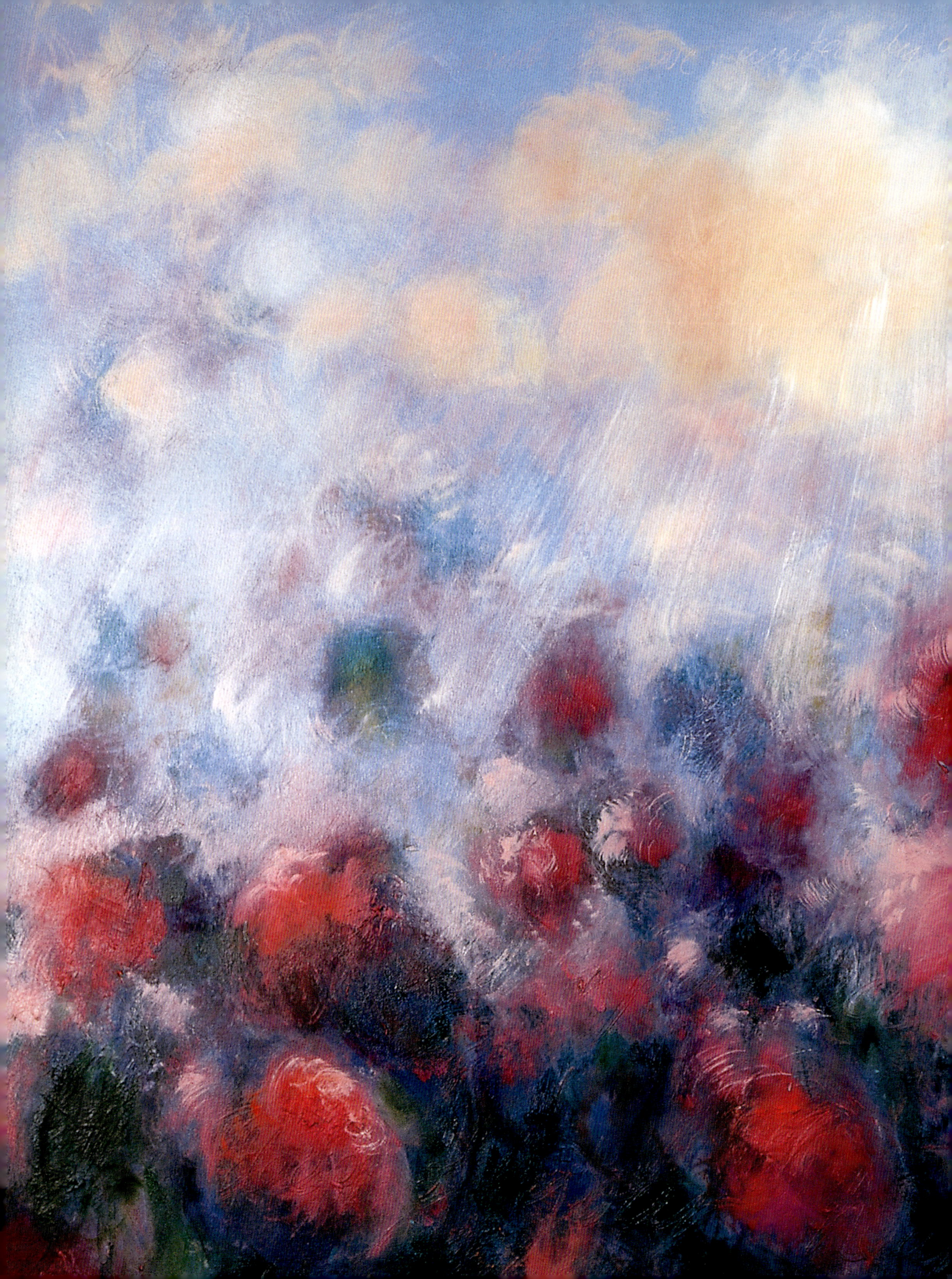

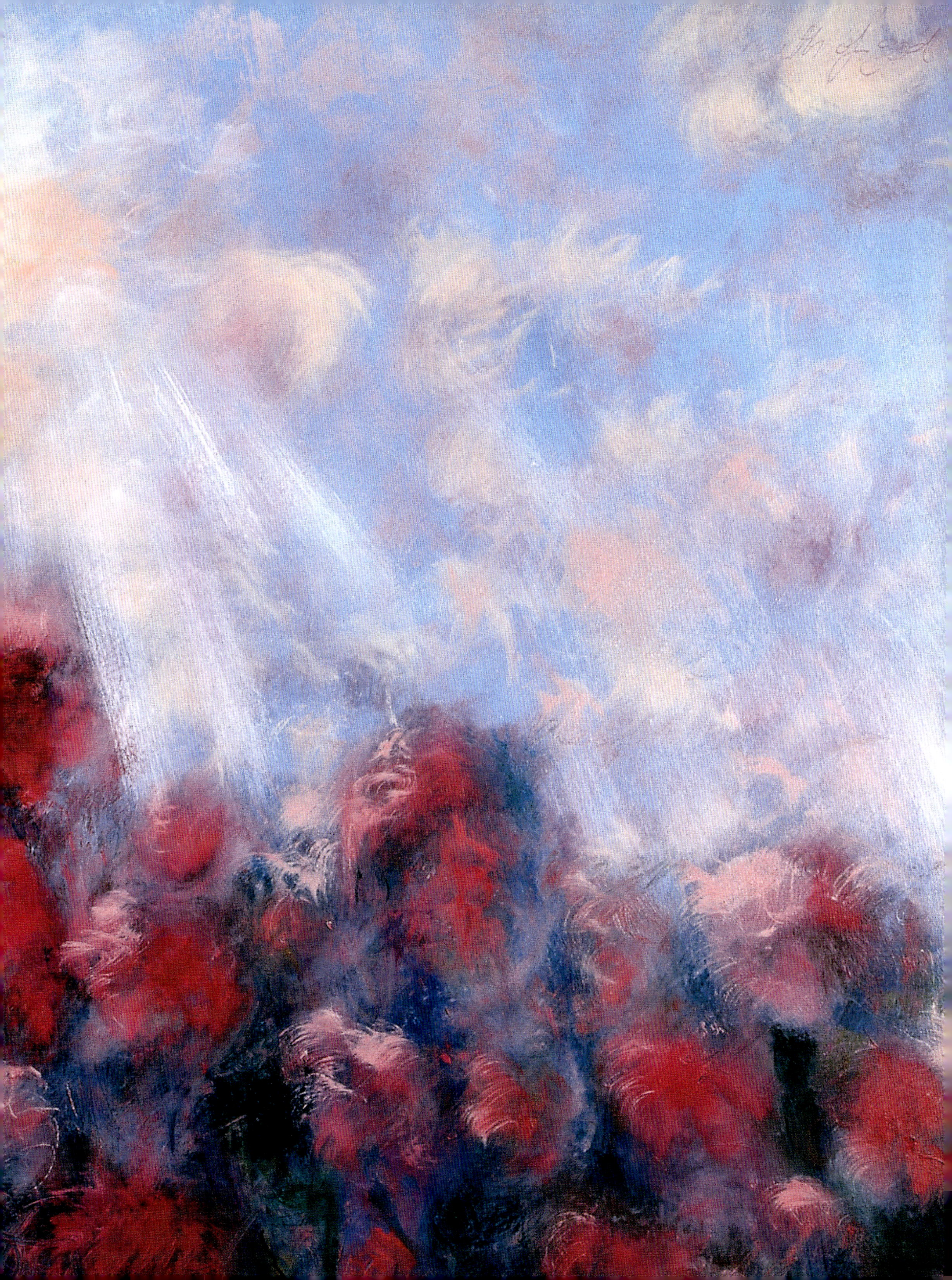

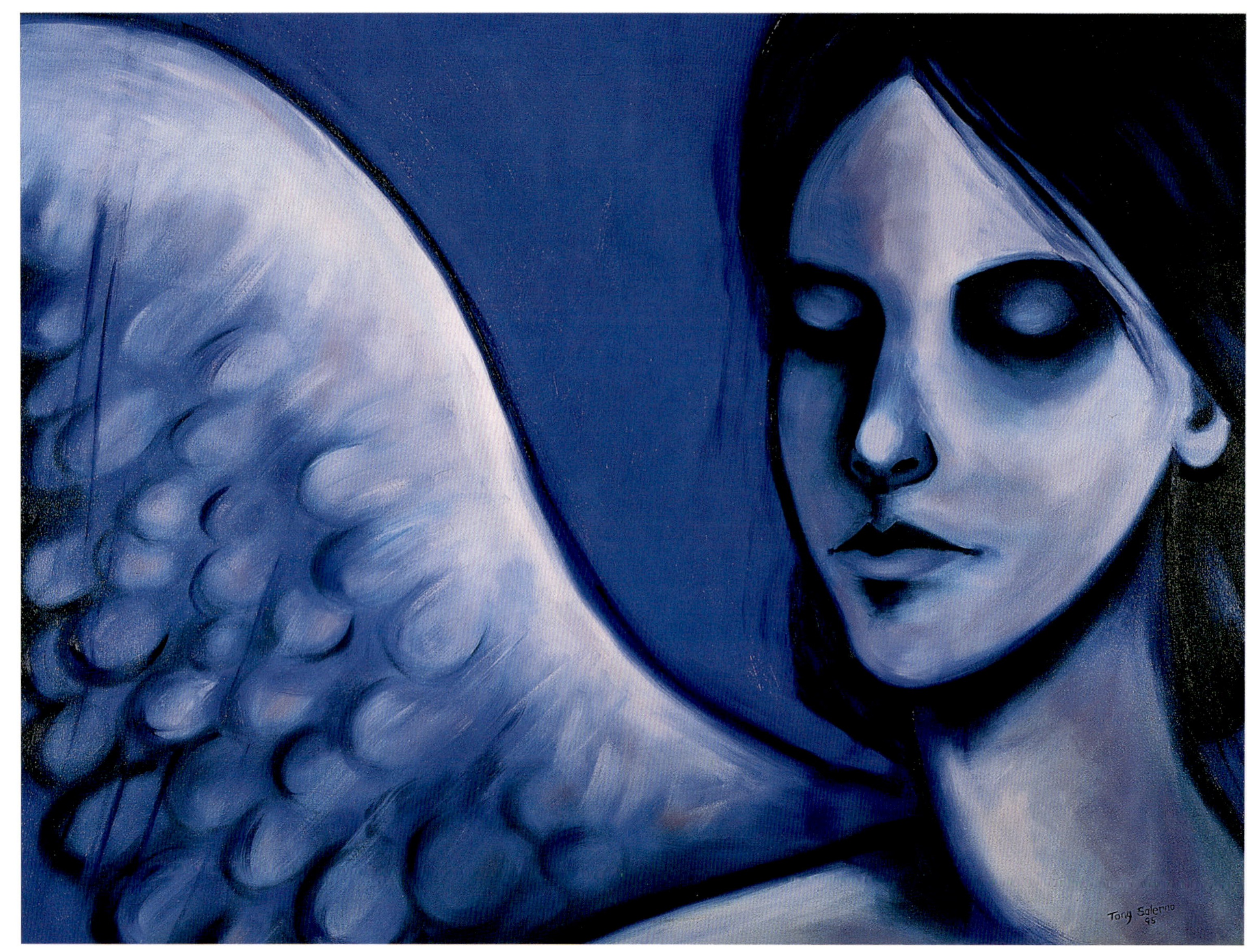

"Blue Angel" *Oil on canvas*
Previous page: *"Heaven On Earth"* *Oil on canvas*
Next page: *"Crimson Gold"* *Acrylic on canvas*

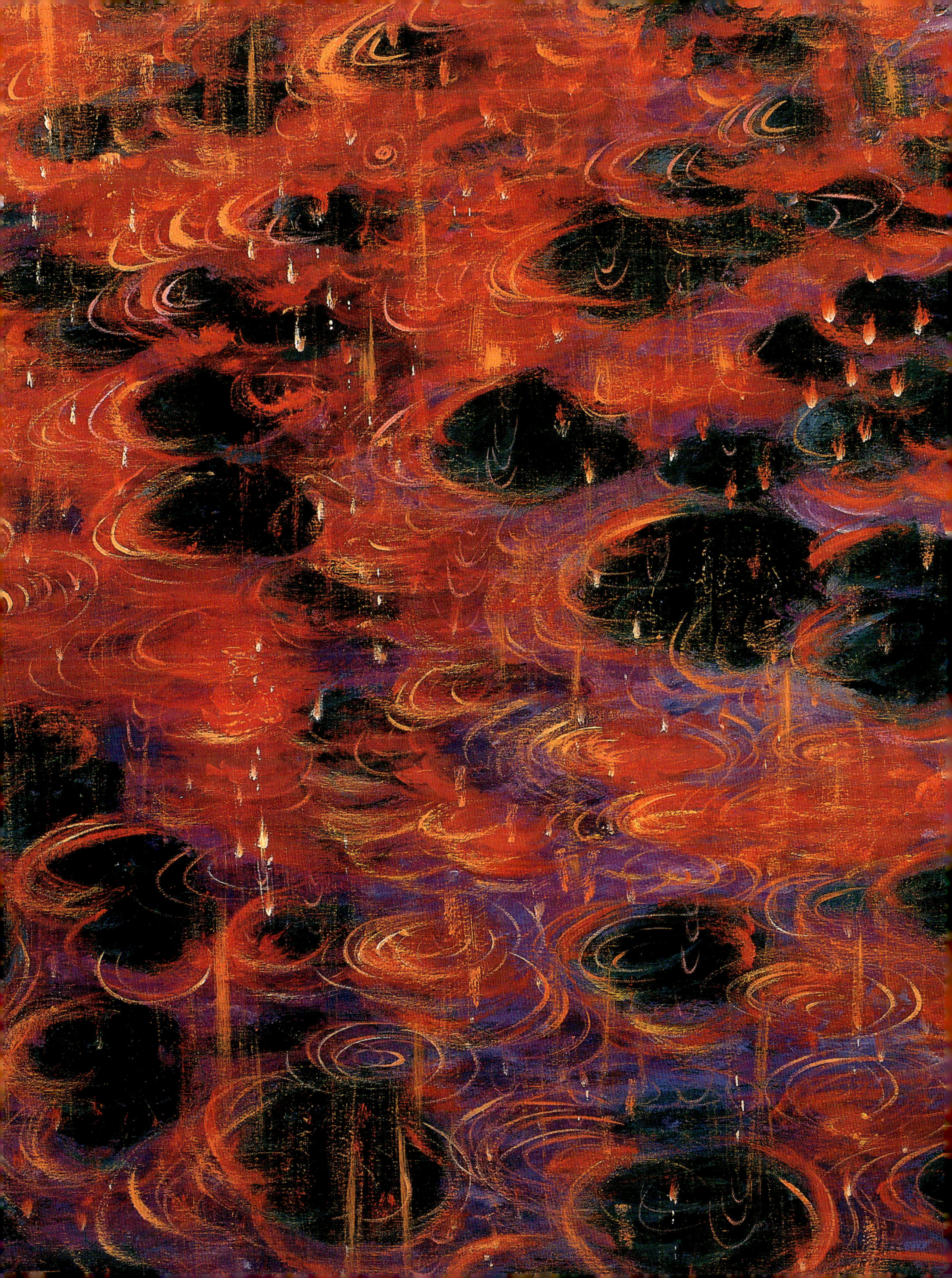

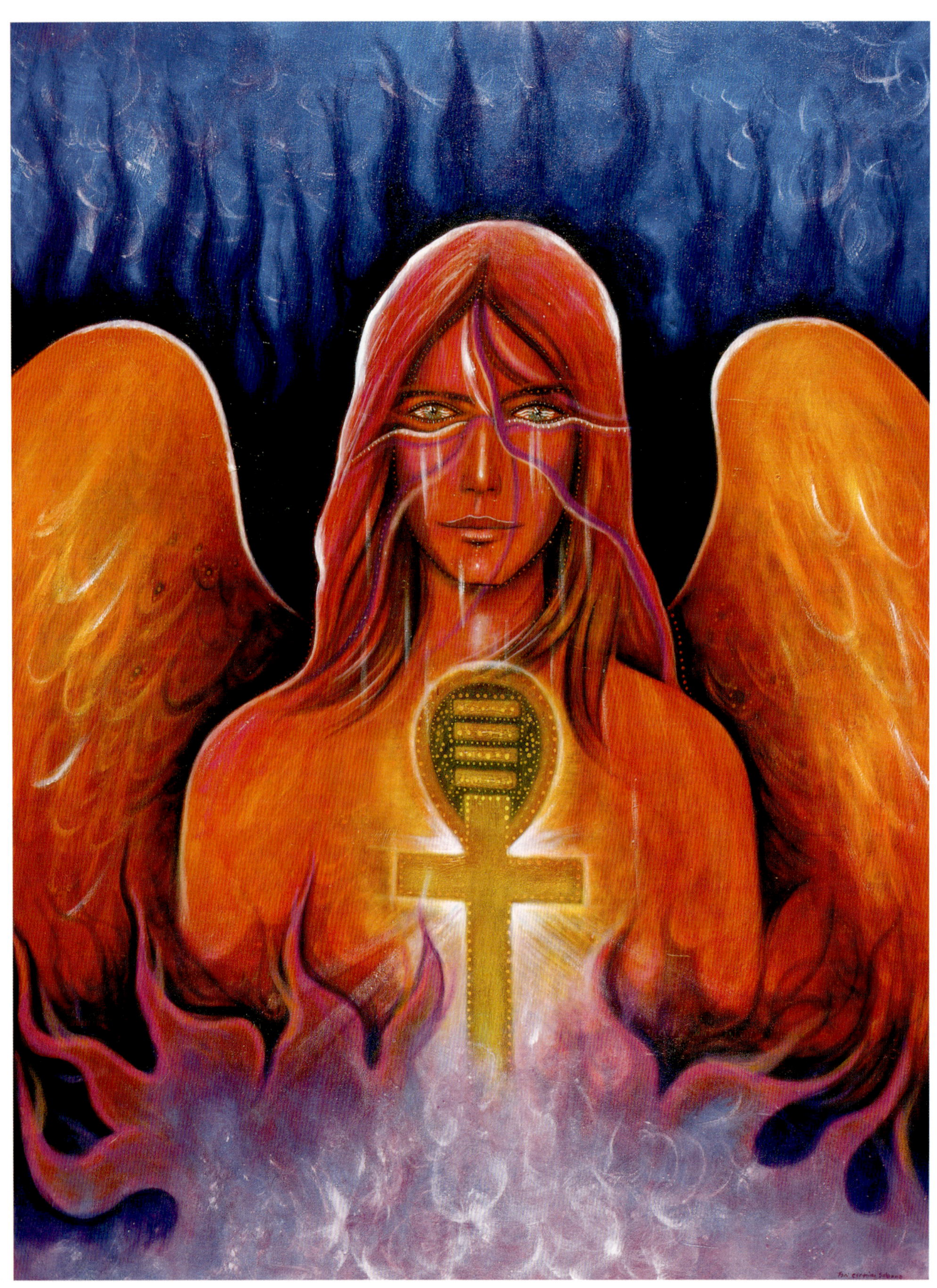

"Archangel Metatron" *Acrylic on canvas*
Next page: *"Tantric Love"* *Acrylic on canvas*

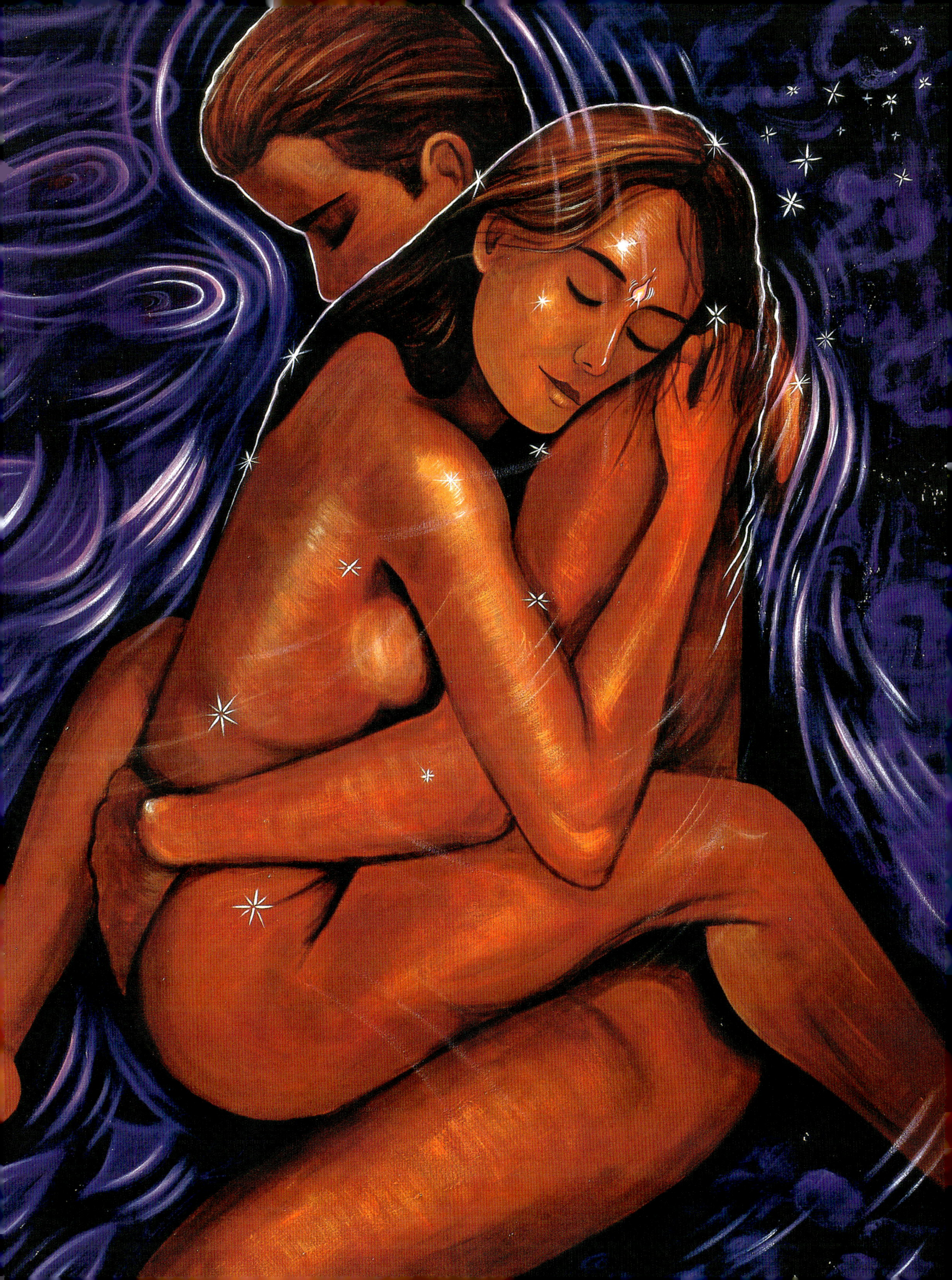

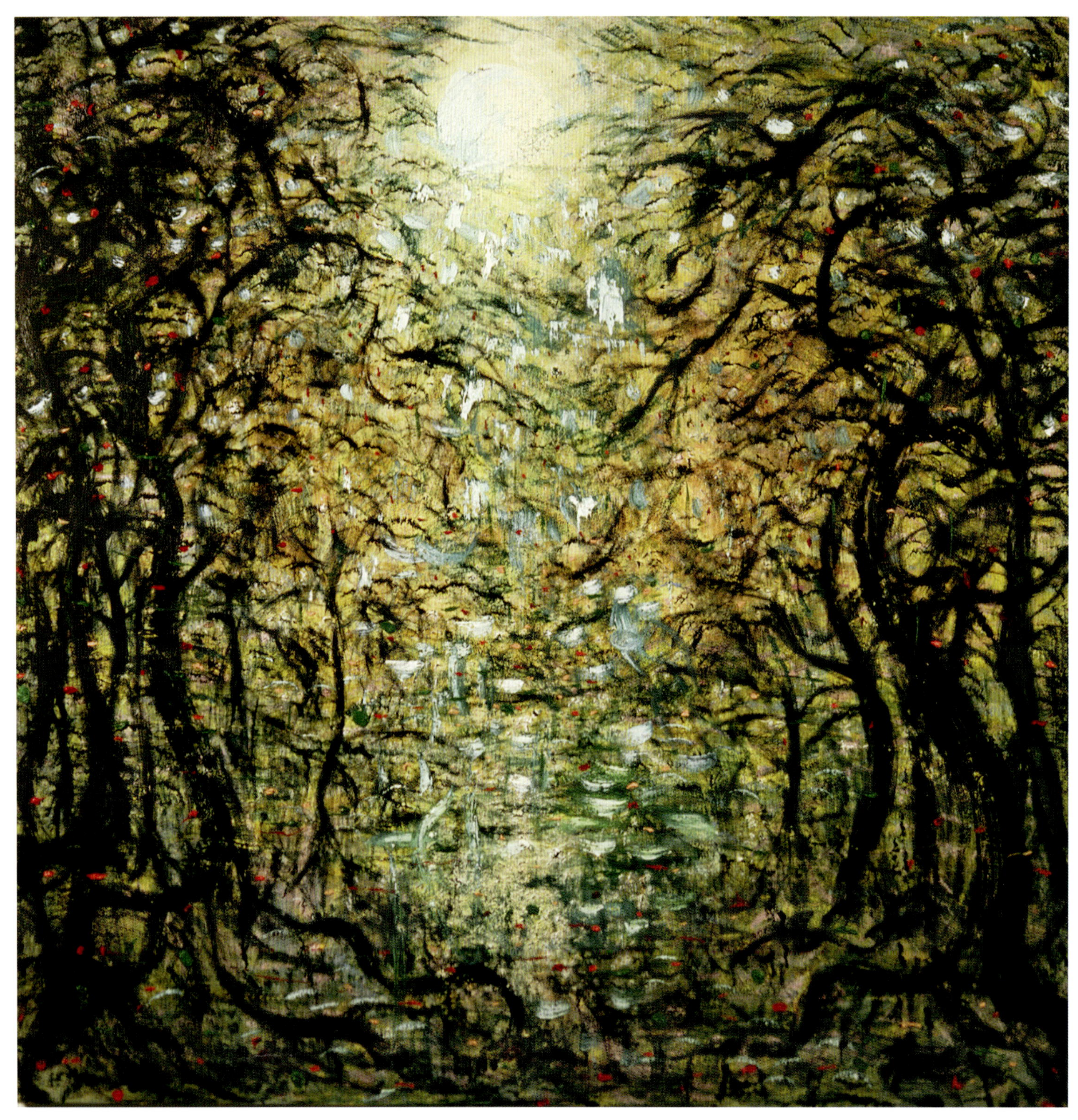

"Una Selva Oscura" *Oil on canvas*
Next page: "A New Day" *Acrylic on canvas*

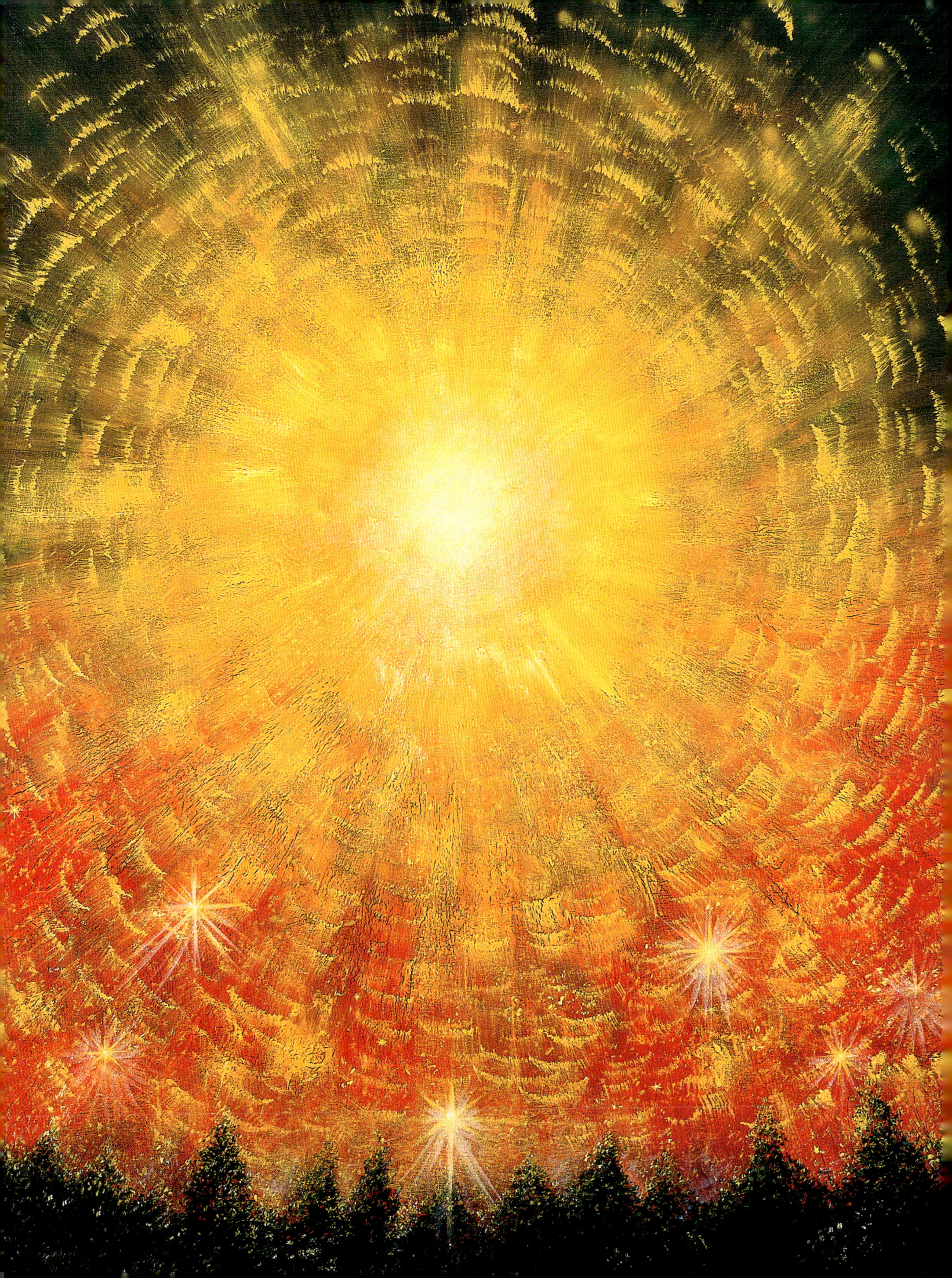

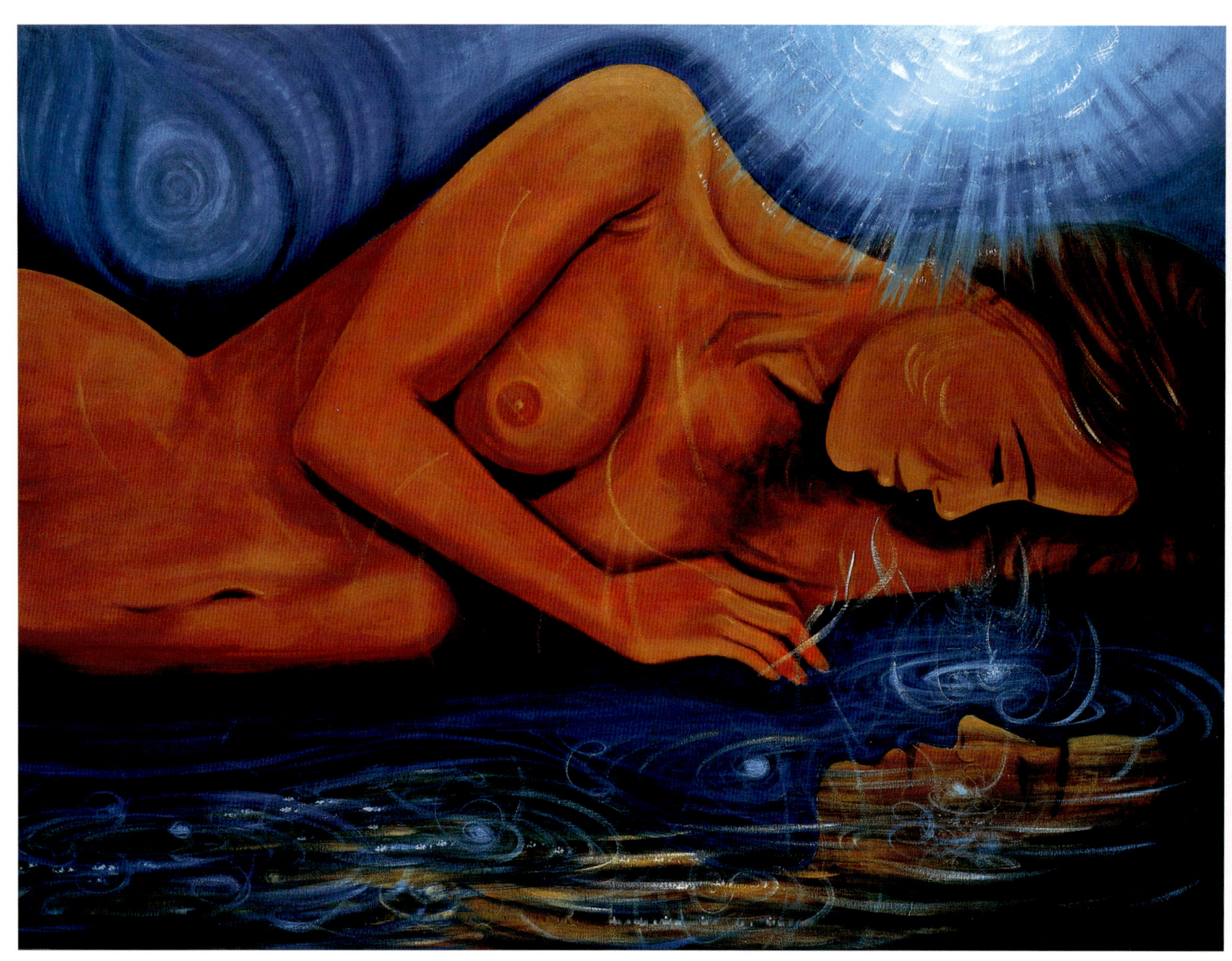

"Sacred Reflection" *Acrylic on canvas*
Next page: "Amethyst" *Acrylic on canvas*

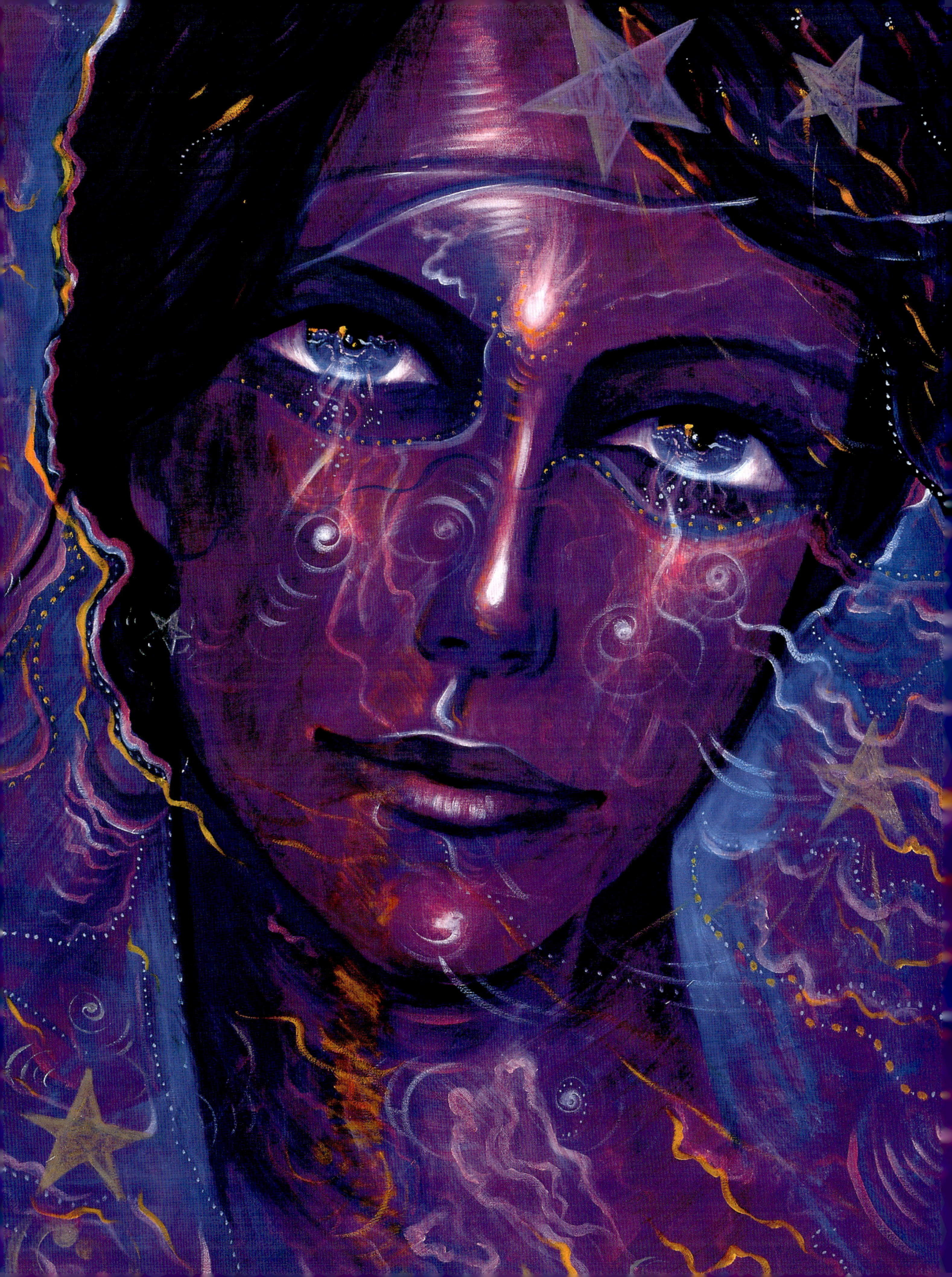

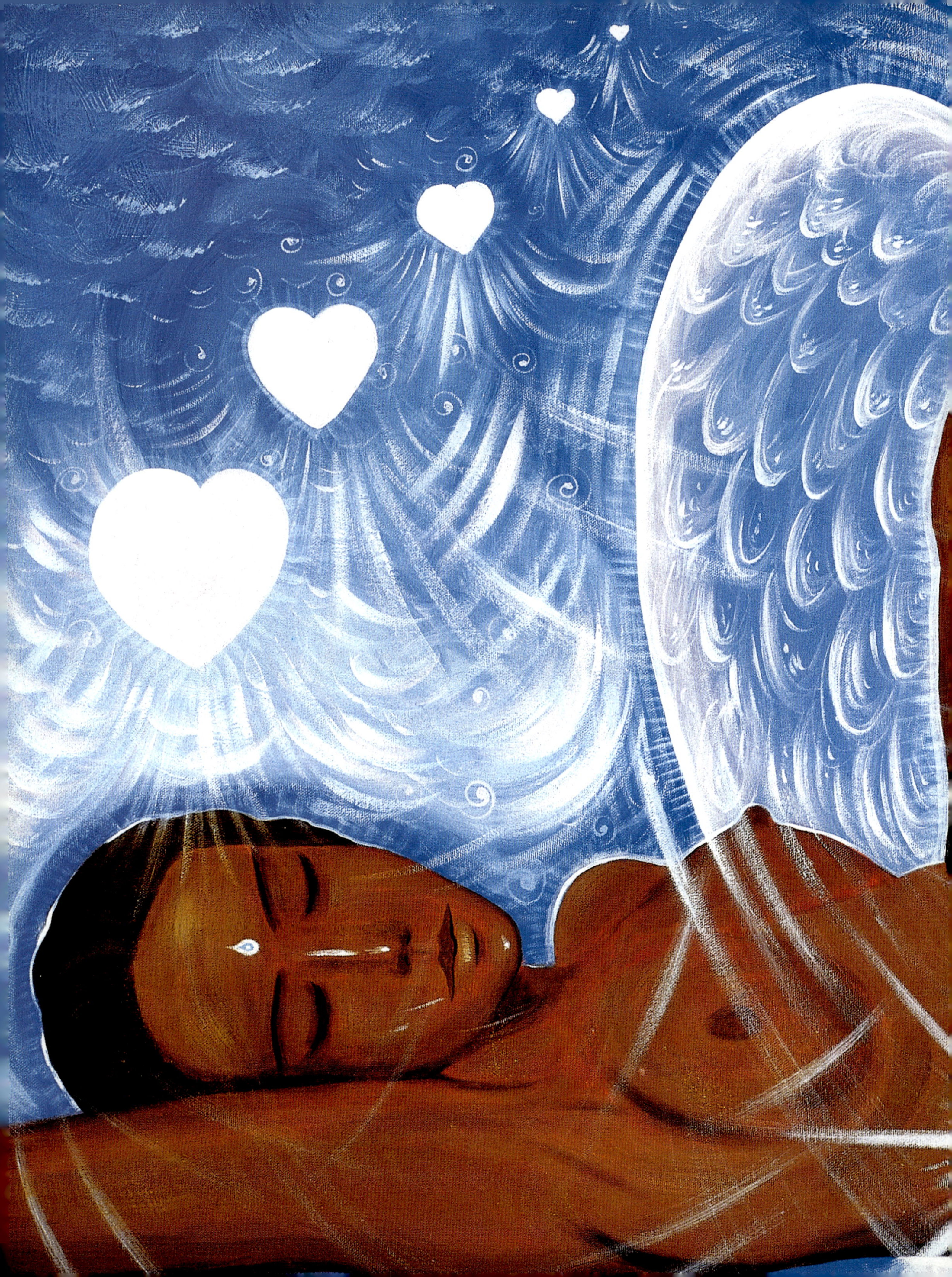

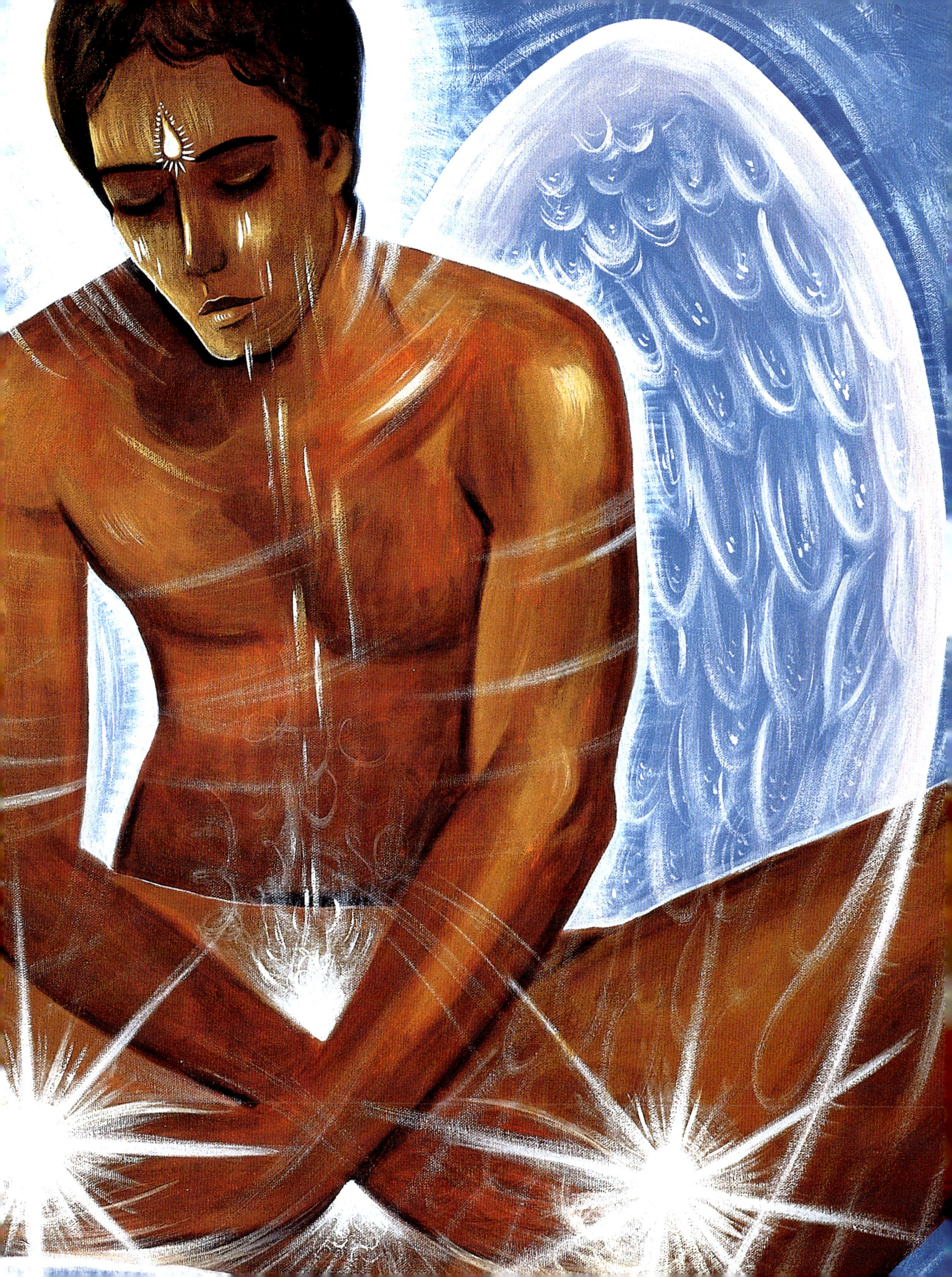

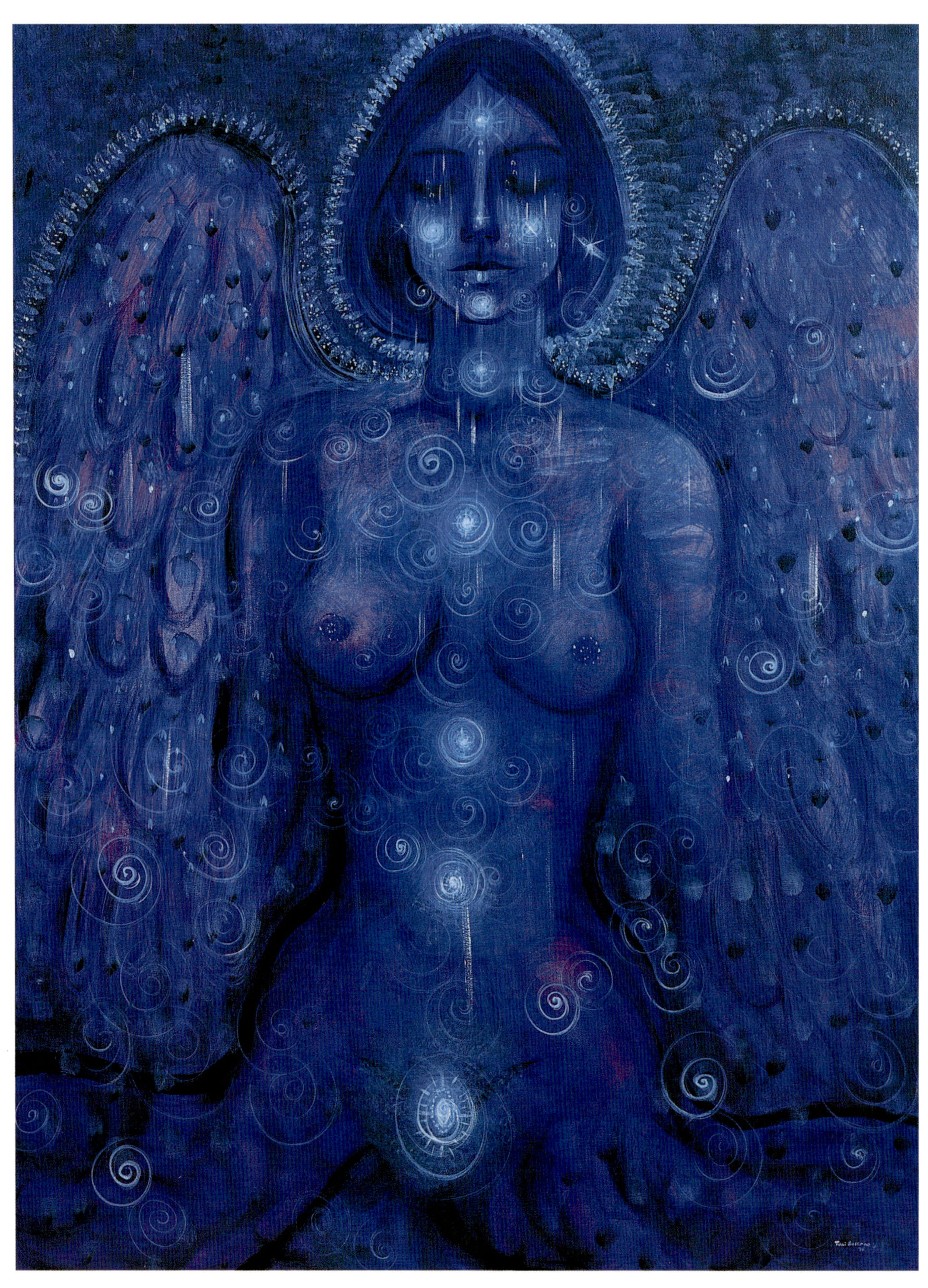

"Amethyst Wings" Acrylic on canvas
Previous page: "Celestial Healing" Acrylic on canvas
Next page: "Meditating Angel" Pastel and pencil on canvas

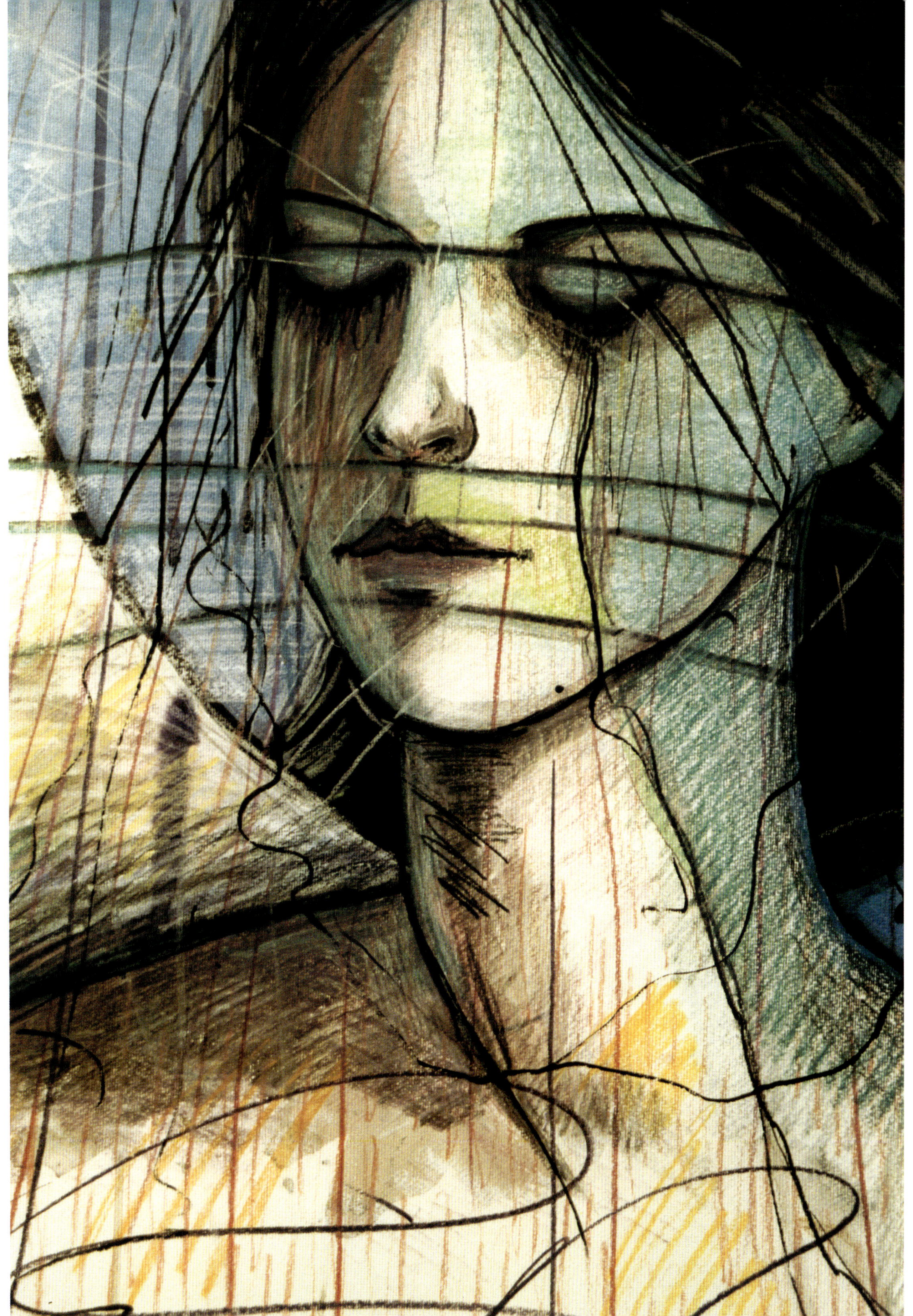

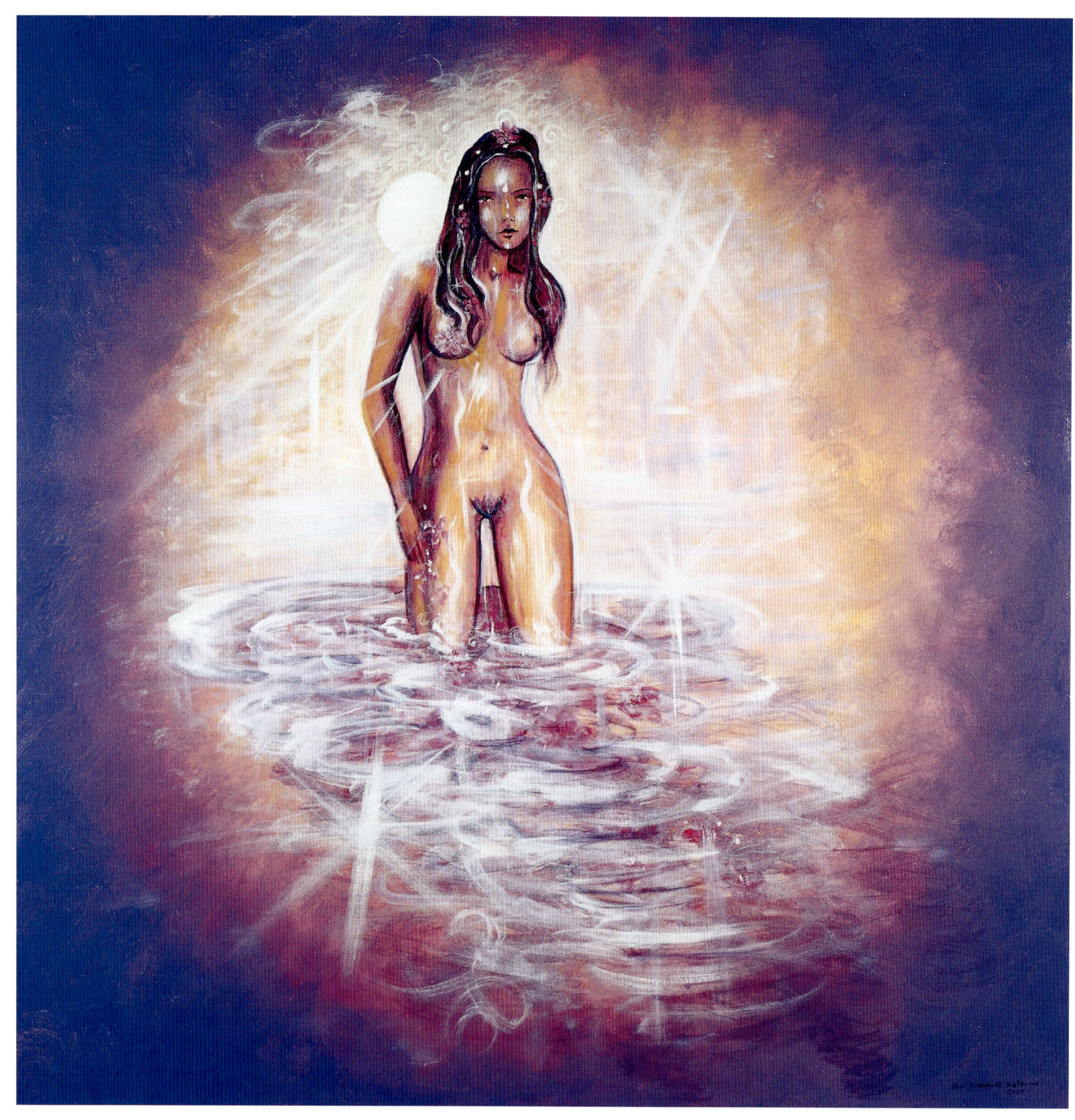

"Remember" *Acrylic on canvas*
Next page: "Rose Quartz" Acrylic on canvas

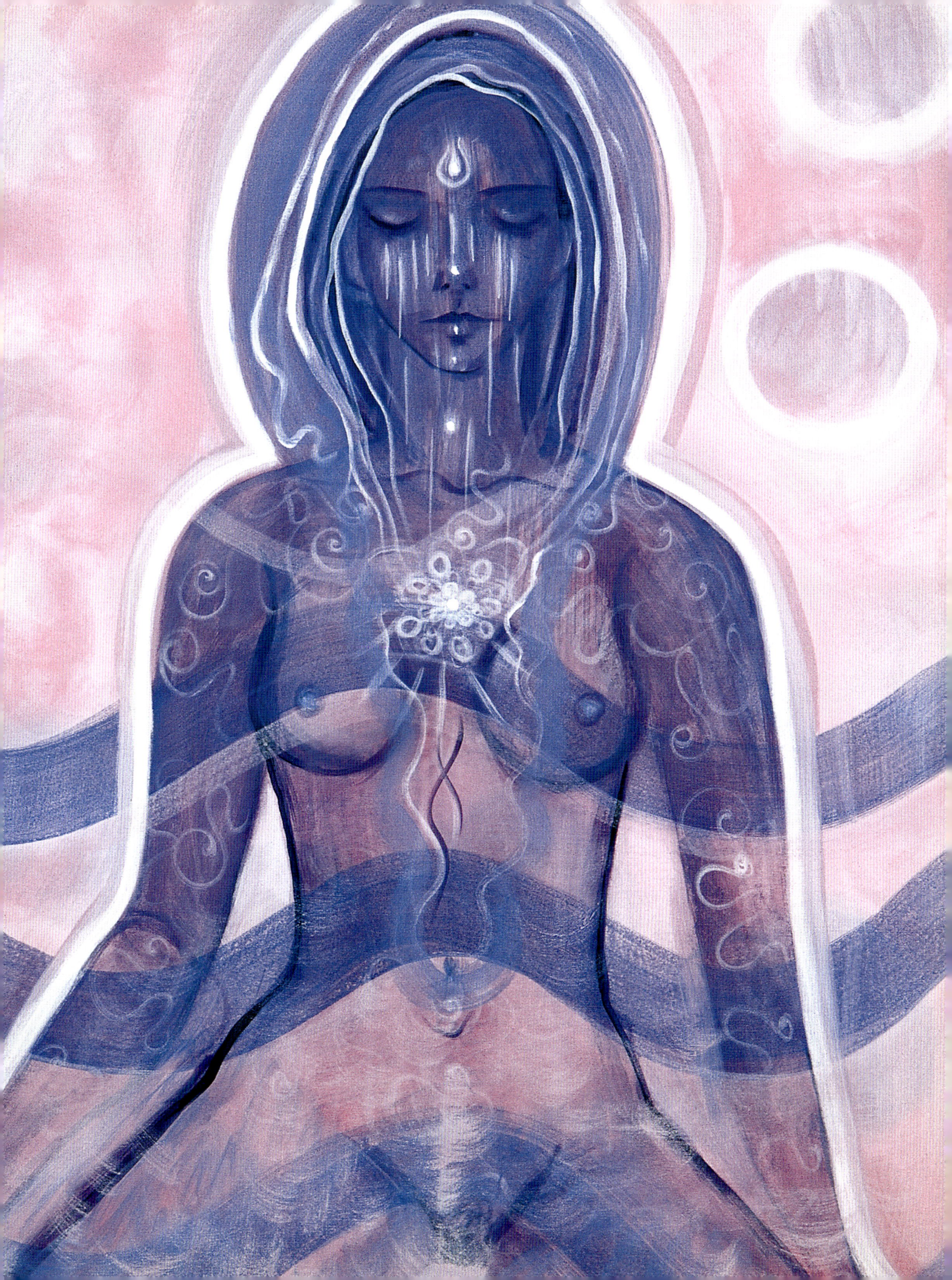

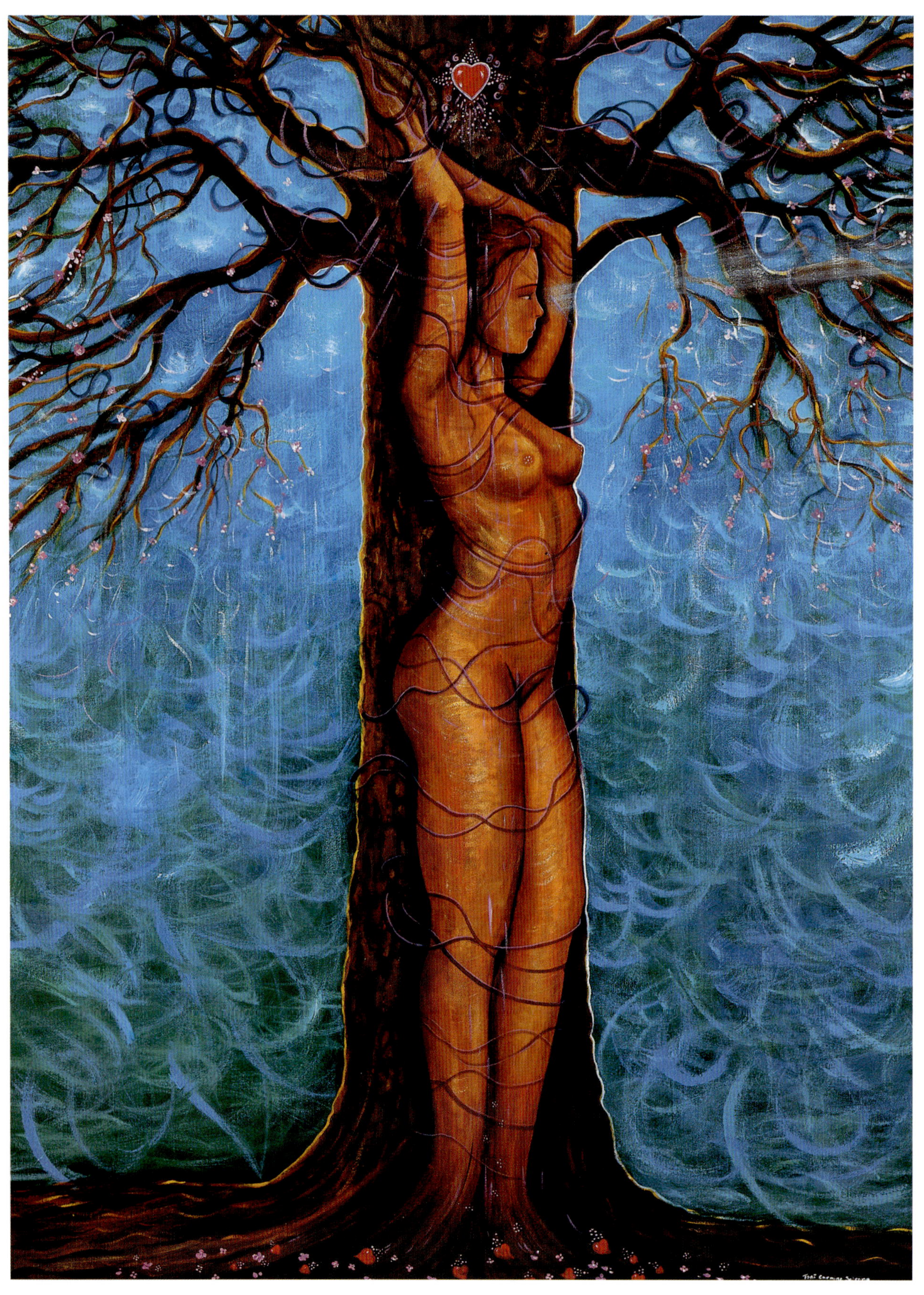

"Captive Heart" Acrylic on canvas
Next page: *"Flames Of Compassion"* Acrylic on canvas

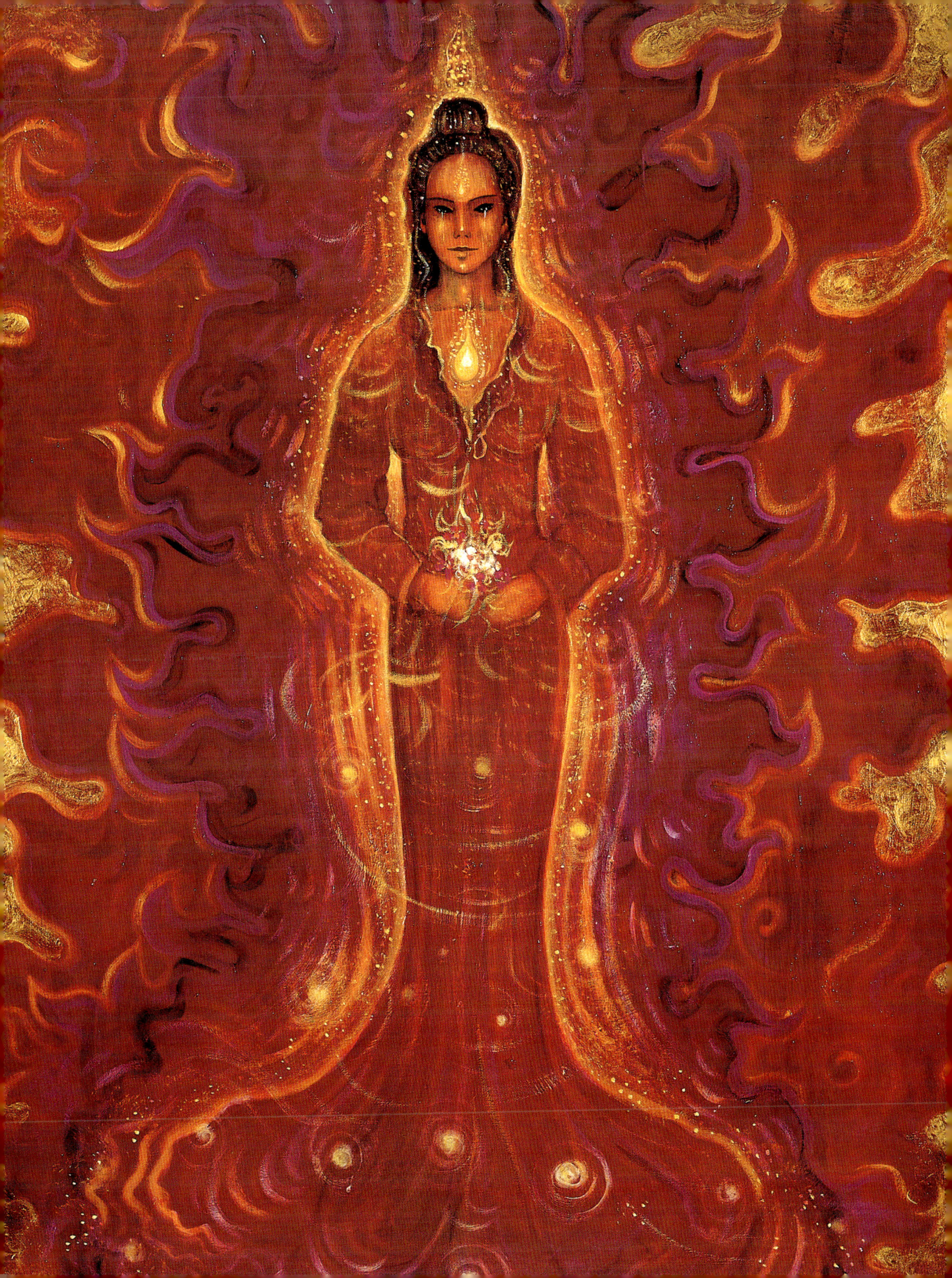

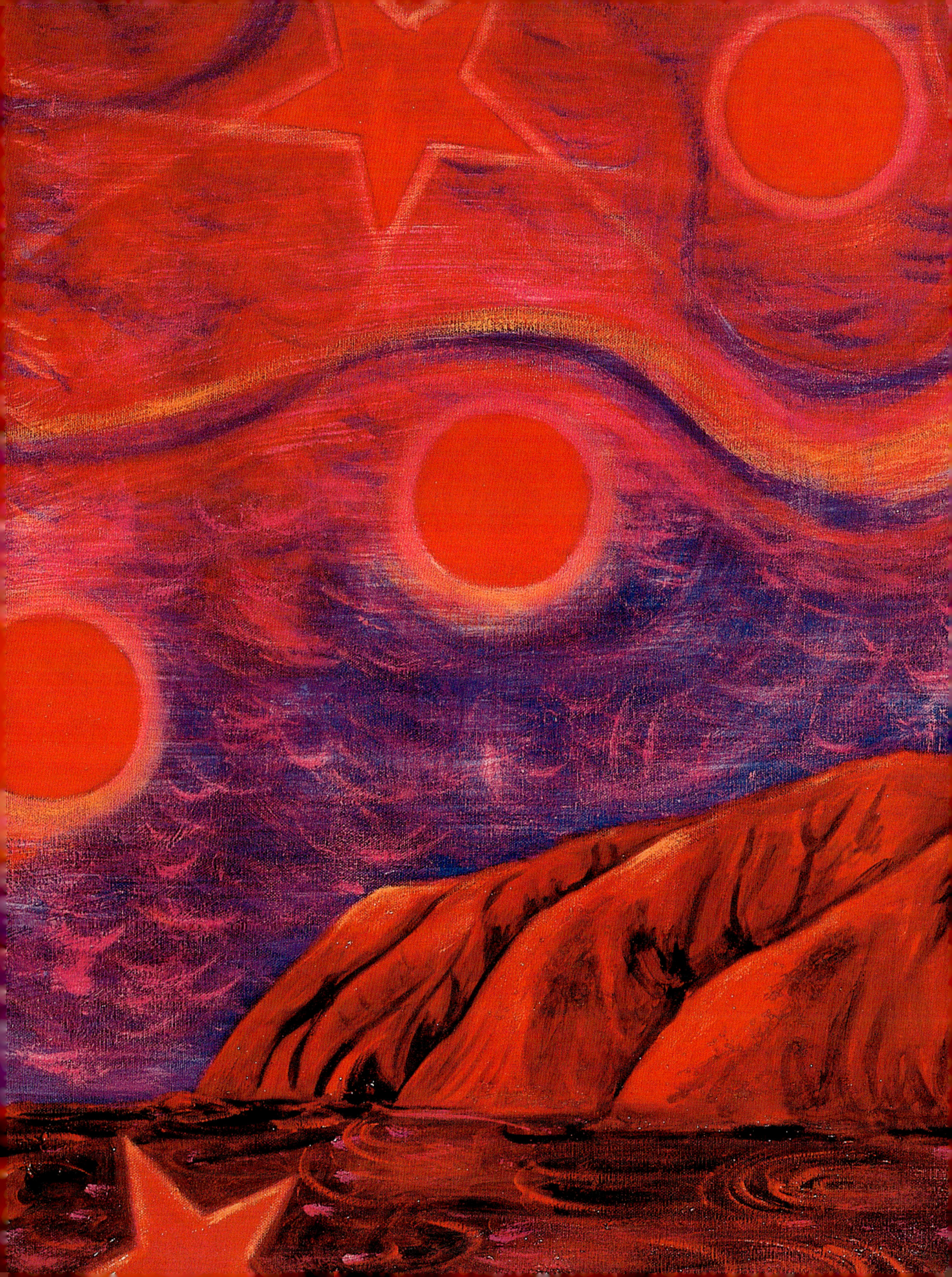

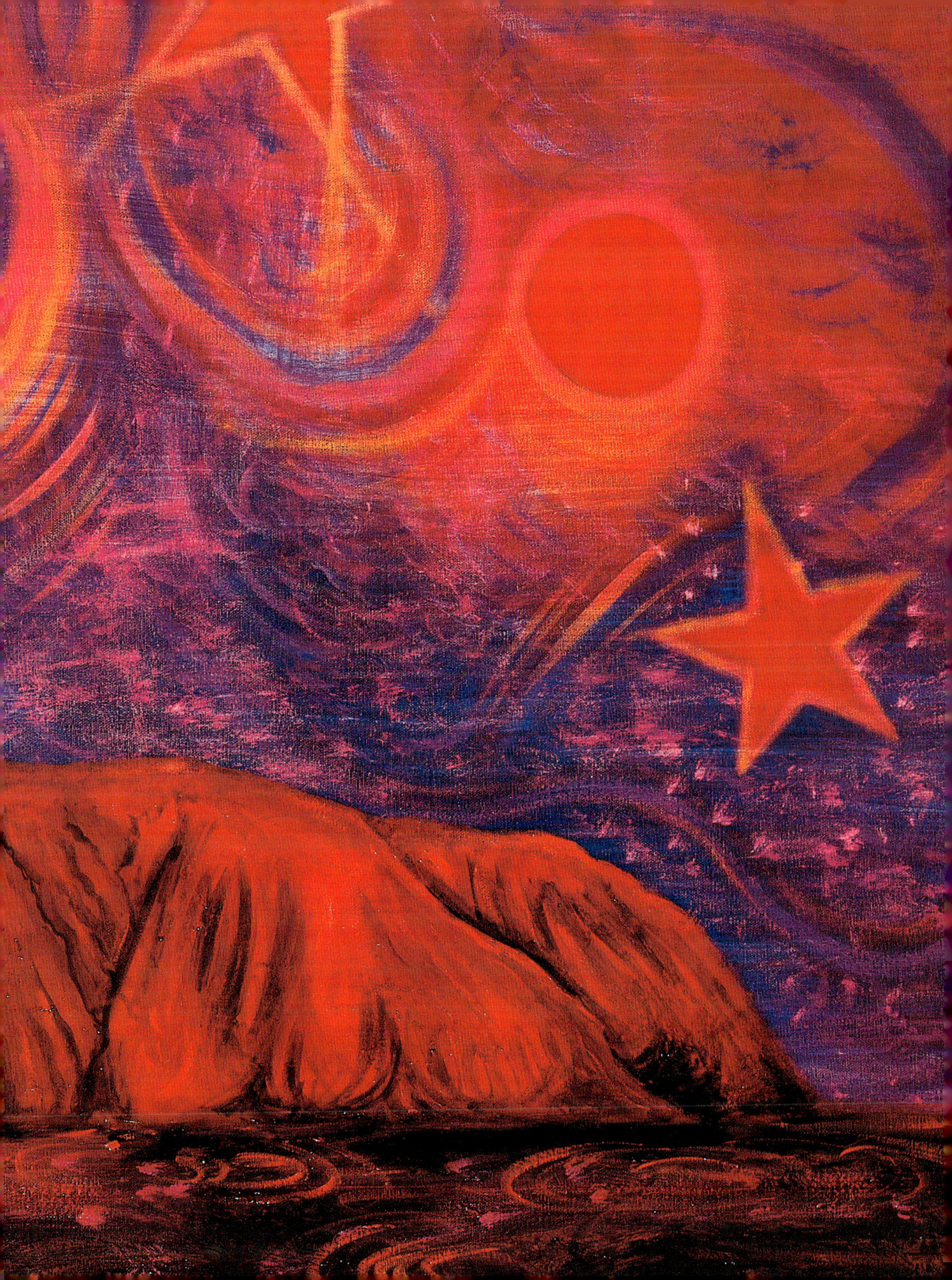

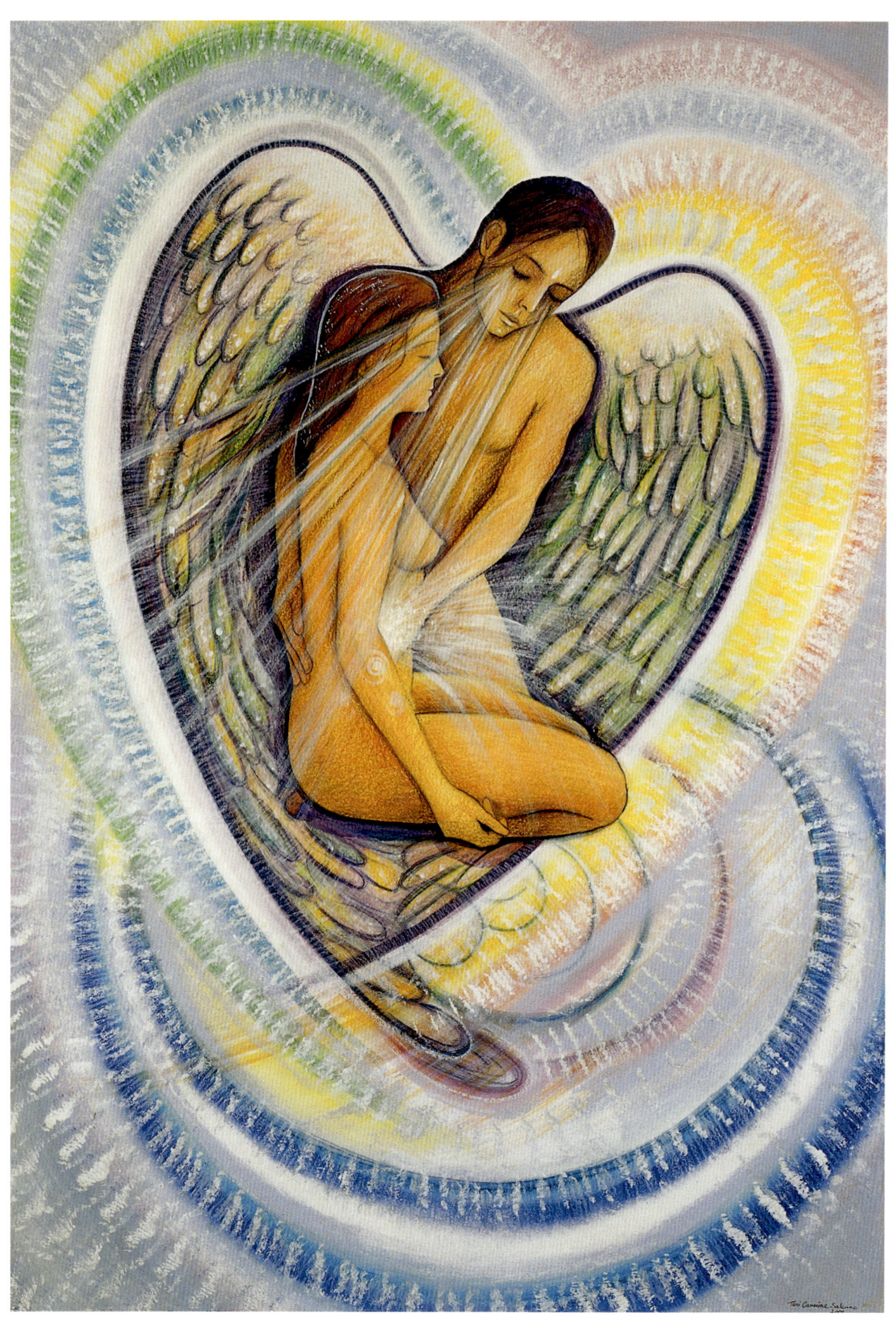

"Diamond Light" *Pastel on paper*
Previous page: "Uluru" Acrylic on canvas

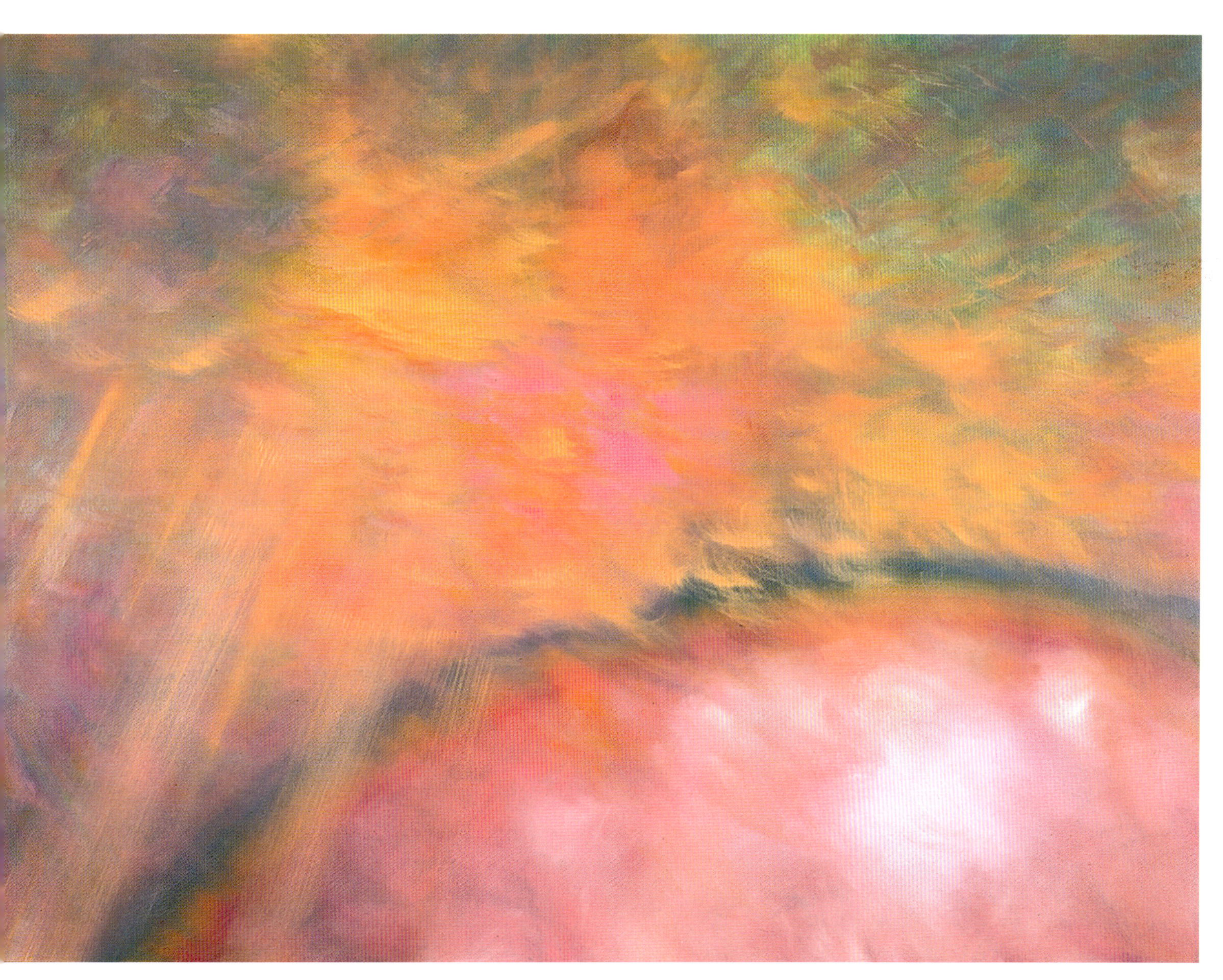

"Celestial Light" *Oil on canvas*

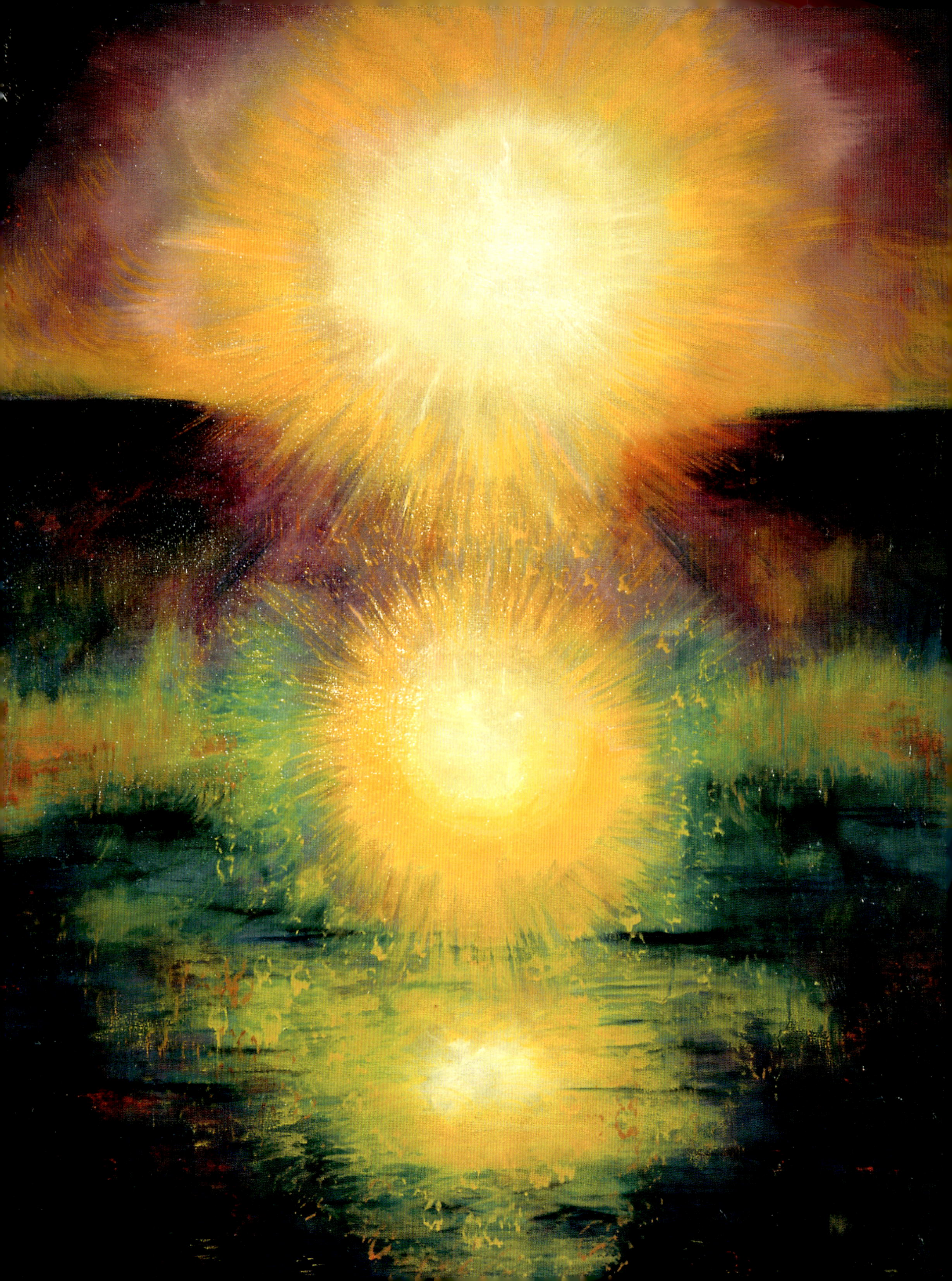

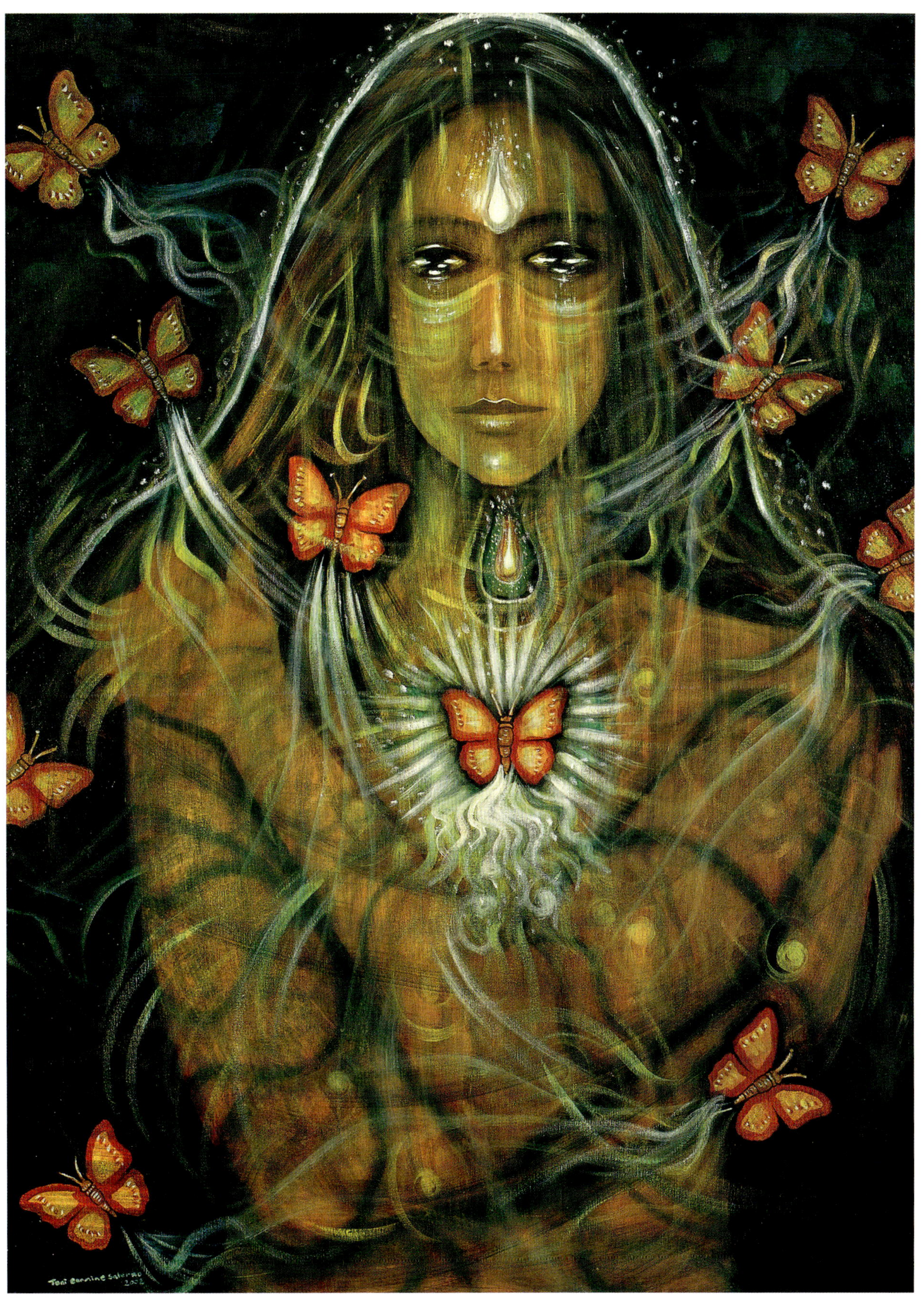

"Goddess" *Acrylic on canvas*
Previous page: *"Trilogy Of Light"* *Oil on canvas*

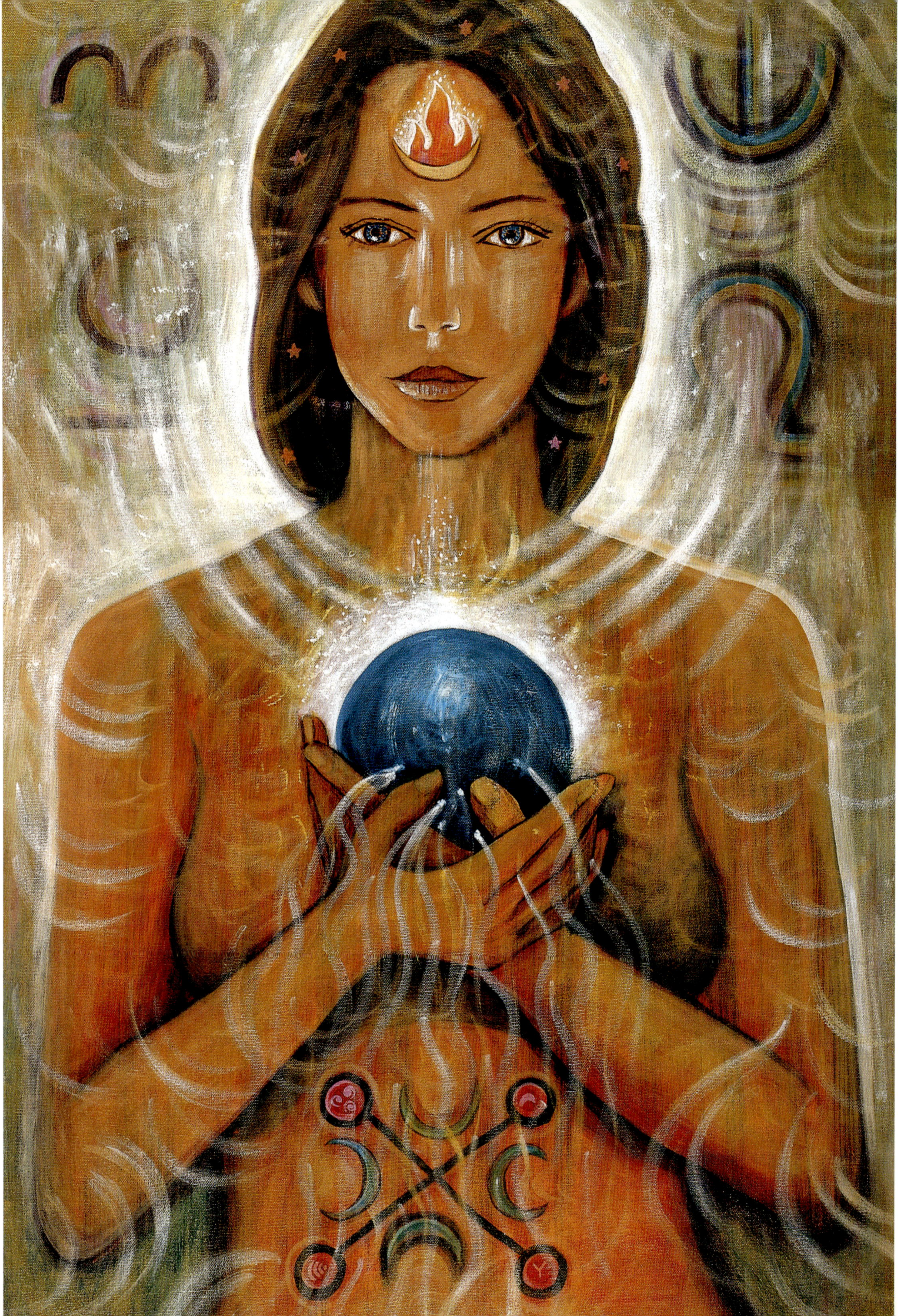

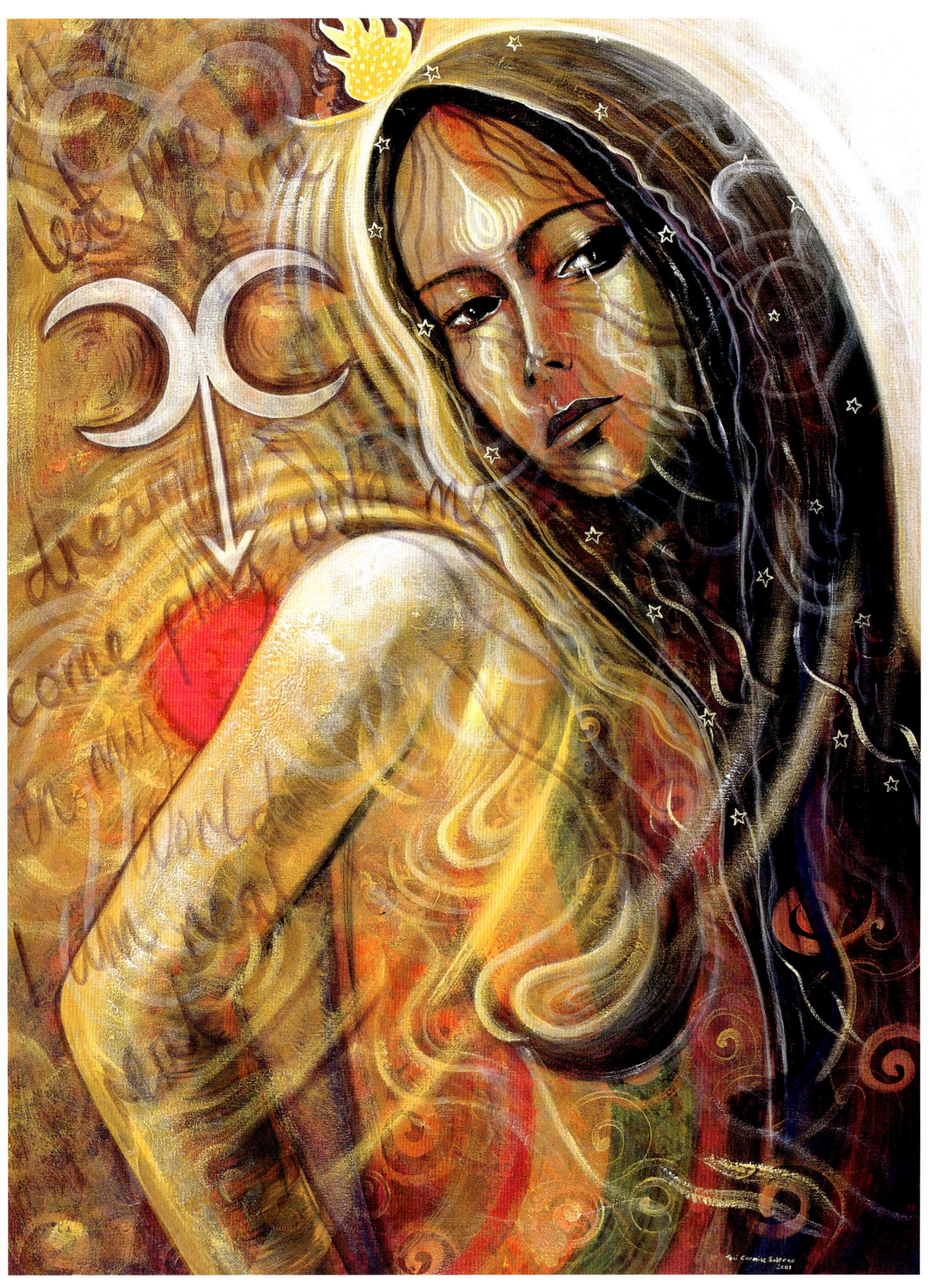

"Amazon Spirit" *Acrylic on canvas*
Previous page: *"Acceptance"* *Acrylic on canvas*

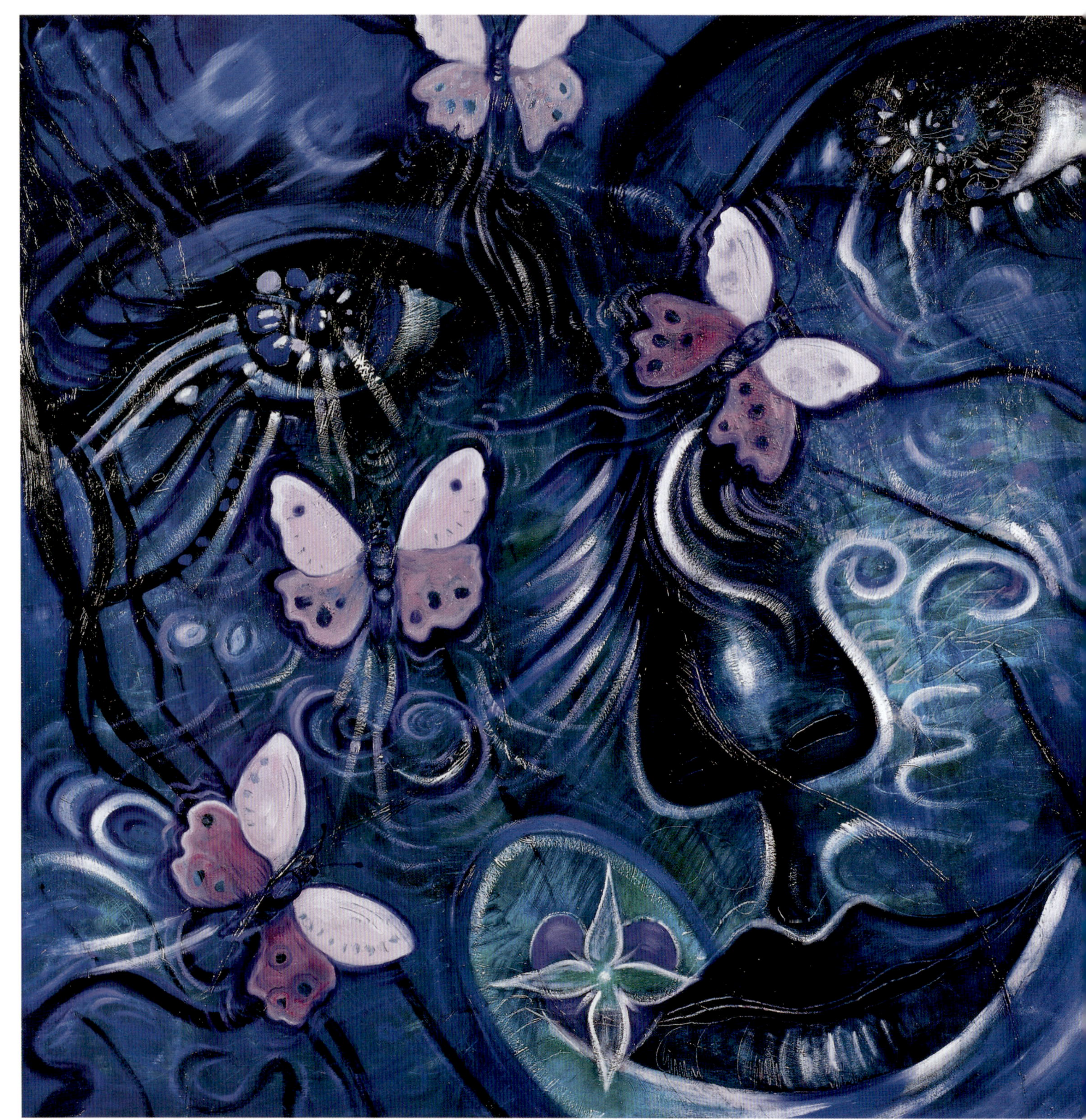

"Butterflies" Acrylic on canvas

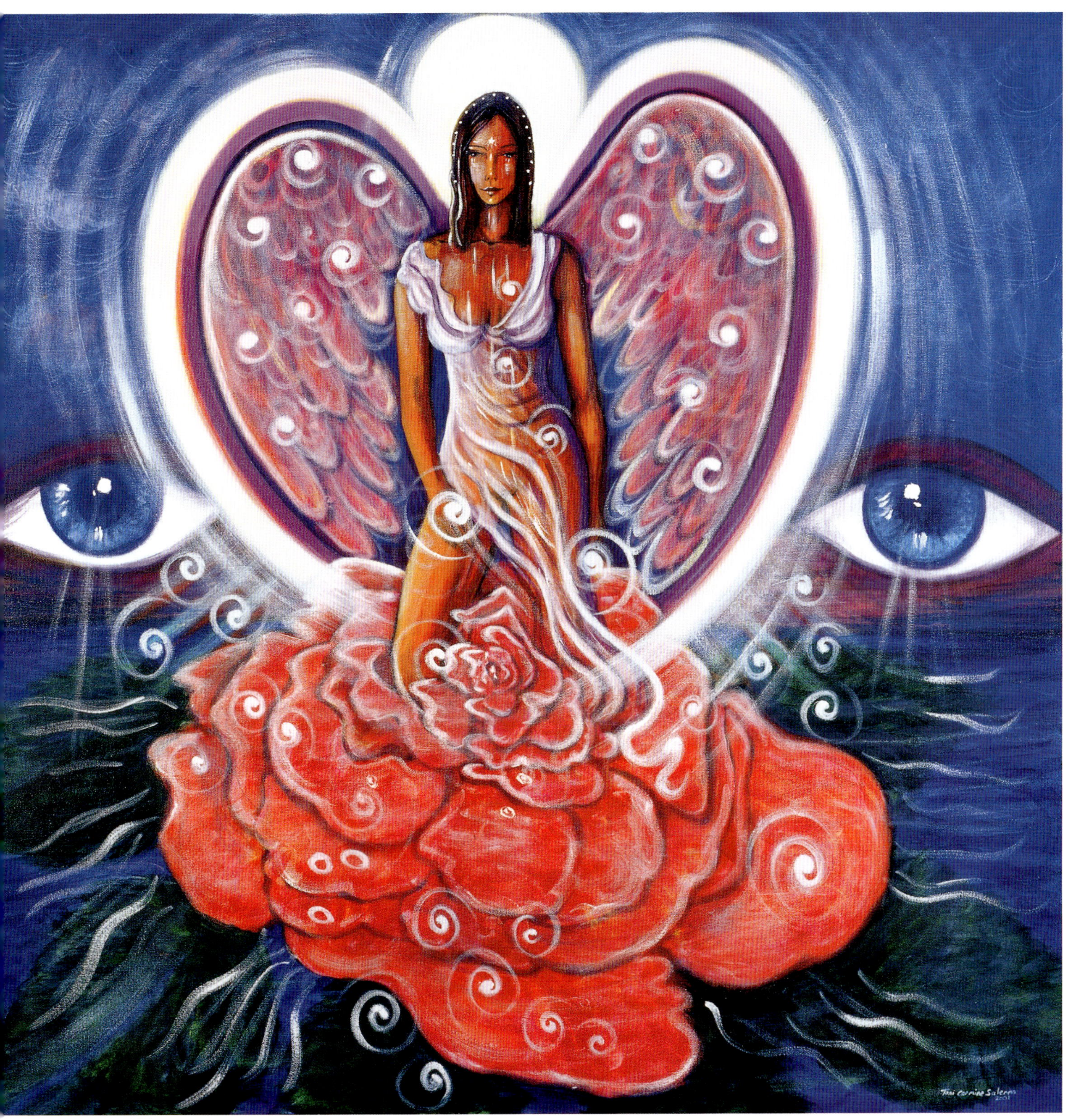

"Chrysalis" *Acrylic on canvas*

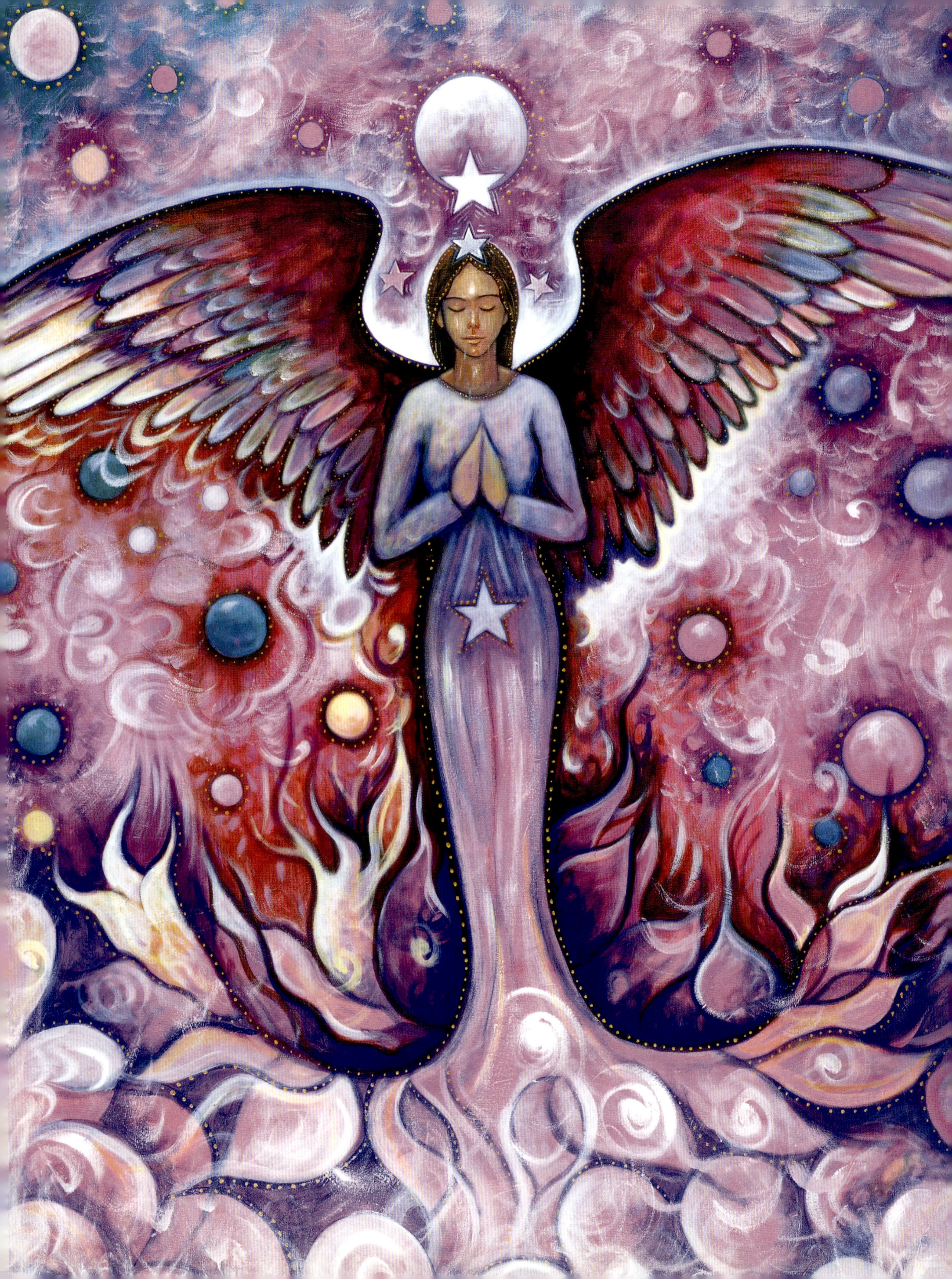

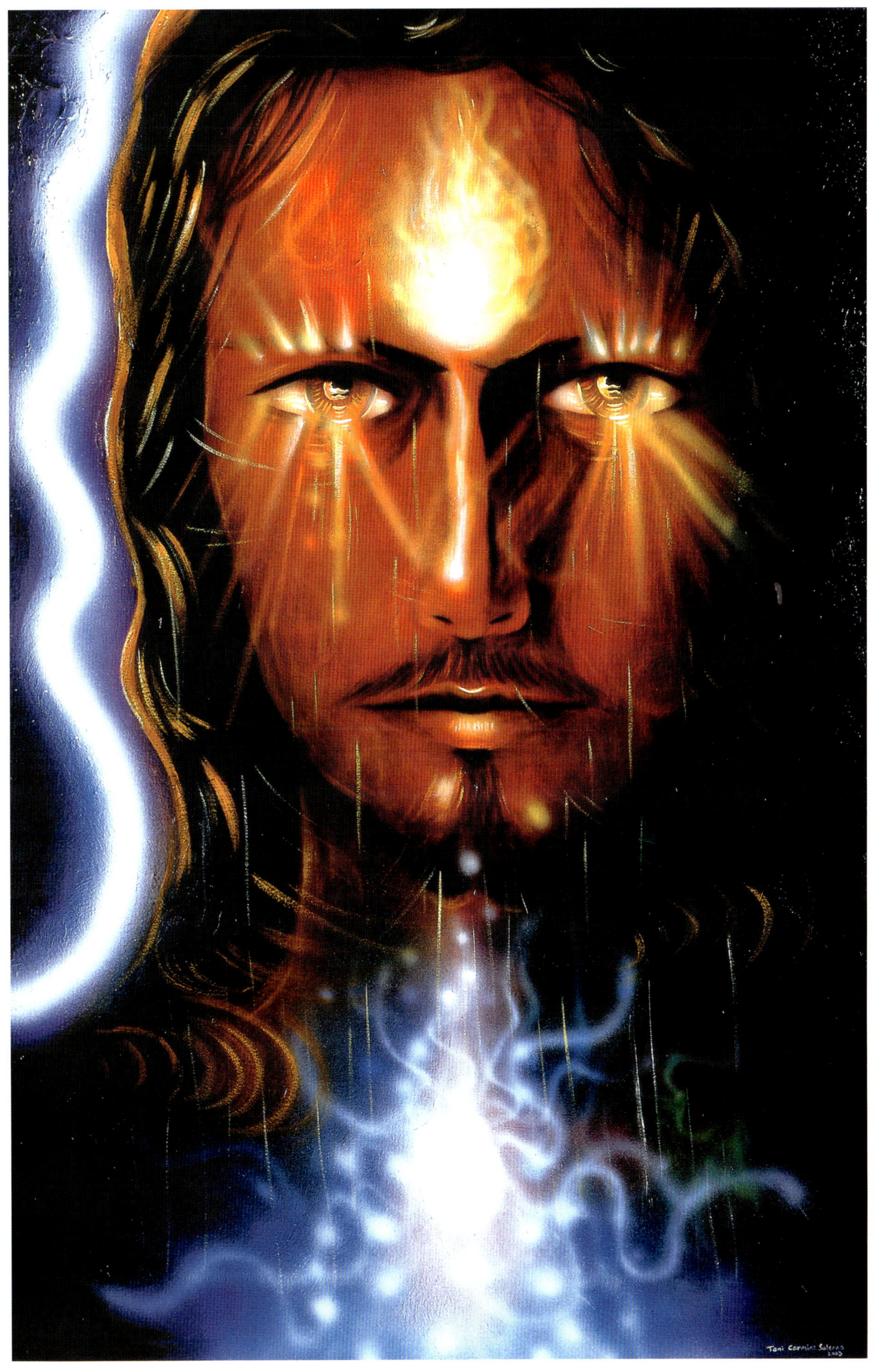

"Hades" *Acrylic on canvas*
Previous page: "The Prayer" Acrylic on canvas

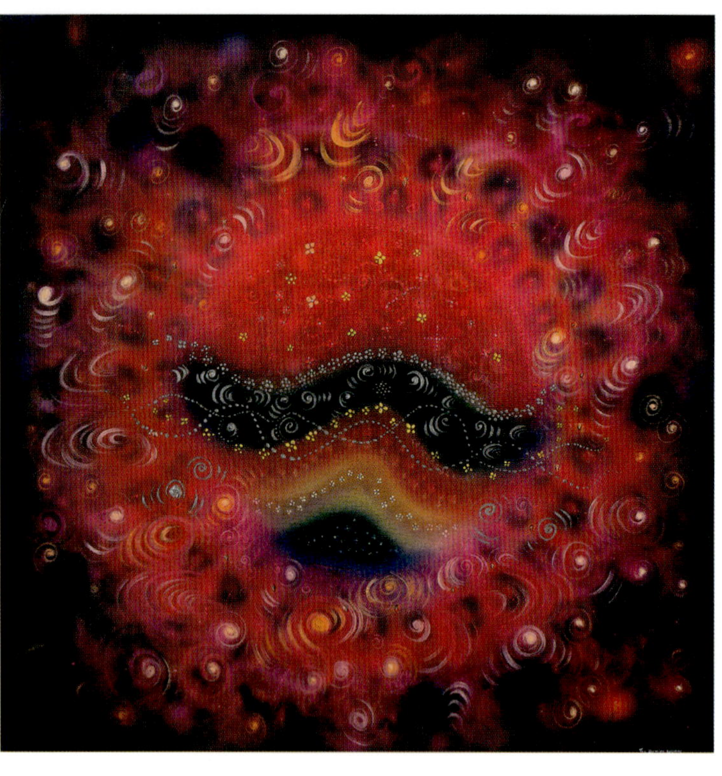

"The Moving Image Of Eternity" *Acrylic on canvas*

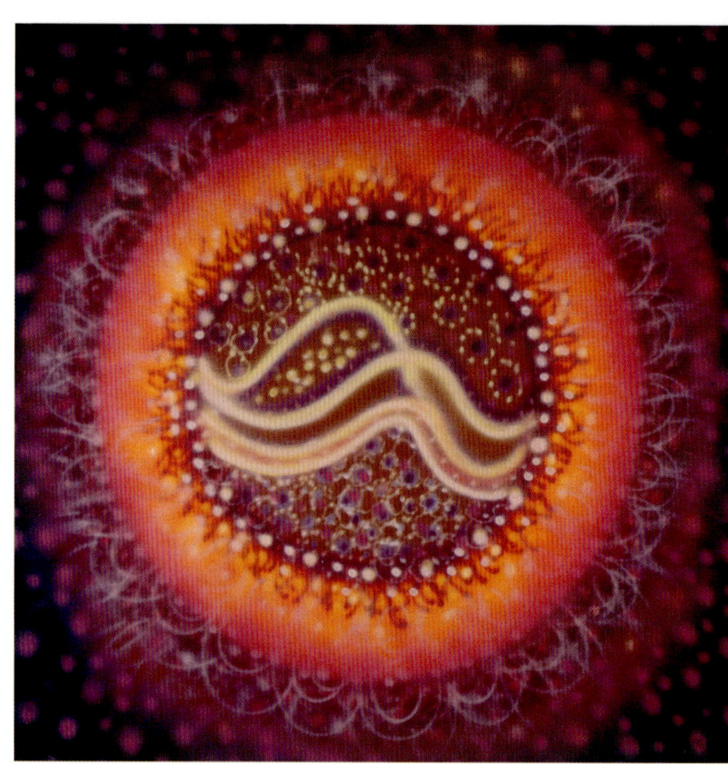

"Beyond The Horizon" *Acrylic on canvas*

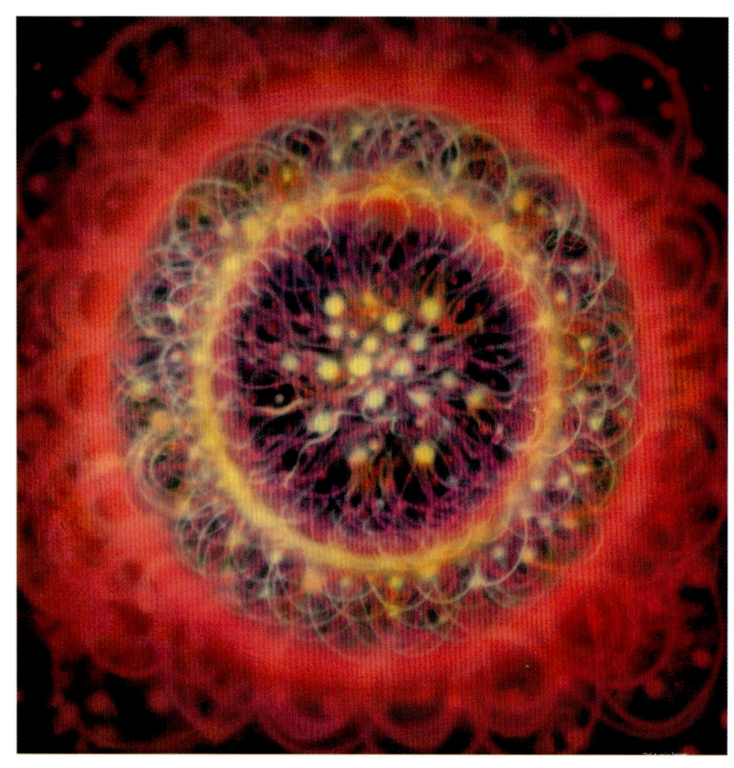

"Cosmology" *Acrylic on canvas*

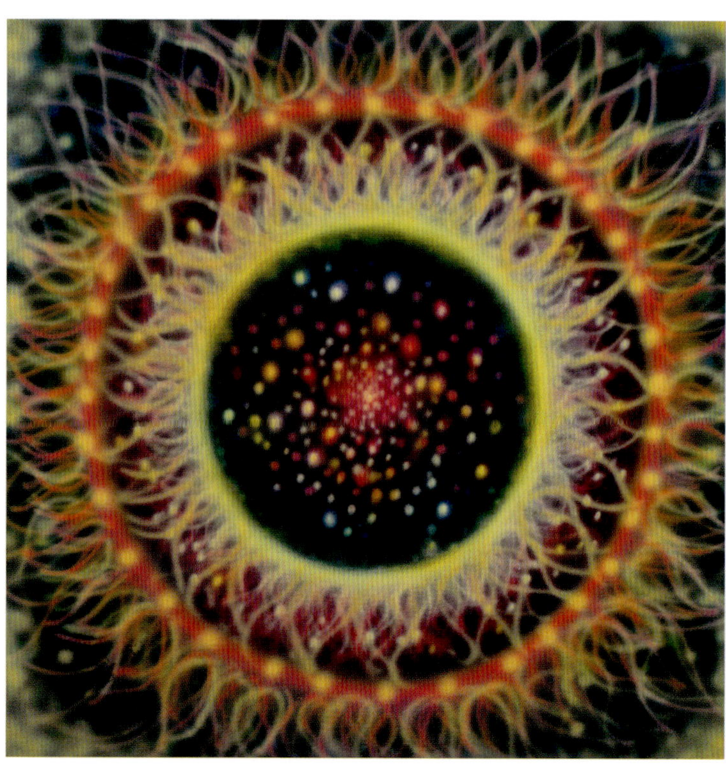

"Inside A Black Hole" *Acrylic on canvas*

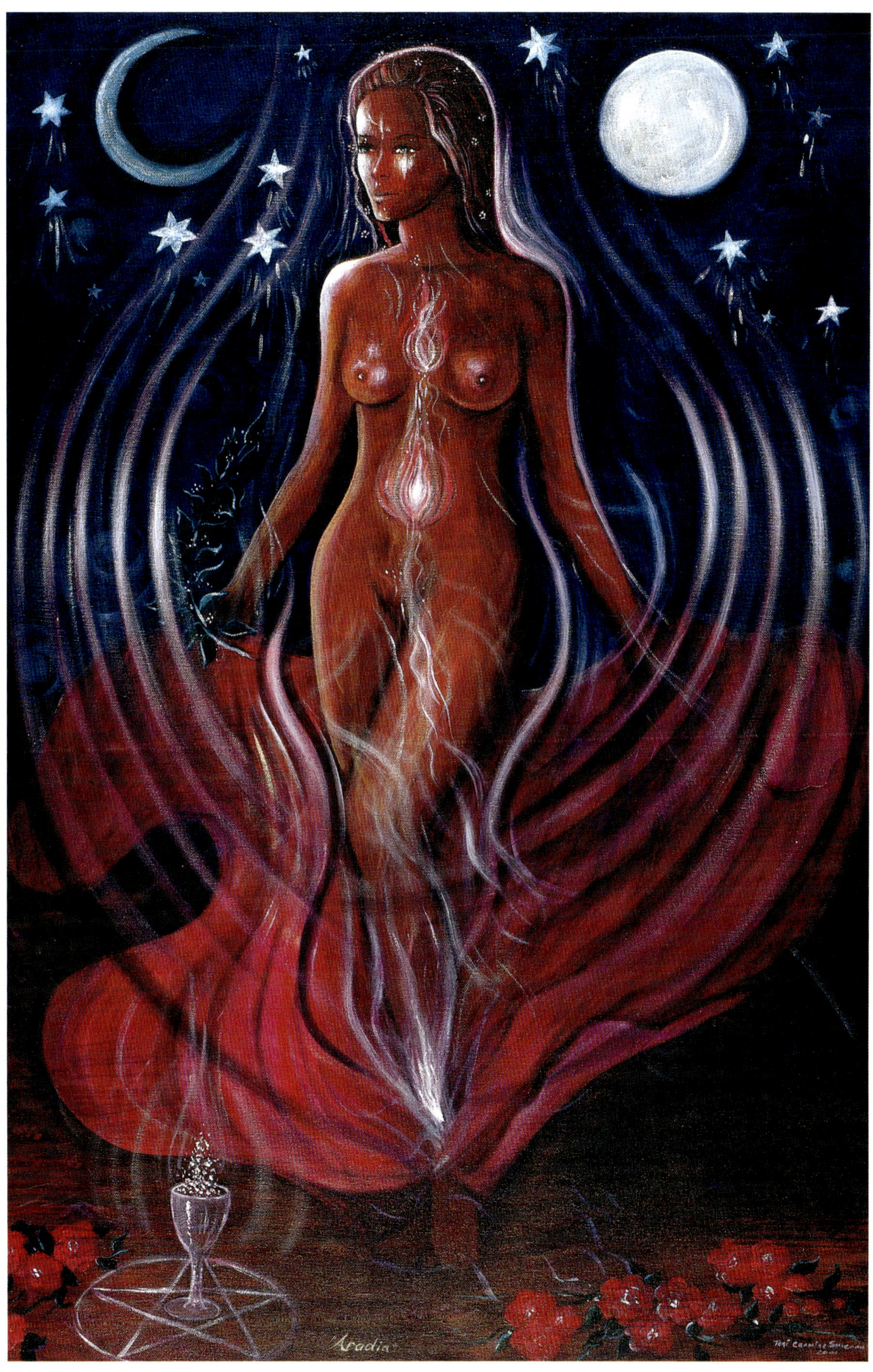

"Purity" *Acrylic on canvas*

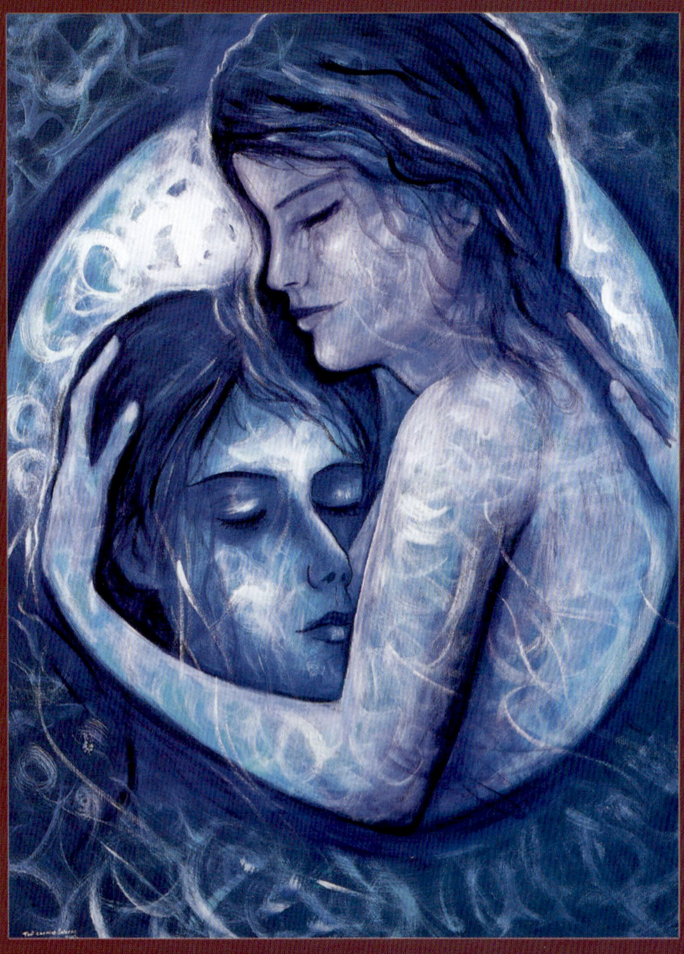

"Embrace" Acrylic on canvas

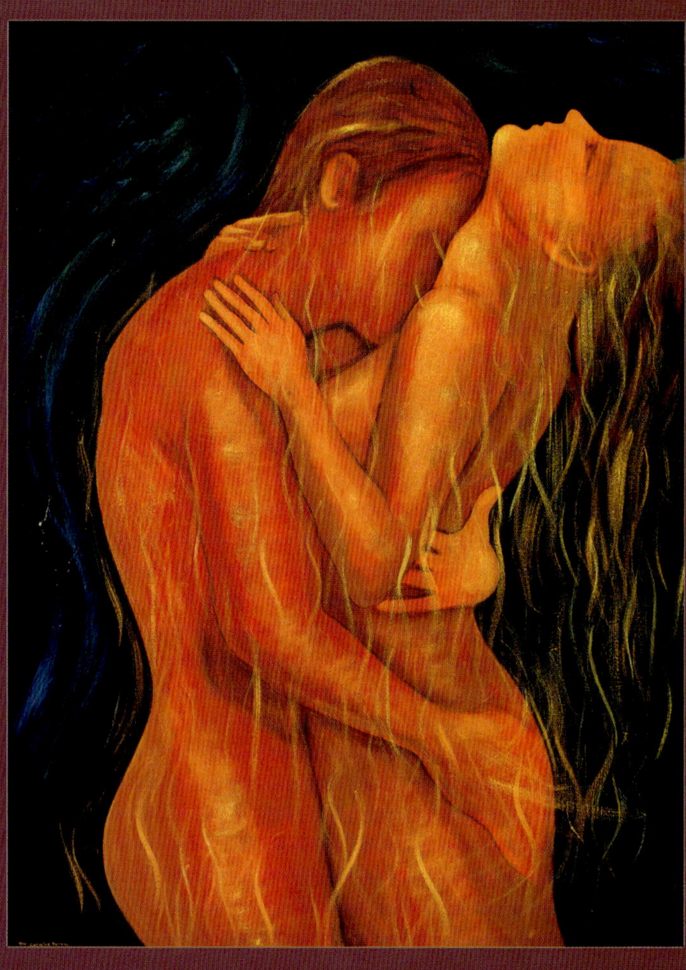

"Tantric Ecstasy" Acrylic on canvas

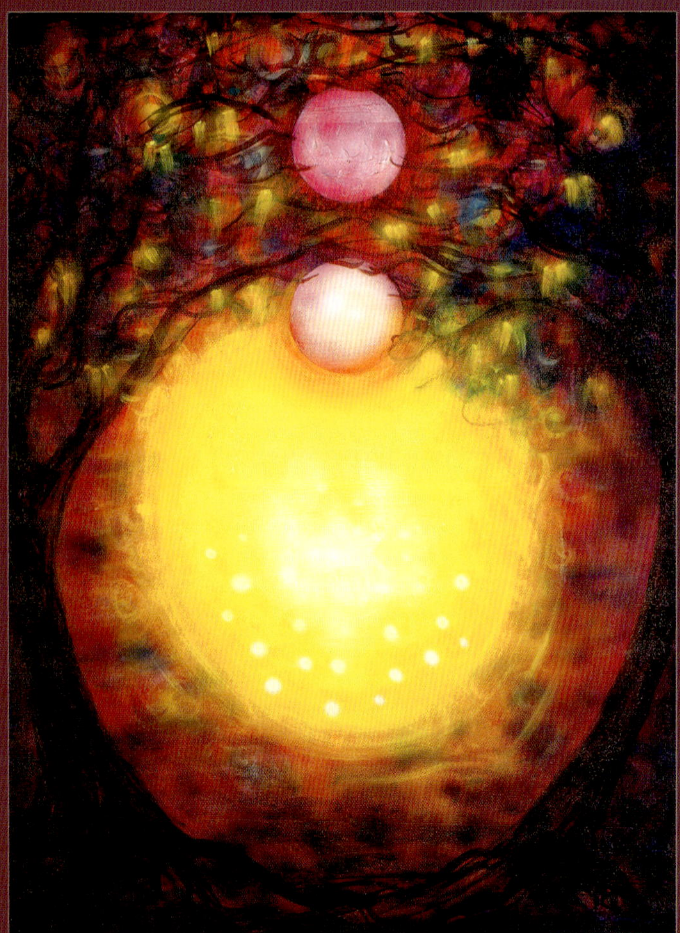

"Golden Vortex" Acrylic on canvas

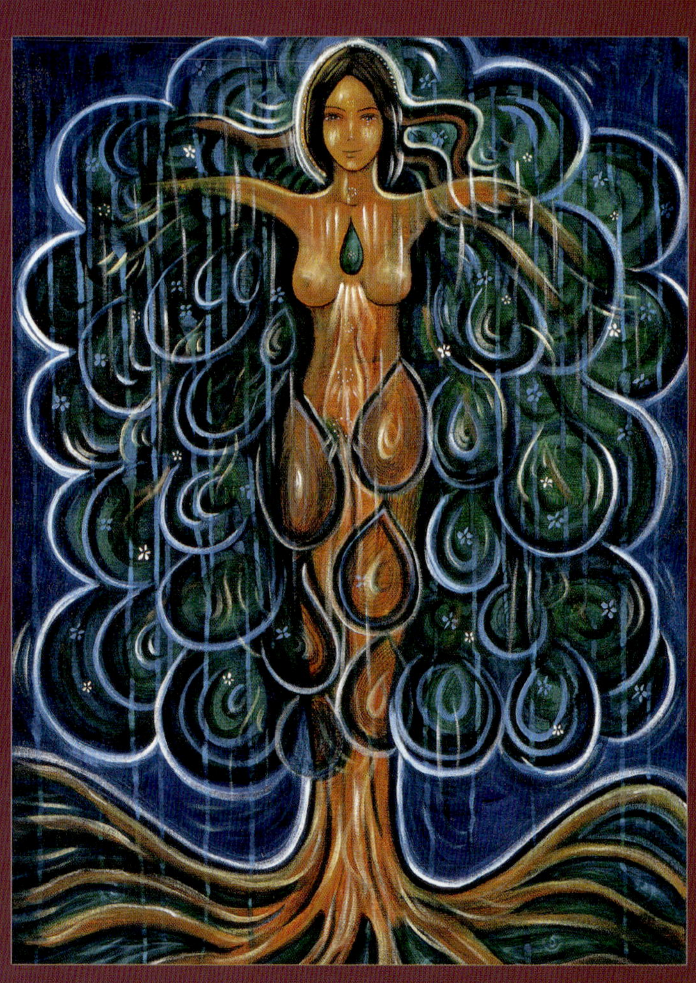

"Tree Of Knowledge" Acrylic on canvas

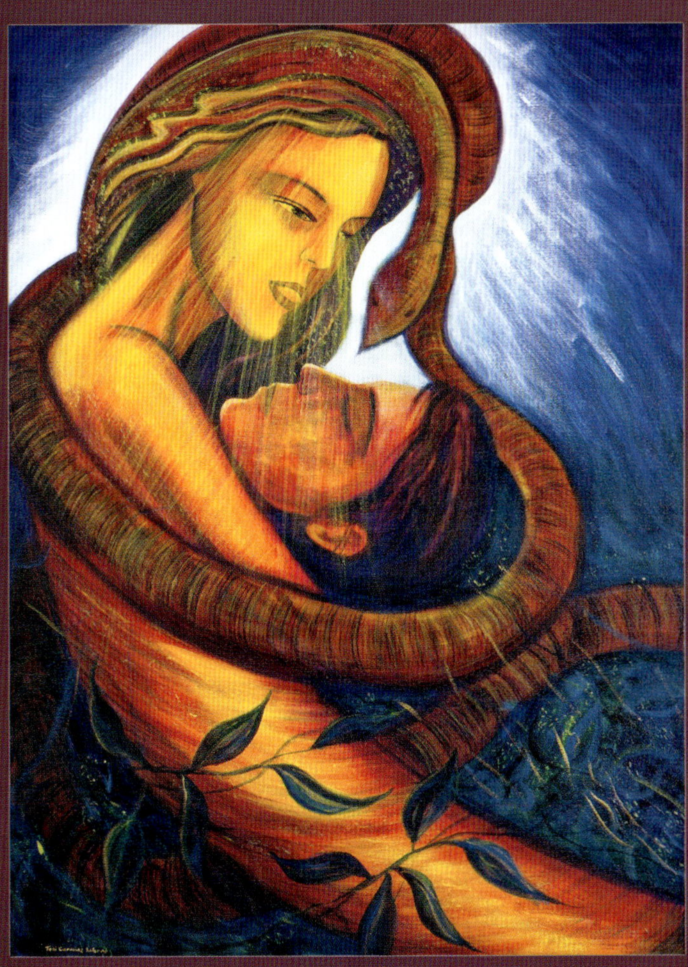

"Can You Feel Me" *Acrylic on canvas*

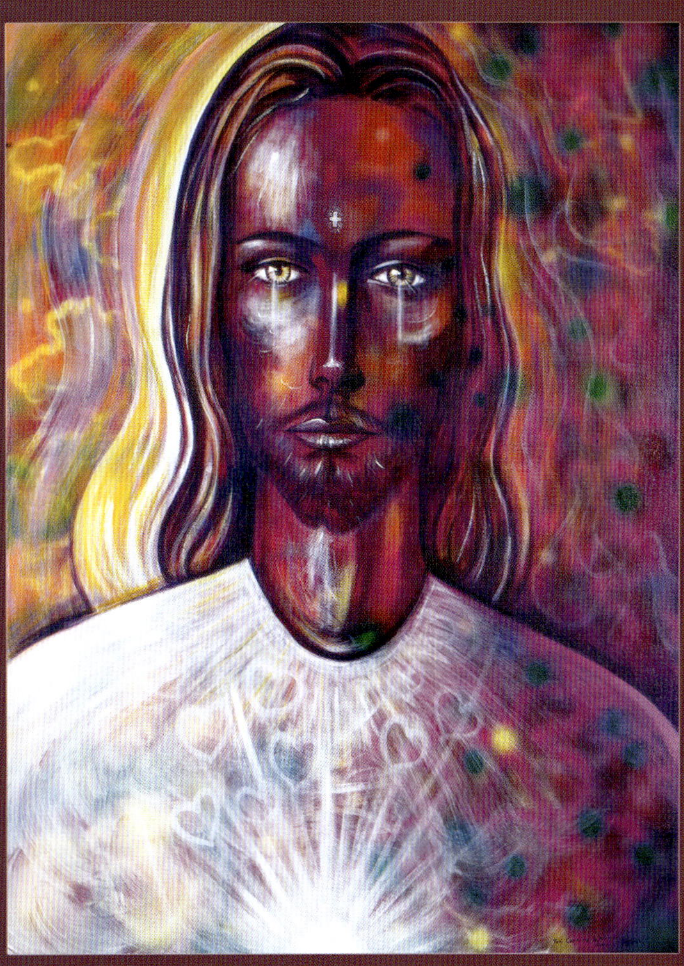

"Christos" *Acrylic on canvas*

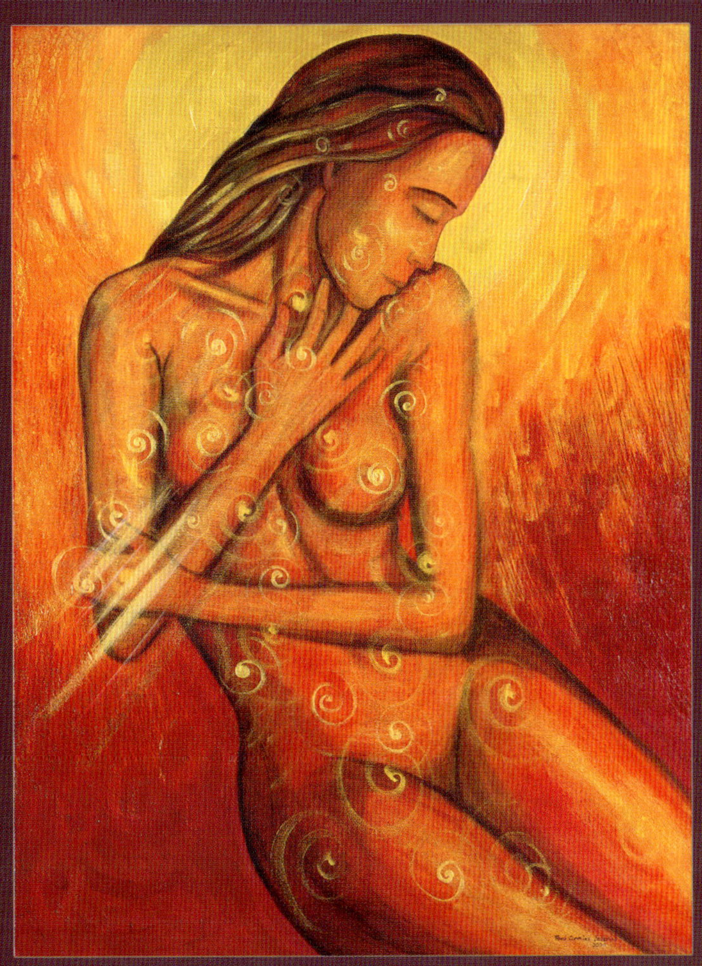

"Harmony" *Acrylic on canvas*

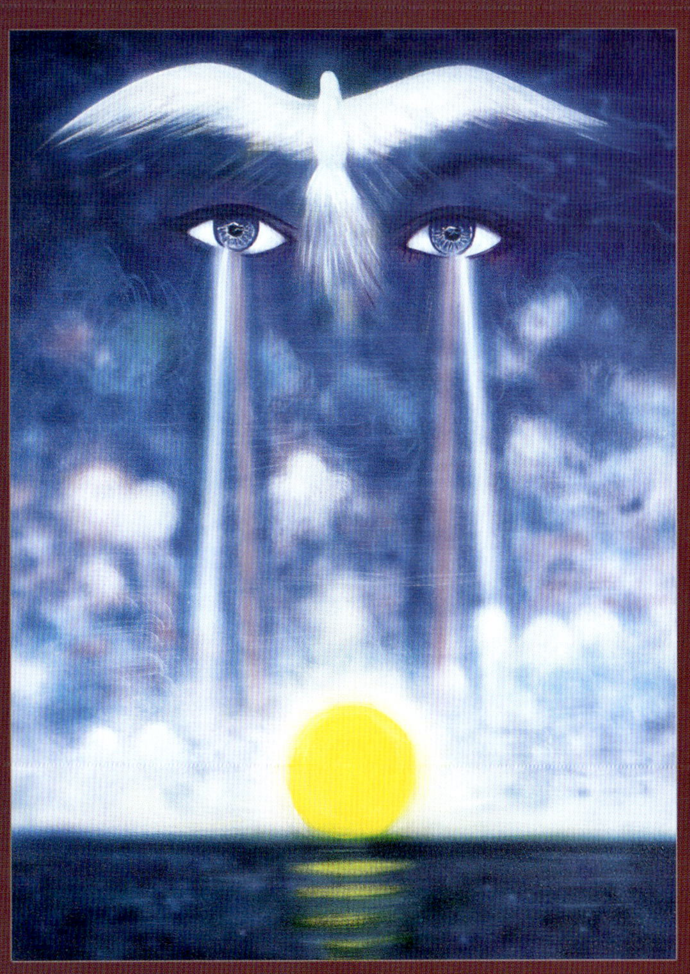

"Amen" *Acrylic on canvas*

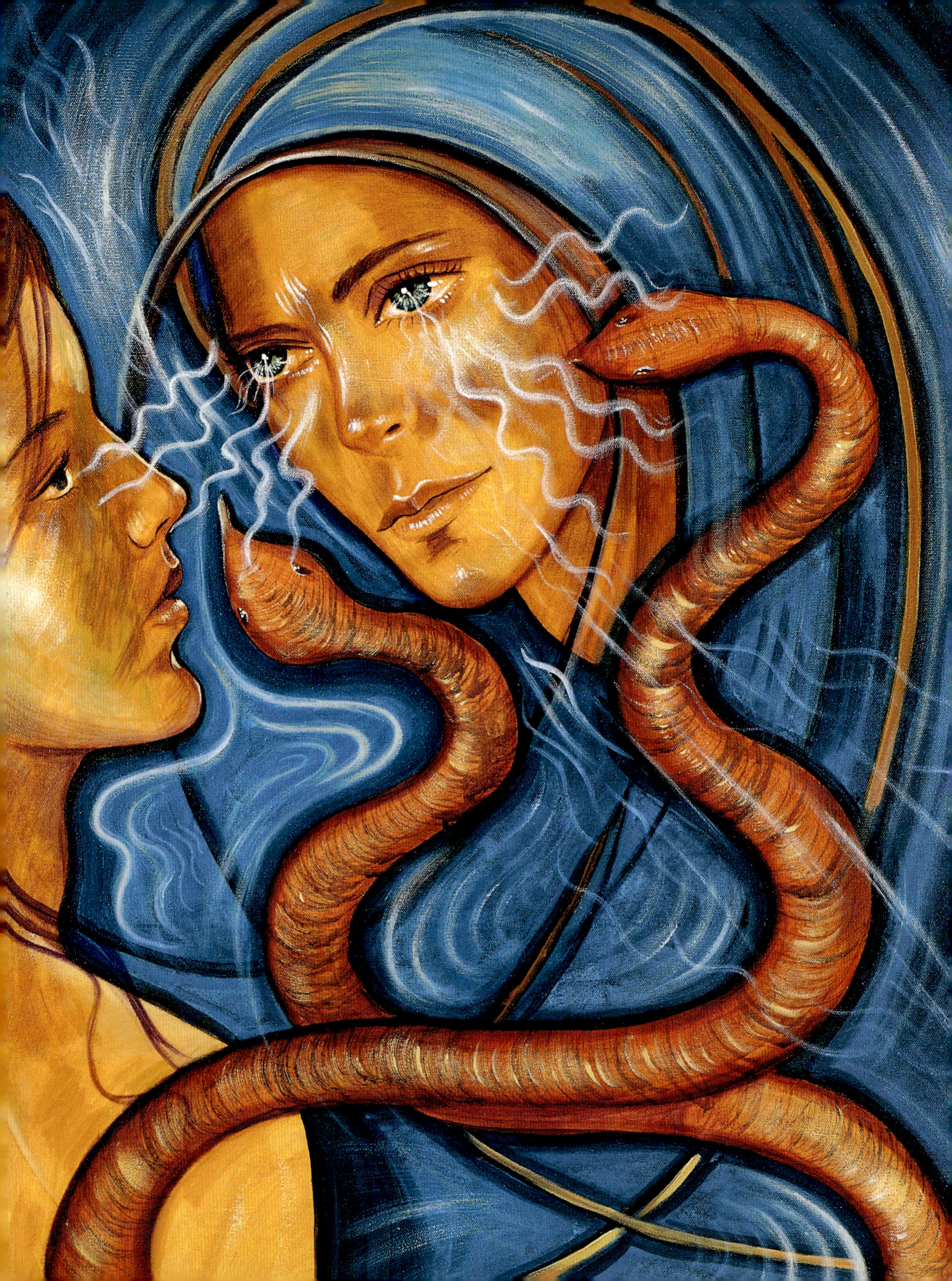

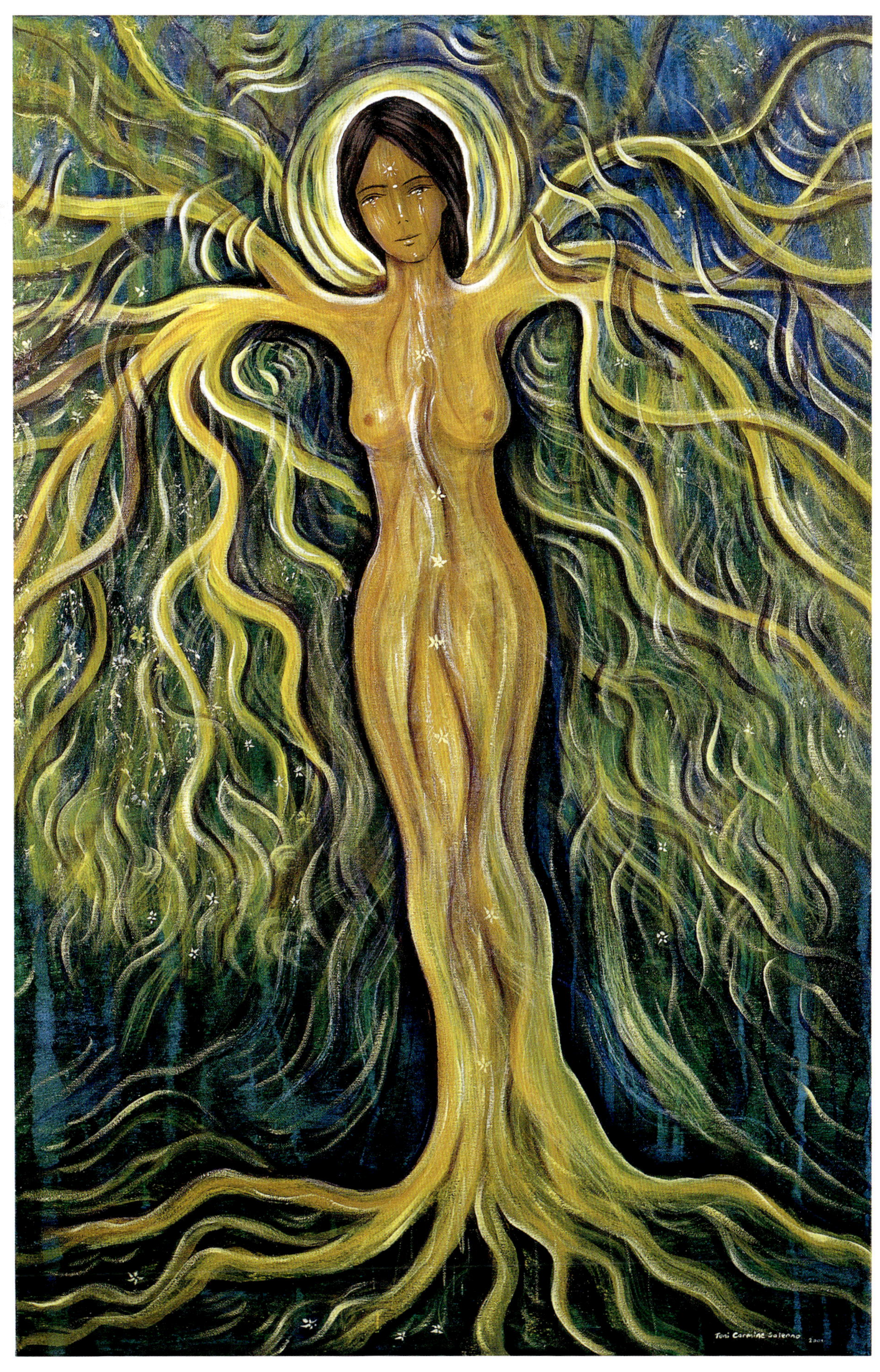

"The Universe" Acrylic on canvas
Previous page: *"Wisdom"* Acrylic on canvas

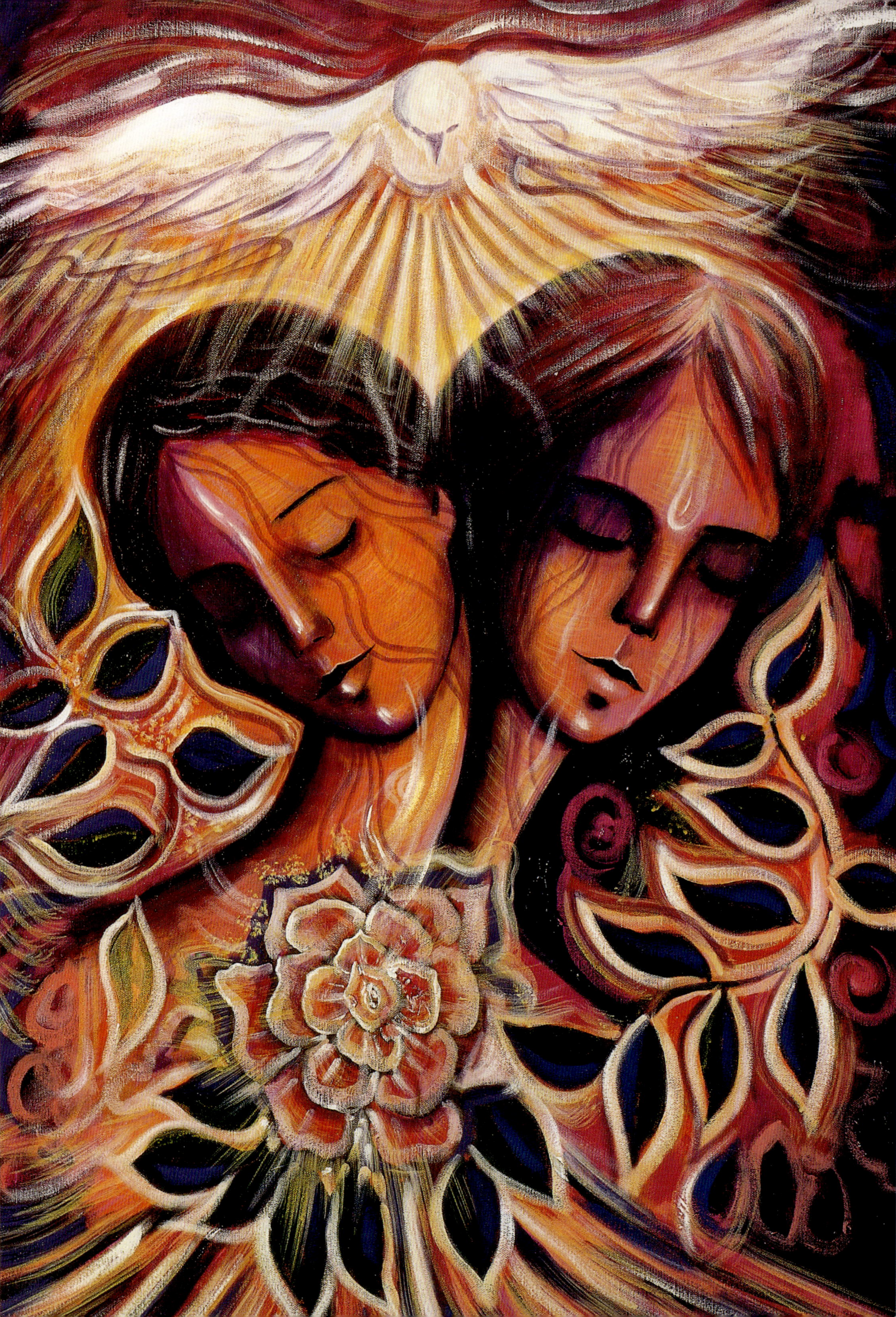

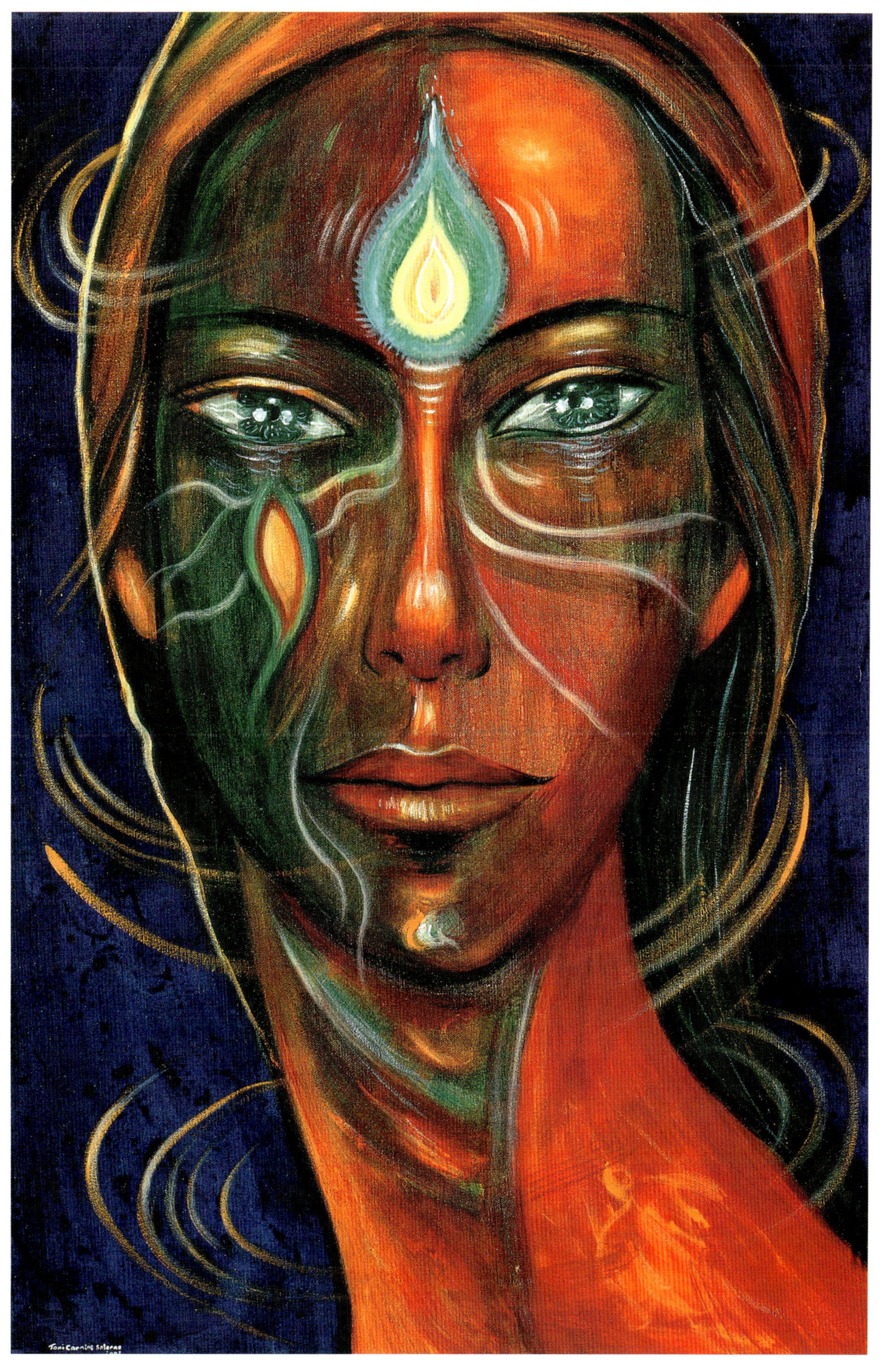

"Blue-Lit Flame" *Acrylic on canvas*

Previous page: *"Willingness To Love"* *Acrylic on canvas*

Next page: *"Mask Of Joy"* *Acrylic on canvas*

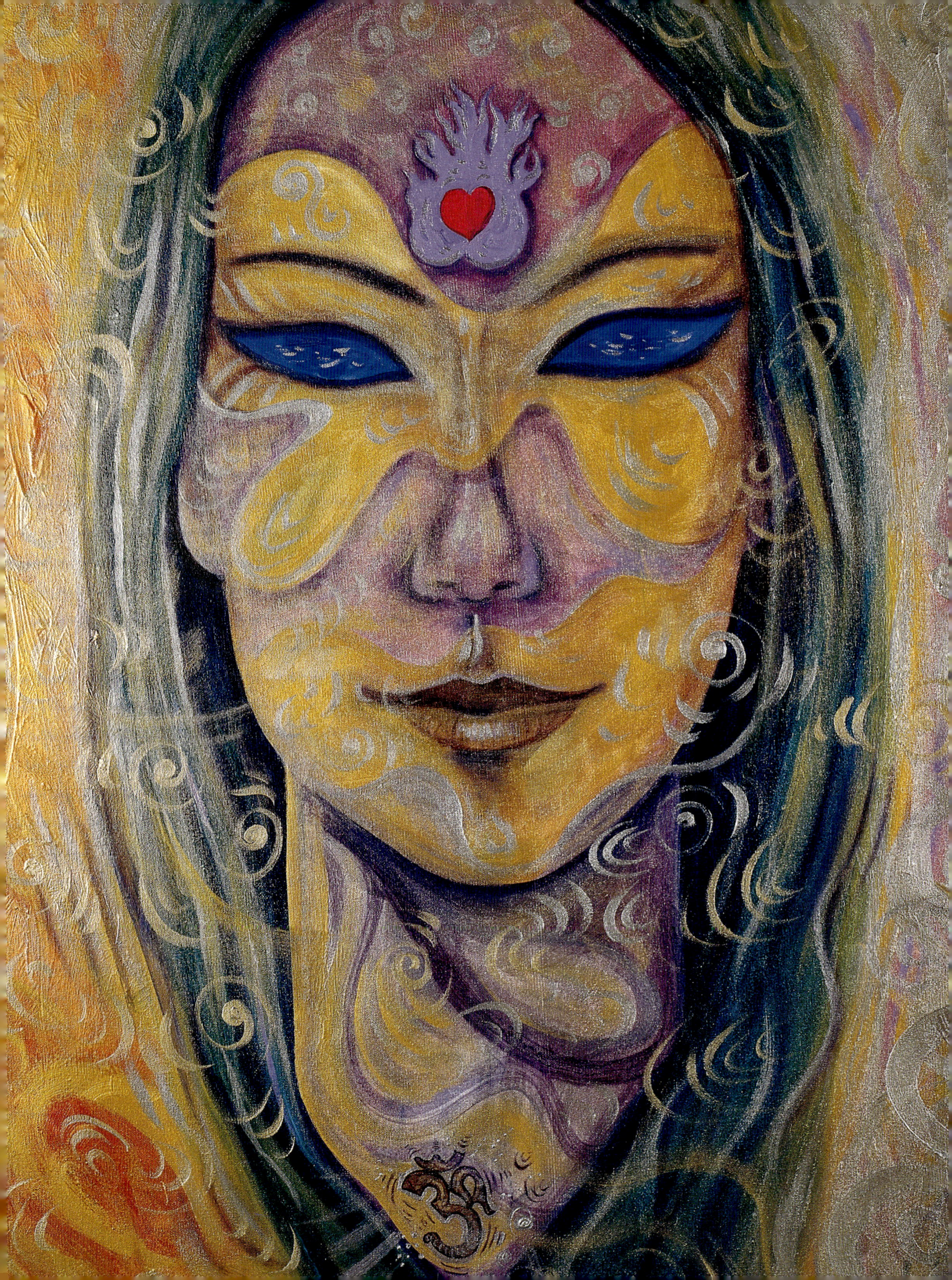

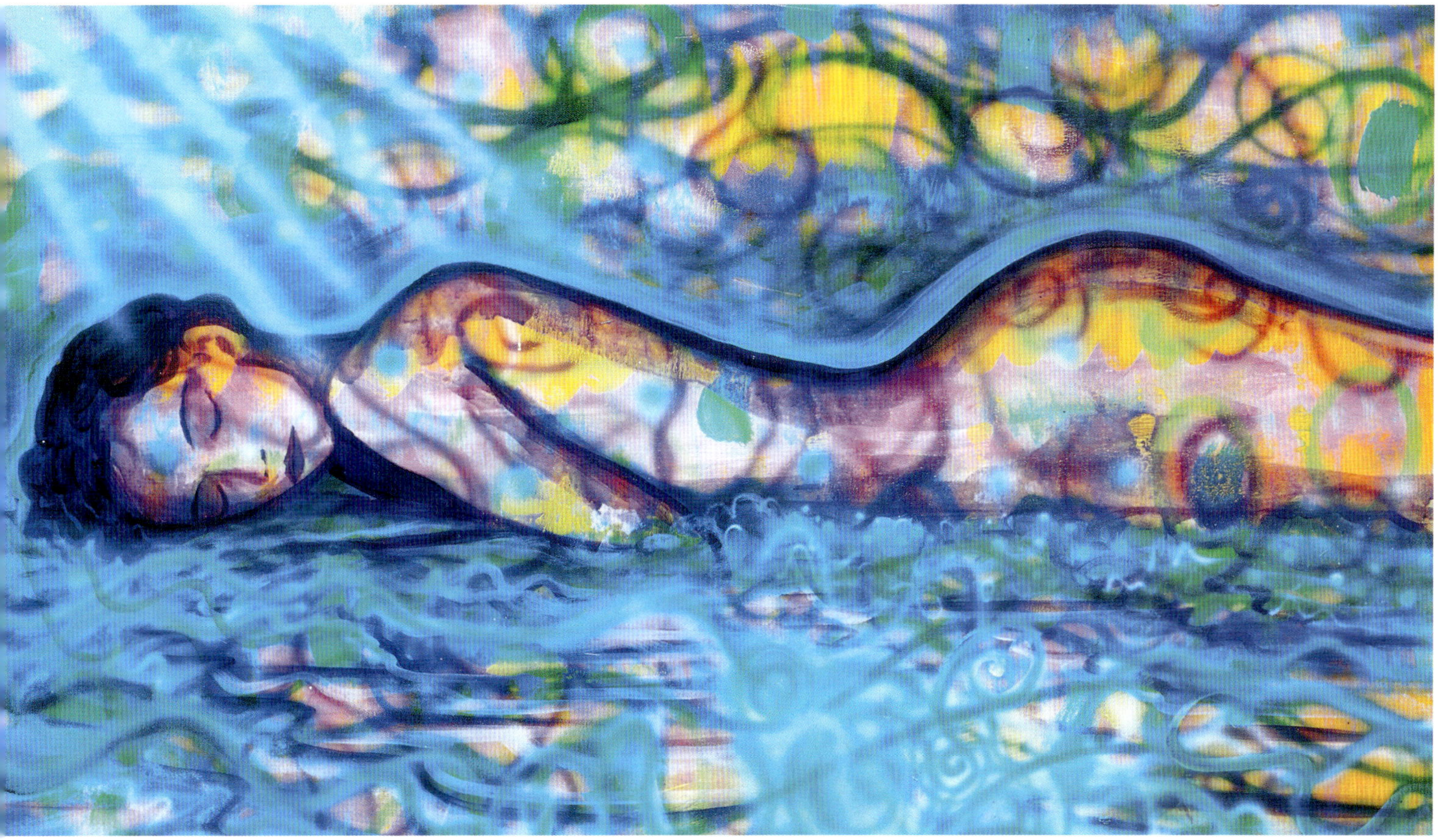

"Turquoise Sea" *Acrylic on canvas*

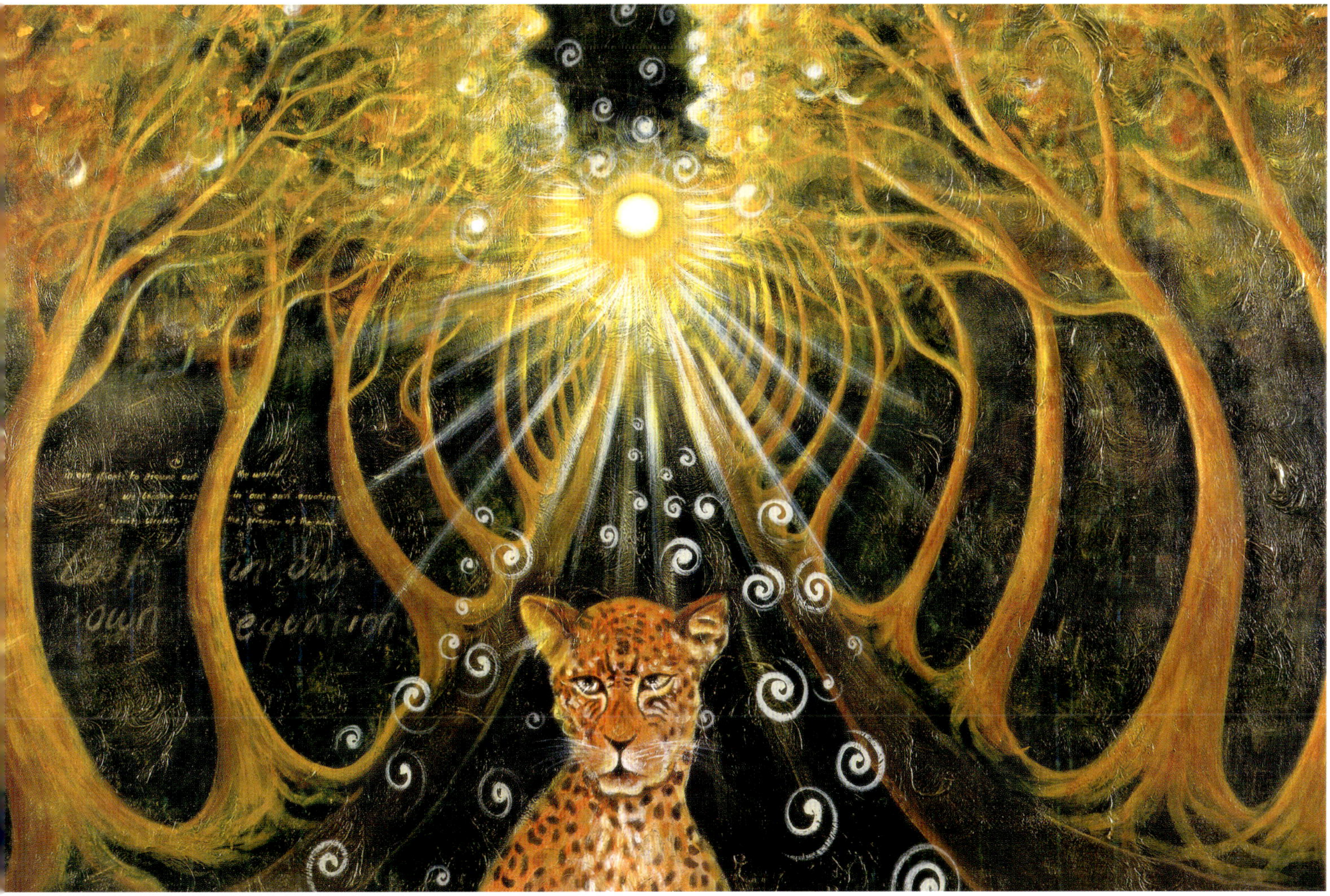

"Lost In Our Own Equations" *Acrylic on canvas*

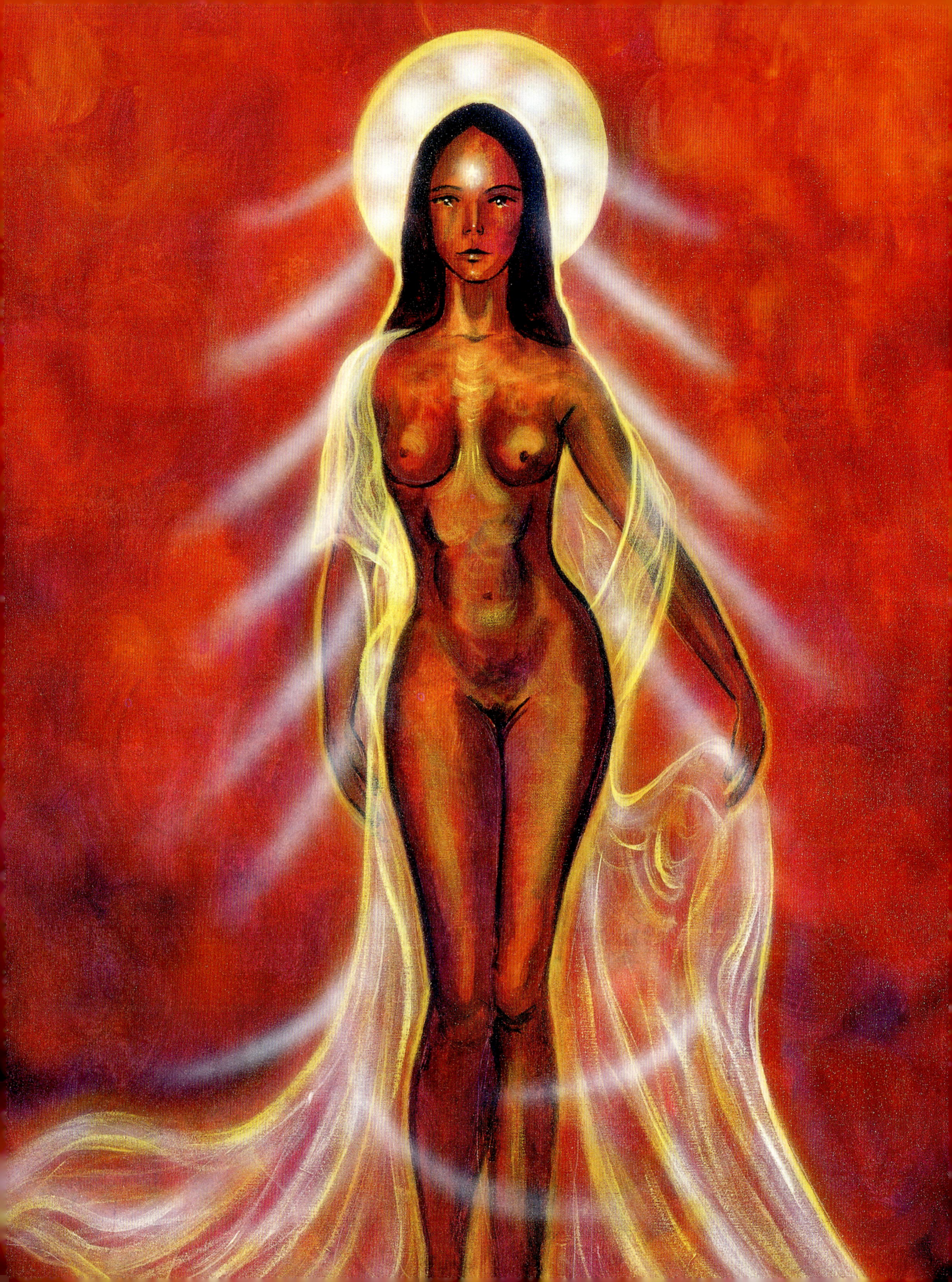

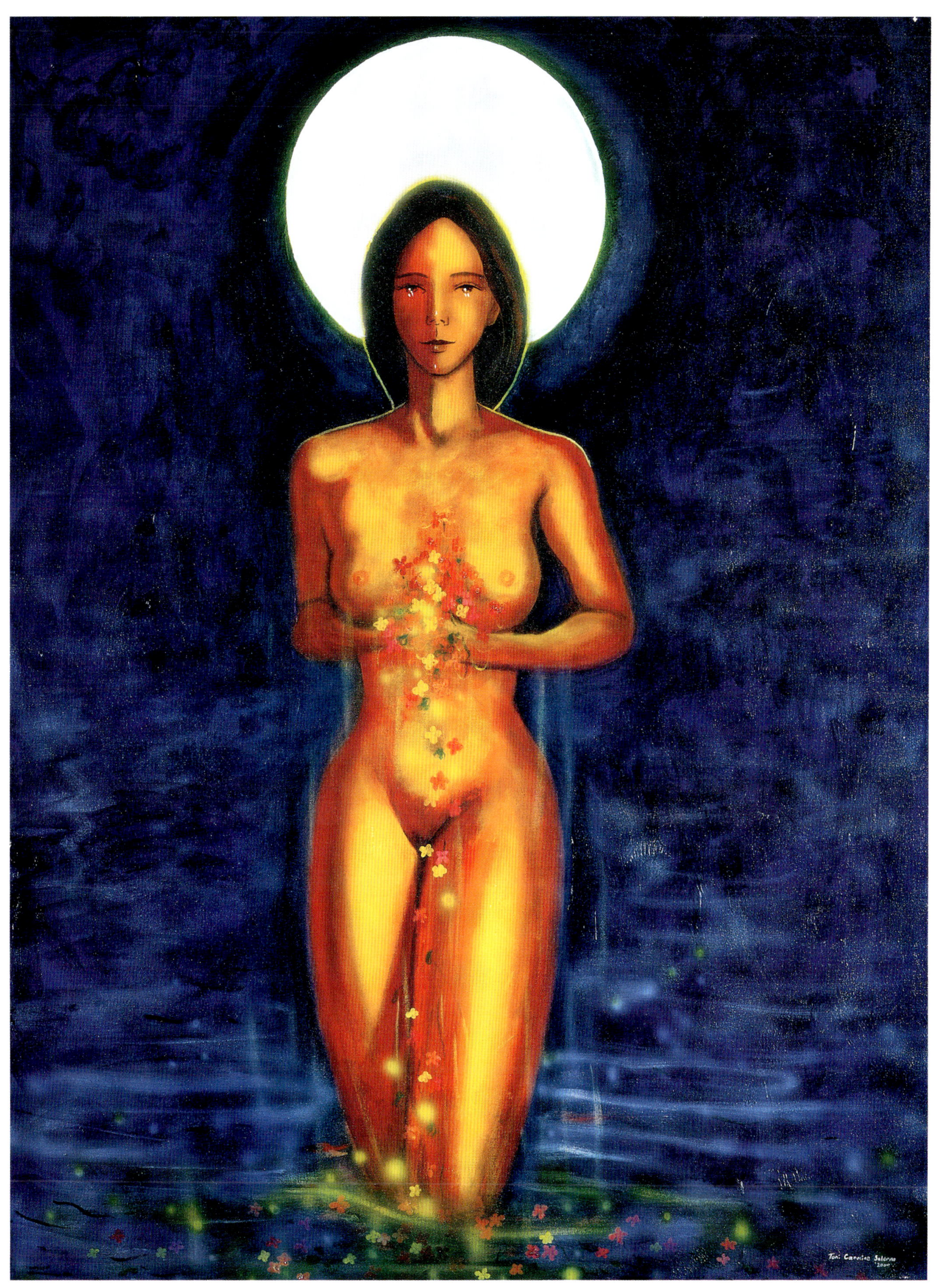

"Luna" *Acrylic on canvas*
Previous page: *"Blaze"* *Acrylic on canvas*

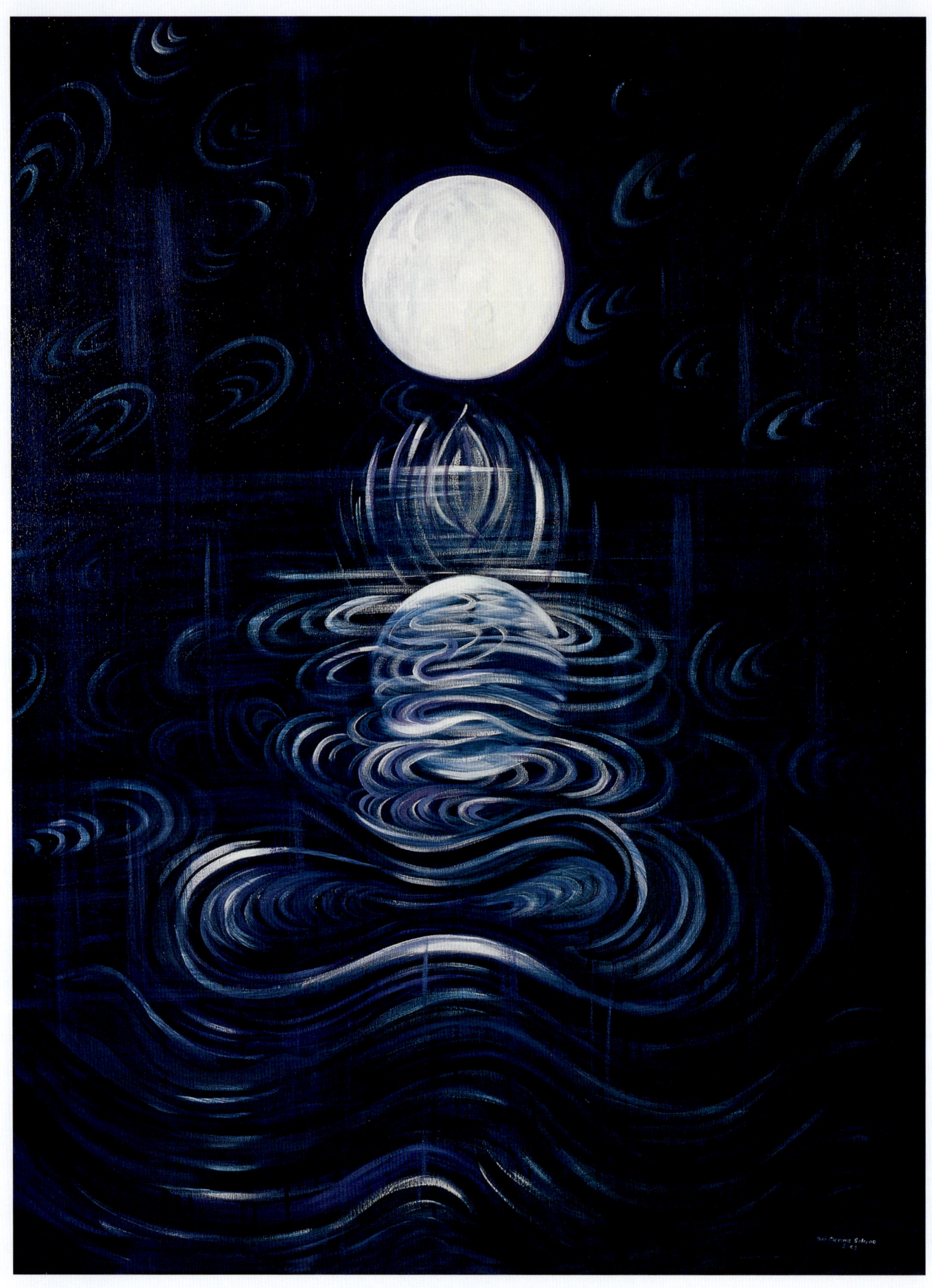

"Moon Glow" *Acrylic on canvas*

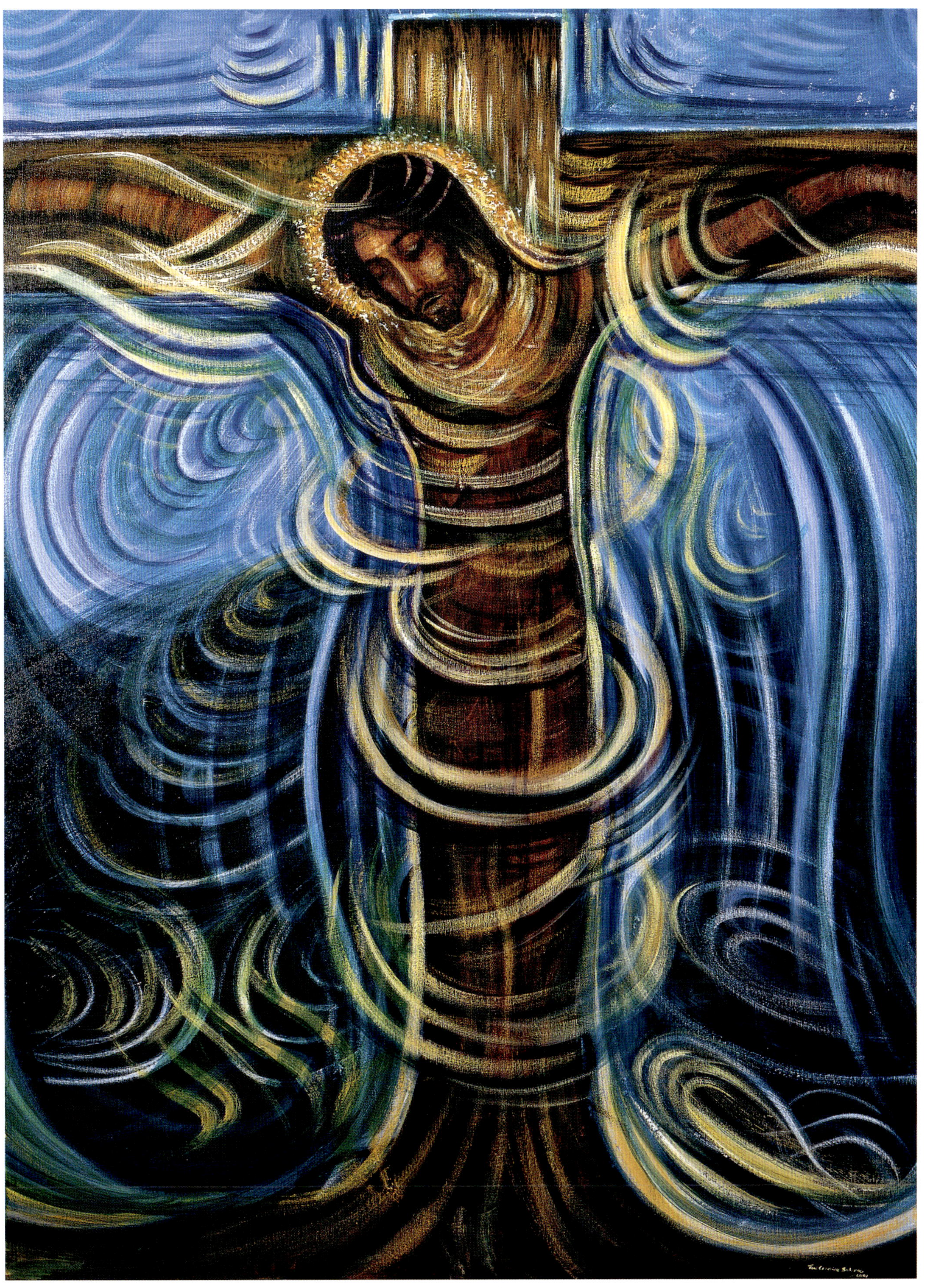

"Forgiveness" *Acrylic on canvas*

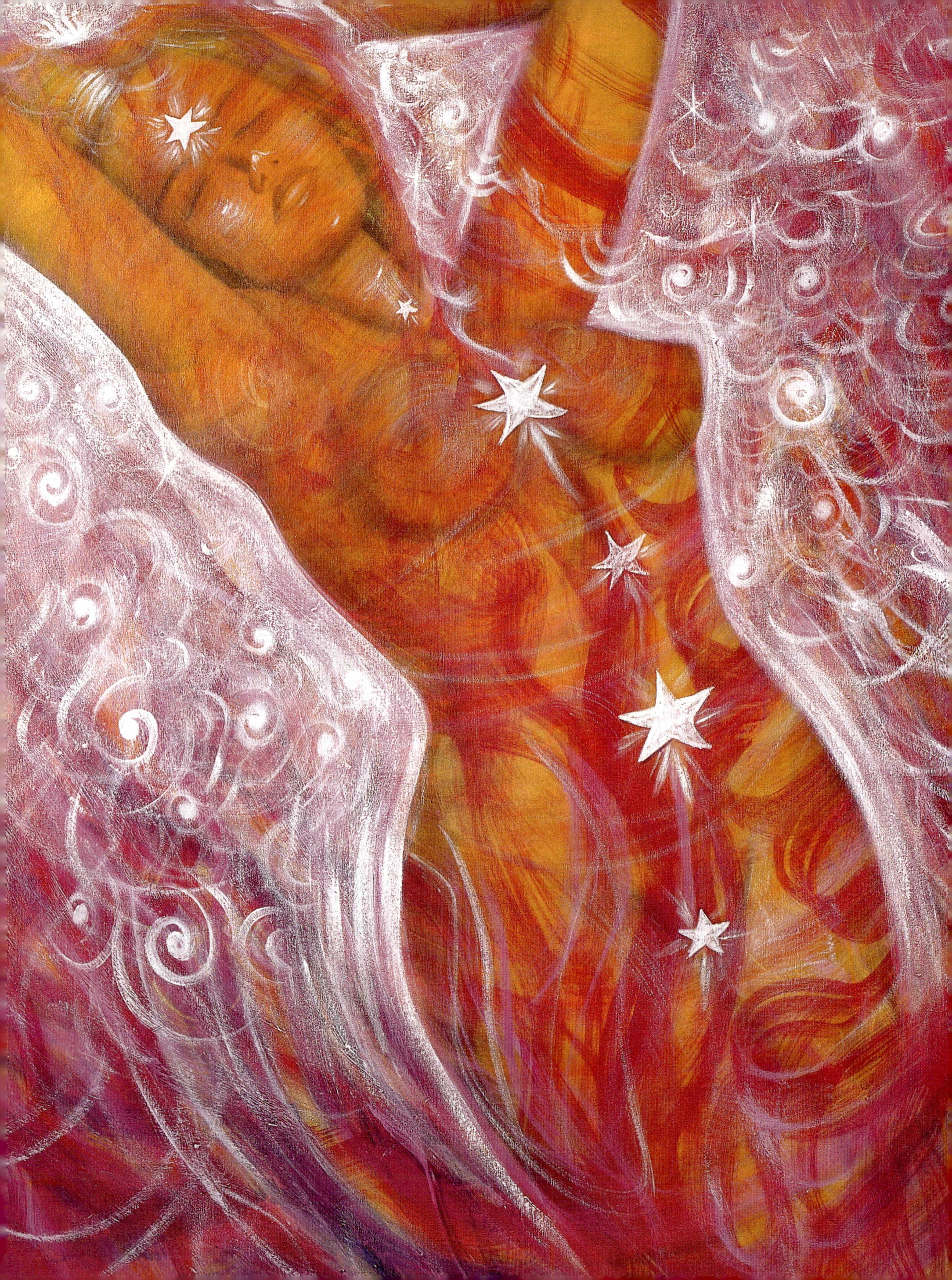

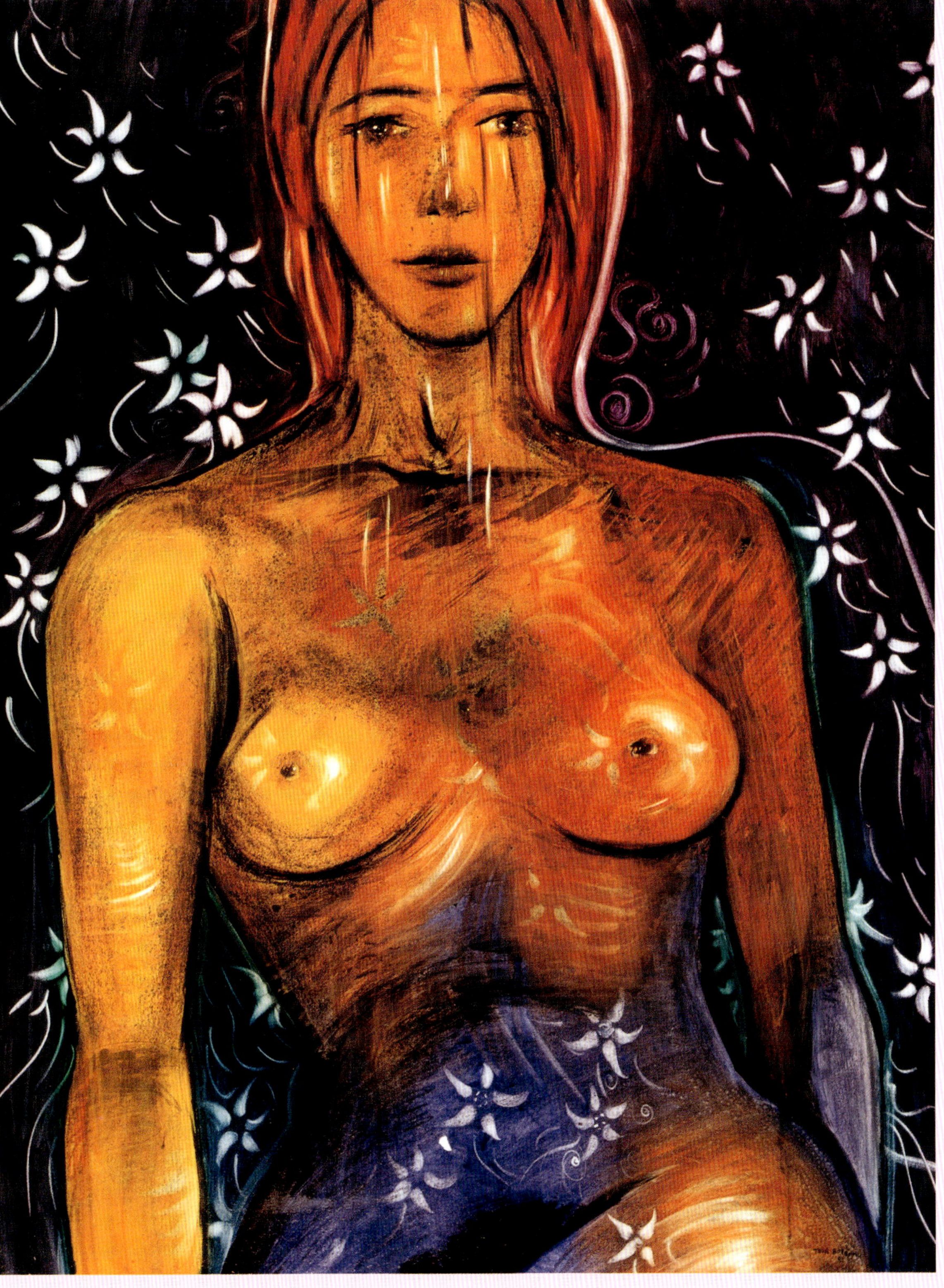

This page: *"Jo"* Oil on canvas / Previous page: *"Crystal Wave"* Acrylic on canvas

Love is a silent state of grace
It is ultimately beyond words, concepts or images
Yet it is possible to convey love through all you do
By doing all you do lovingly

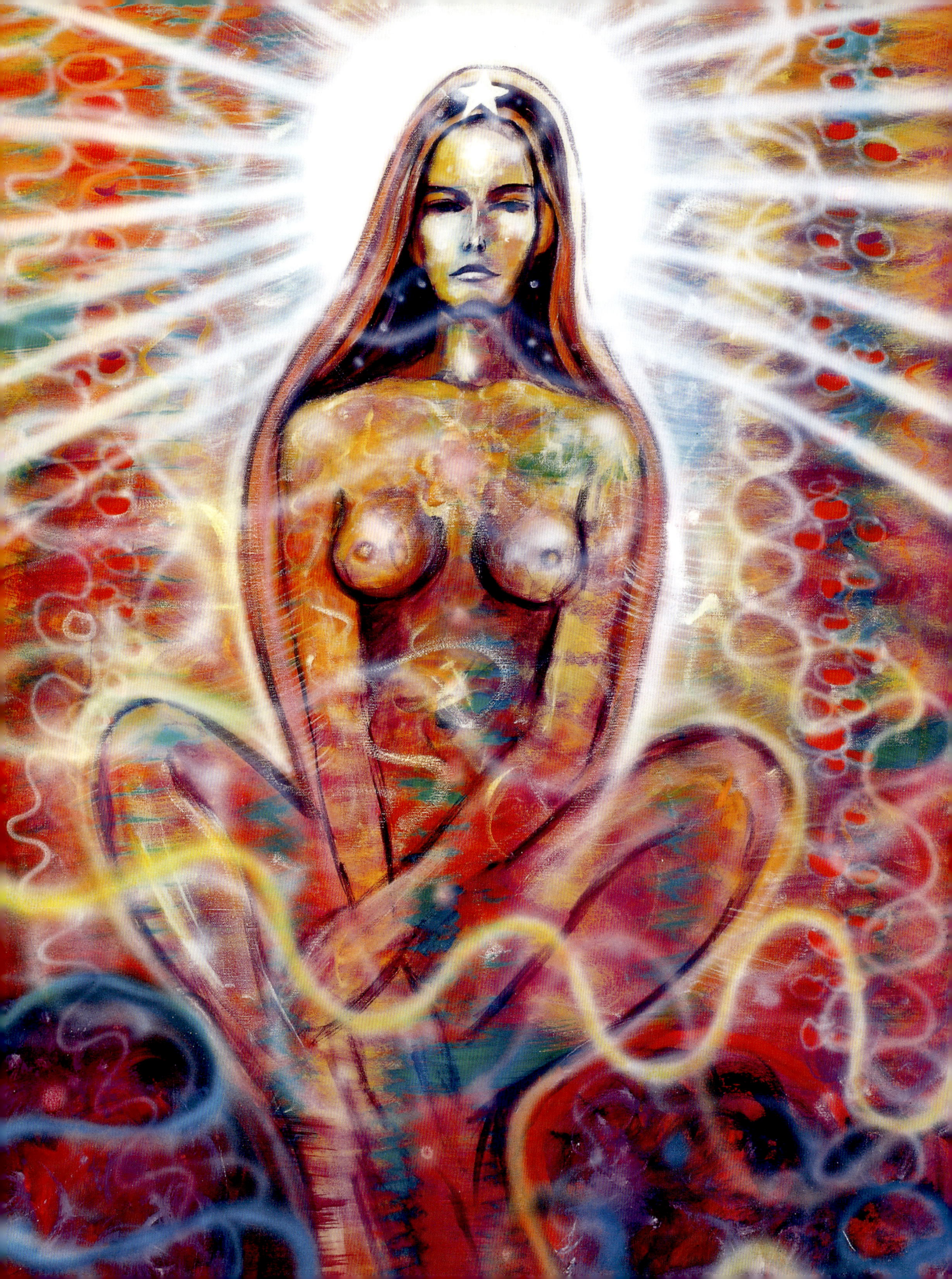

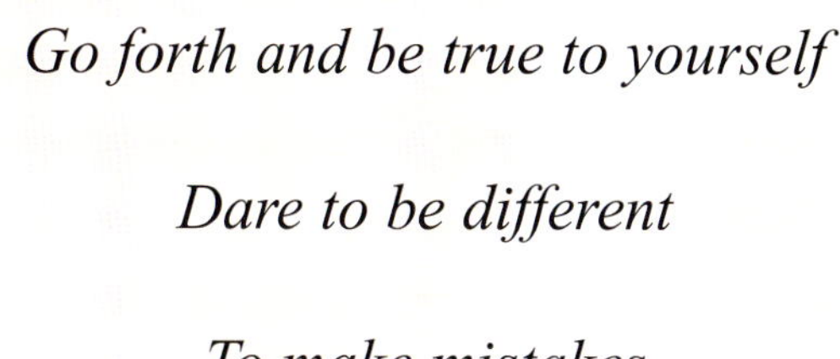

Go forth and be true to yourself

Dare to be different

To make mistakes

Create, for it is in creation that you exist

In a world full of dreams that stem from your heart

In oneness, love and hatred

Wonder and awe, softness and pain, joy and light.

In the stillness the unknown awaits

A void wanting to be filled.

Step into it with courage and strength

Like a budding rose reaching for the light

Love will lead you to greener pastures

Keep your pockets full of dreams

For life is a test of faith.

Allow your light to shine

There is no beginning or end,

There is only love!

"Moon Goddess" *Acrylic on canvas*

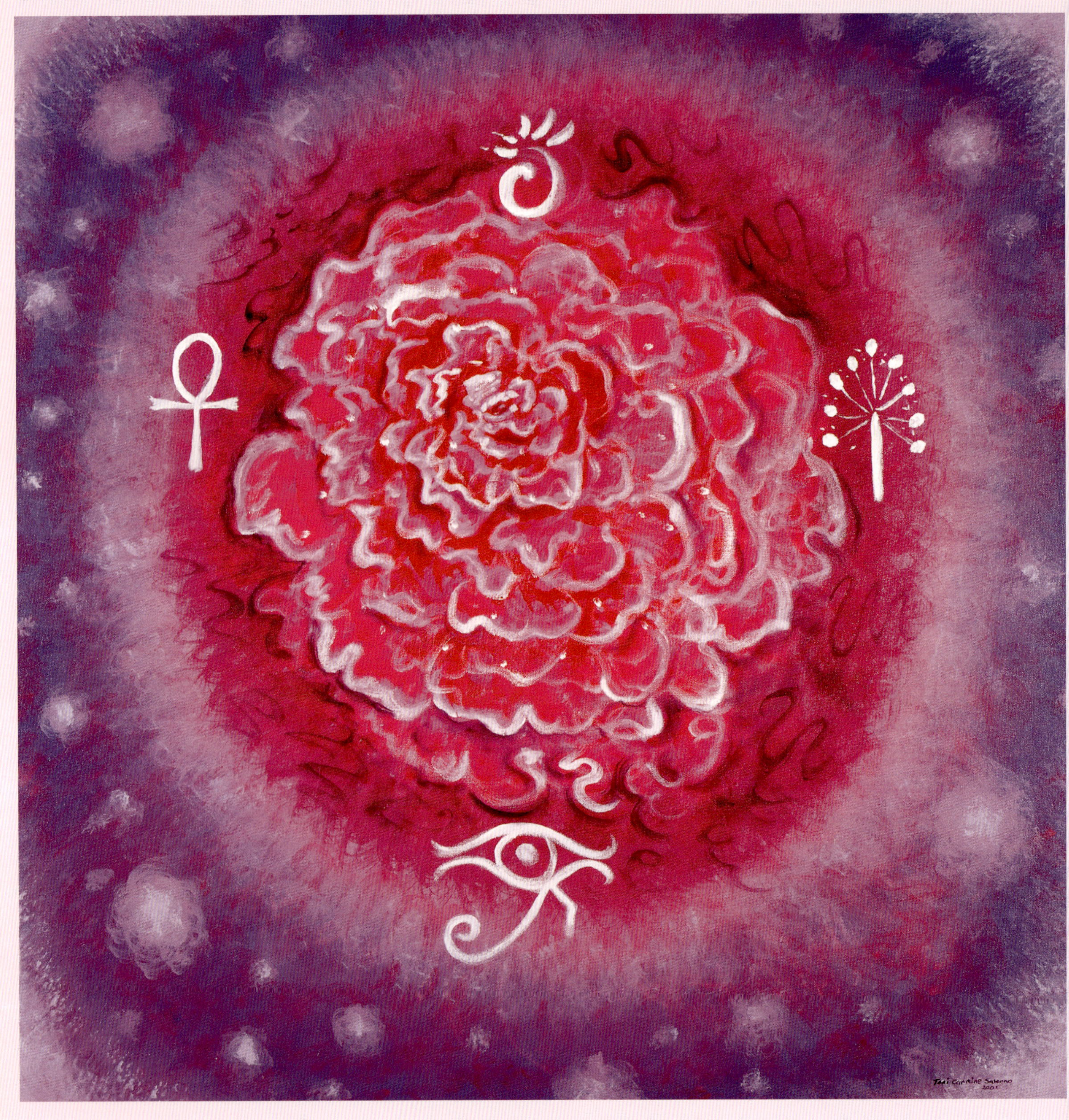

Notions of good and bad,
right and wrong
exist only in our minds.
Deep inside each heart
there is only love.

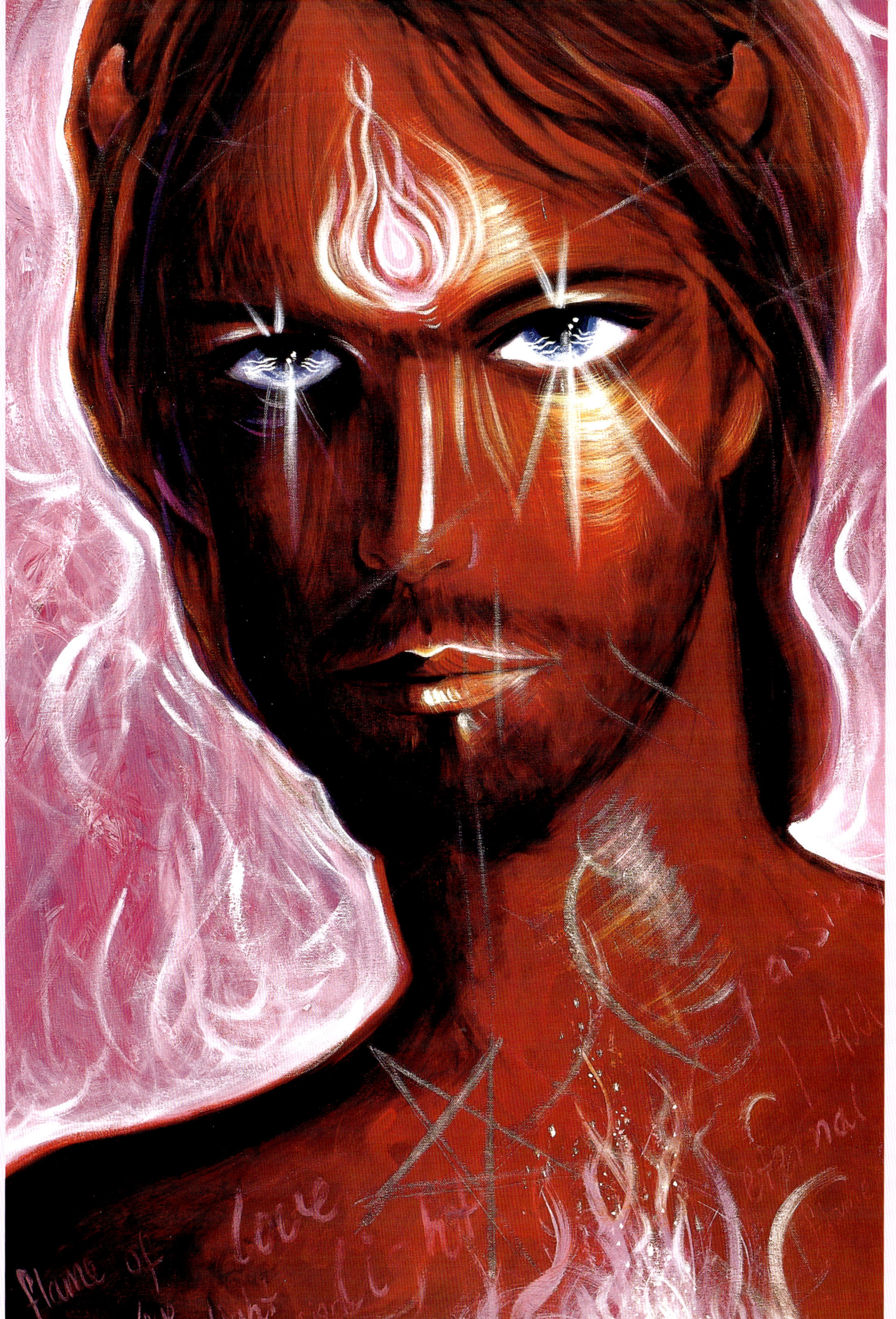

"Diavolino" Acrylic on canvas / Previous page: *"Expectancy"* Acrylic on canvas

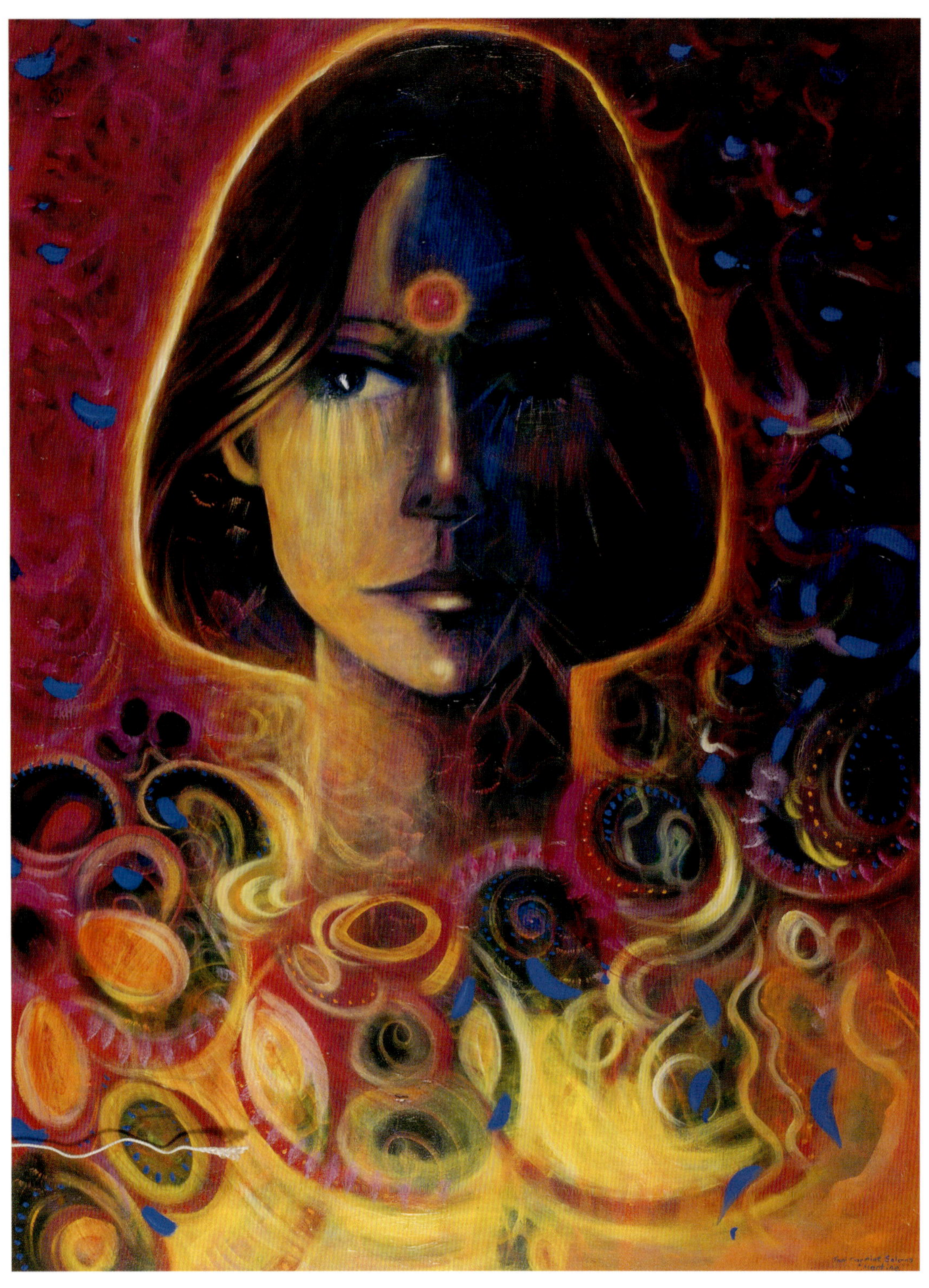

As if in a dream, you shall drift beyond the horizon
Through the ancient mists of time,
Then awaken within the womb
To a new day full of beautiful things.
And you shall not remember what came before
... but for a stirring in your heart.

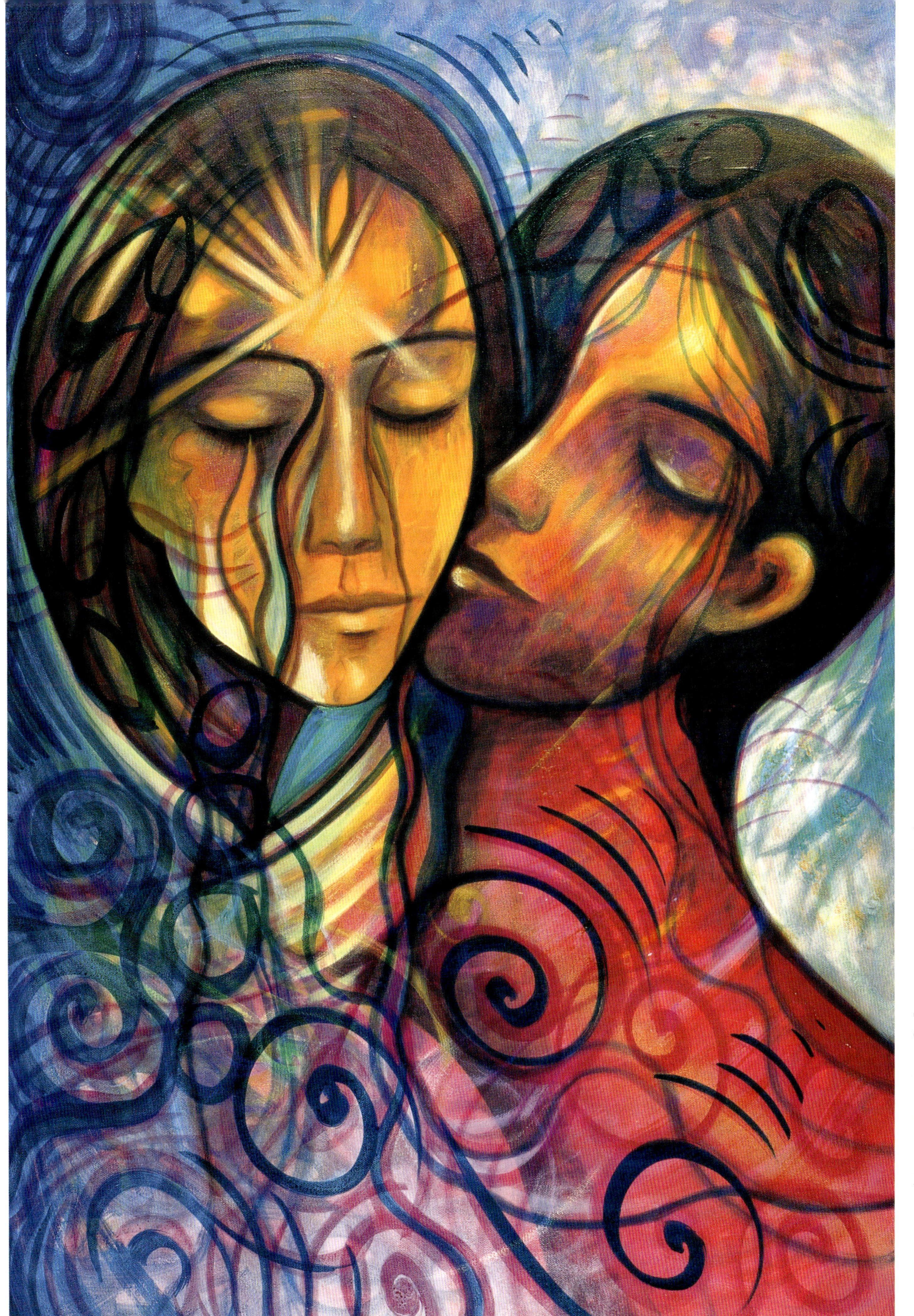

"Anima Animus" Acrylic on canvas / Previous page: *"Martine"* Acrylic on canvas

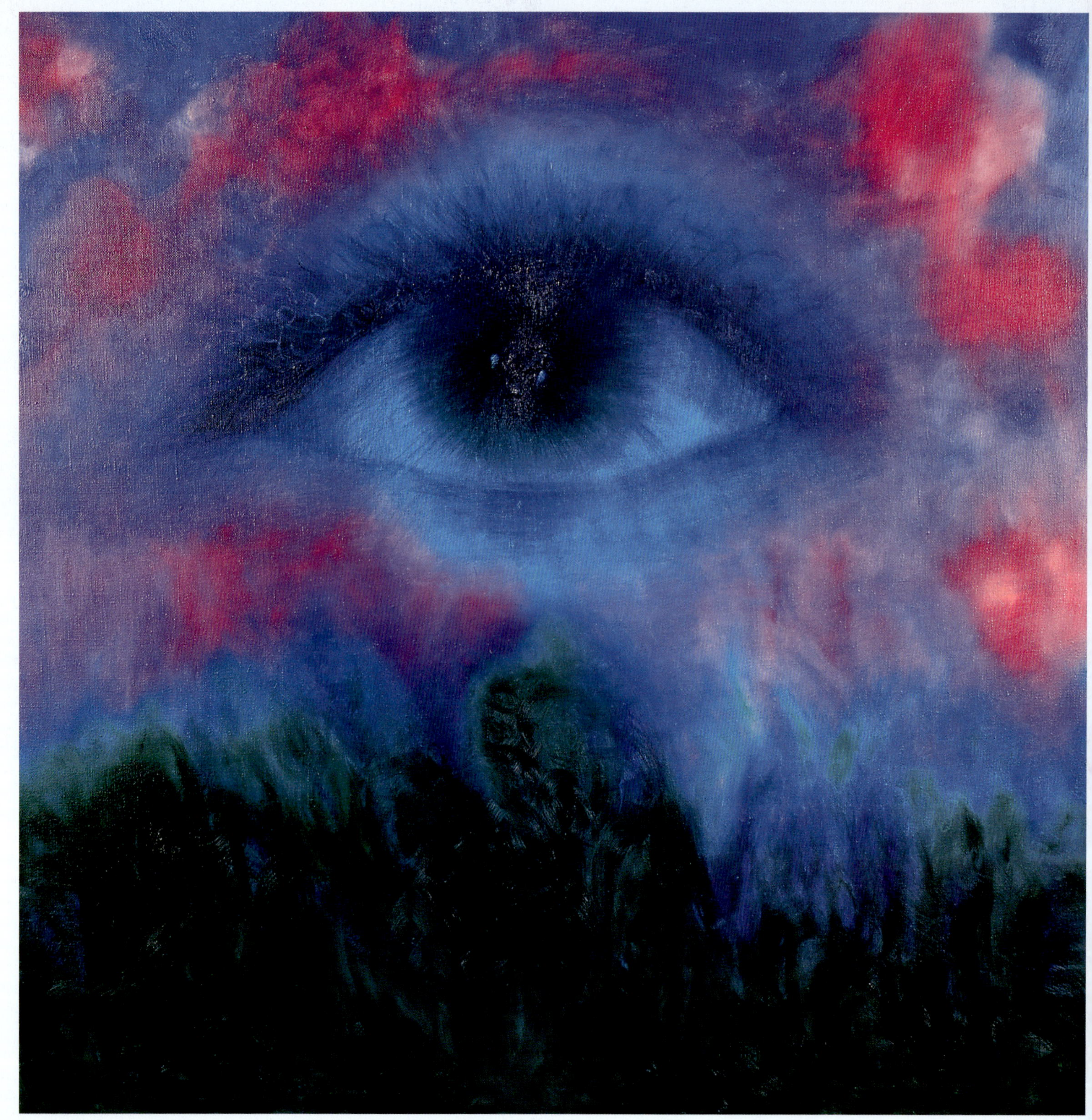

"Eye Of God" *Oil on canvas* / *Next page:* *"Cara"* *Acrylic on canvas*

Life is a luminous gift, forever present, even in the midst of darkness.

When all hope seems lost, delve to the innermost depths of your heart,

for there you will discover the true miracle of life.

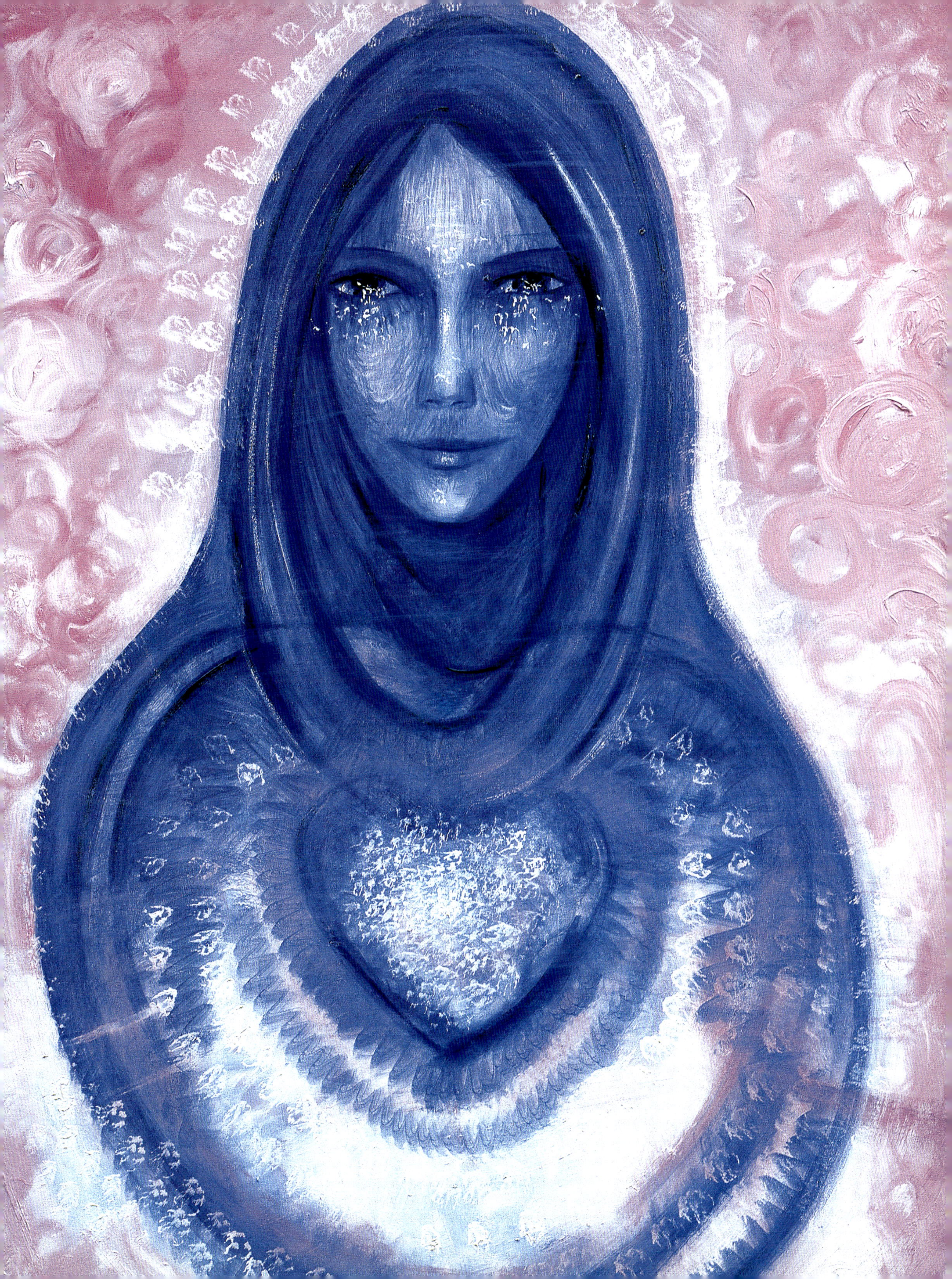

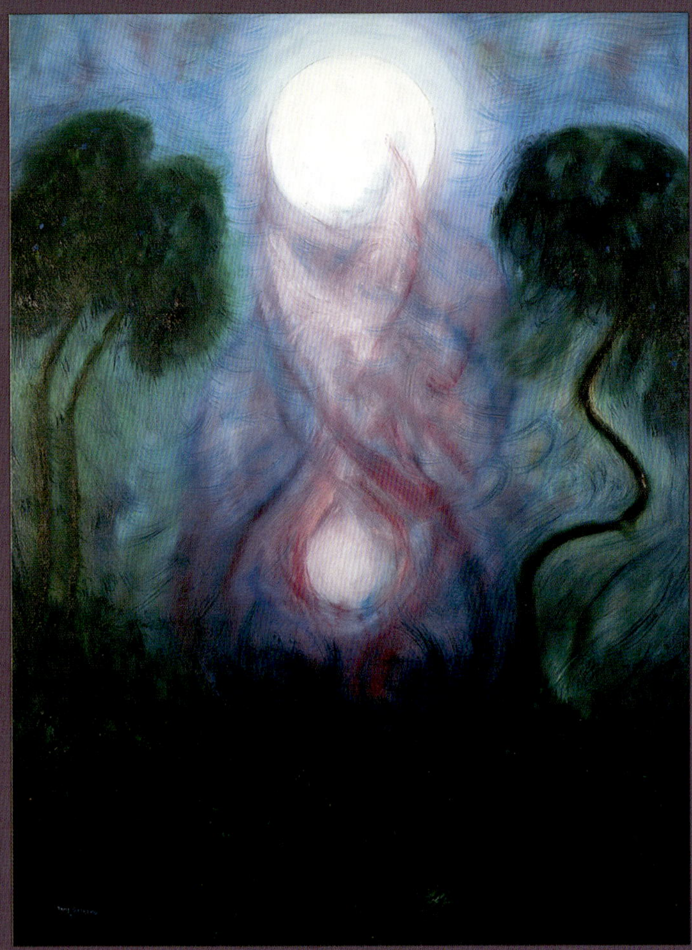

"Higher Self" Oil on canvas

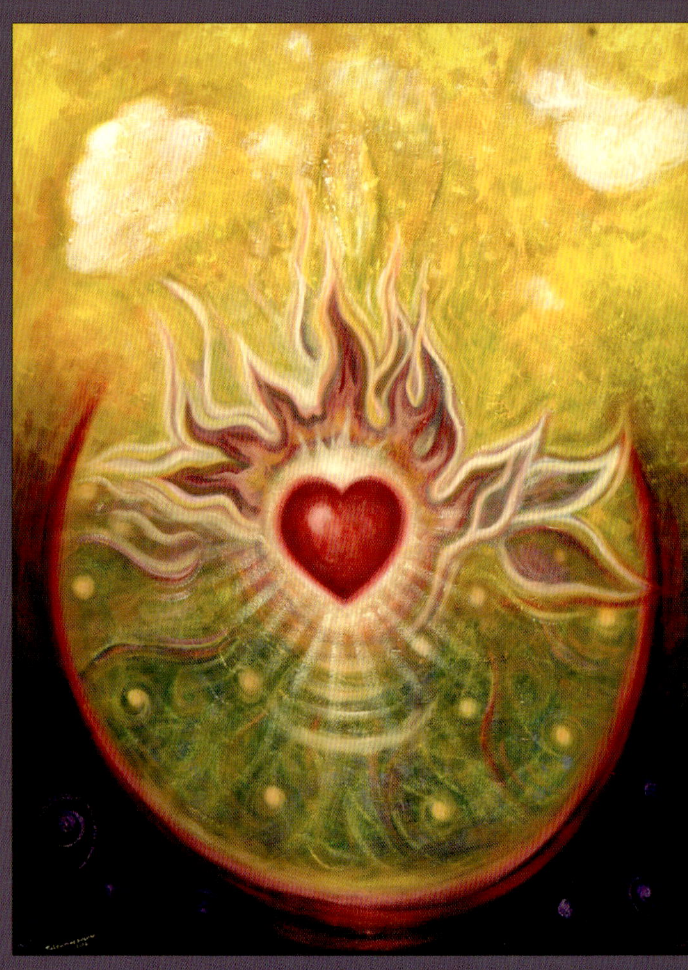

"Sacre Coeur" Acrylic on canvas

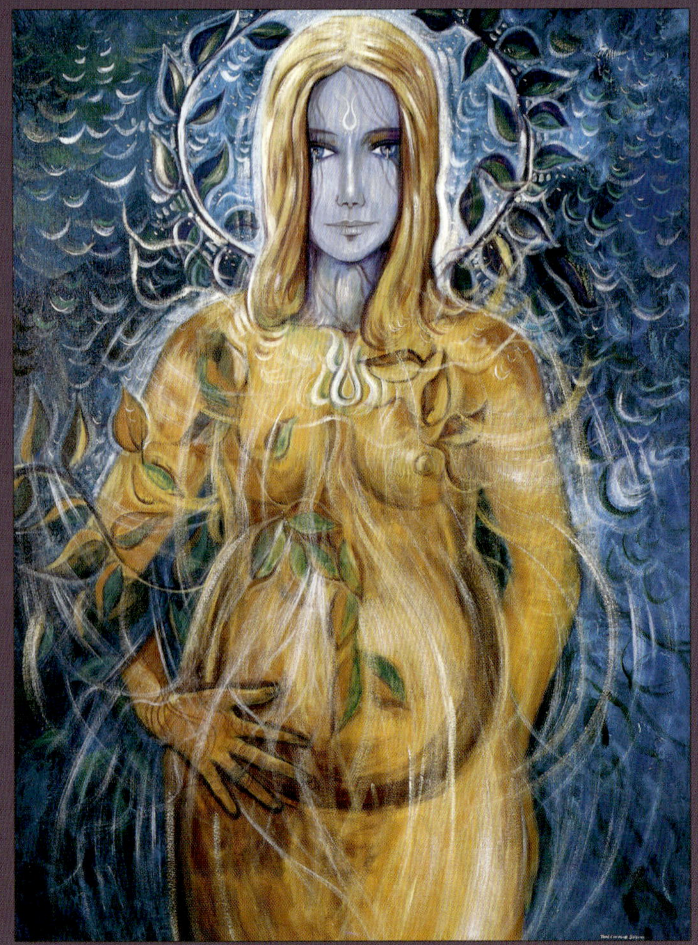

"La Natura" Acrylic on canvas

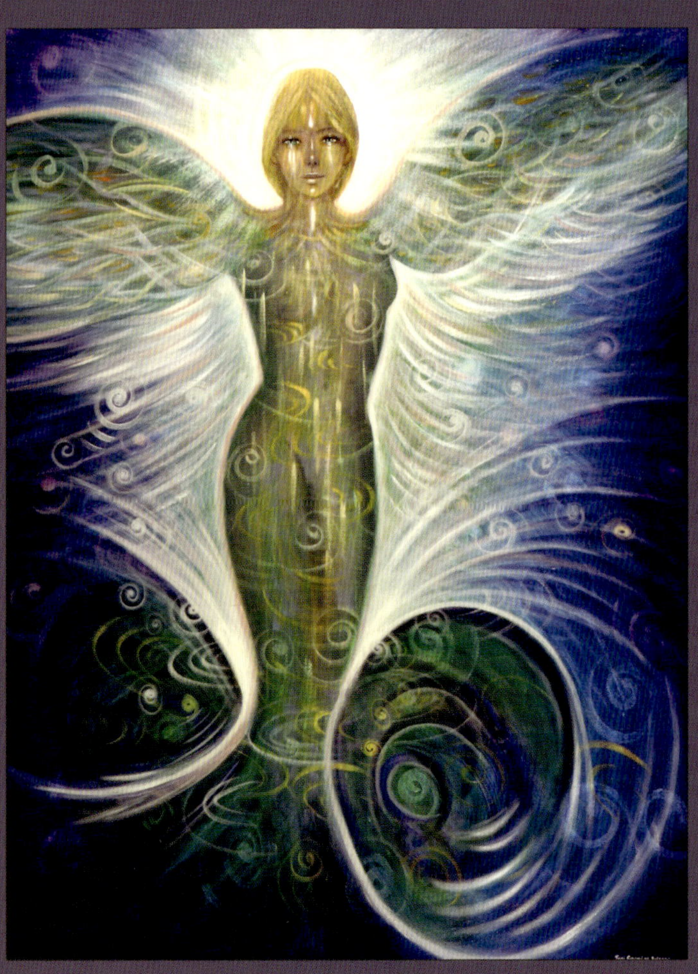

"The Poetry Of Space" Acrylic on canvas

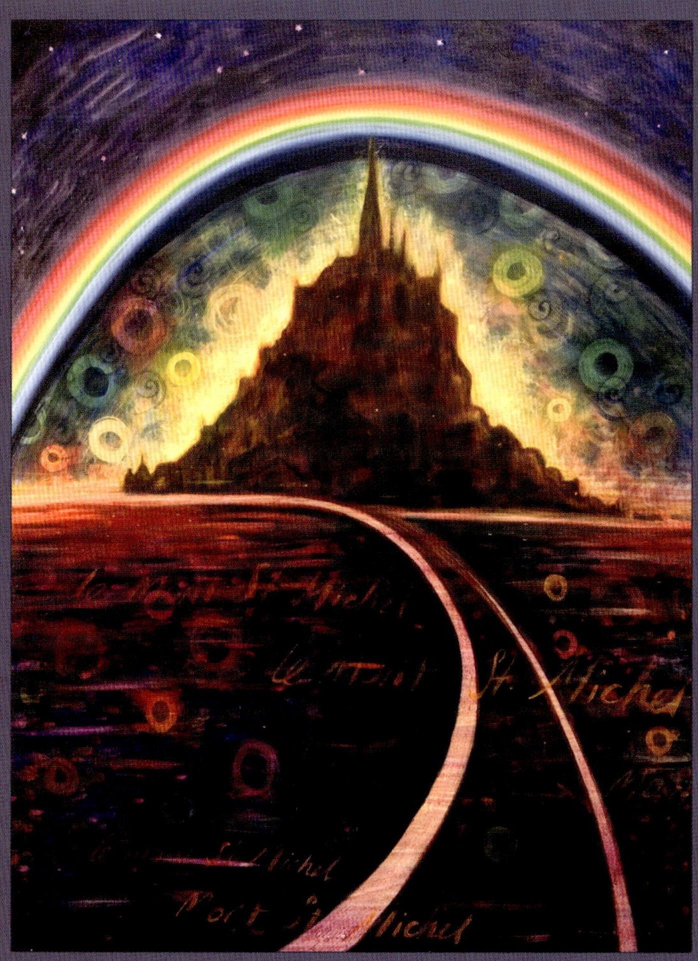

"Mont St. Michel" Acrylic on canvas

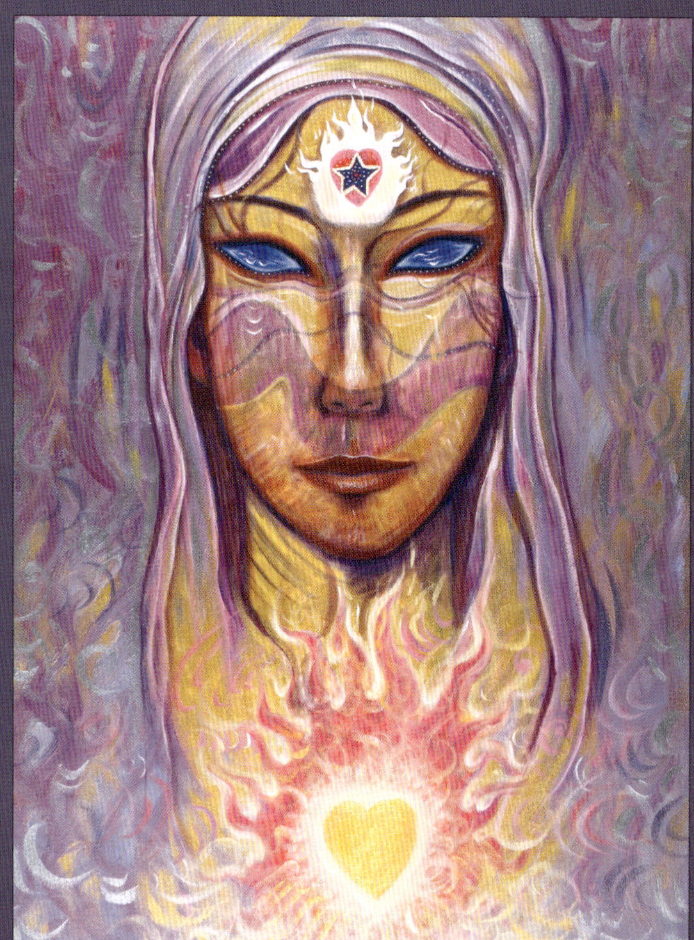

"Anima" Acrylic on canvas

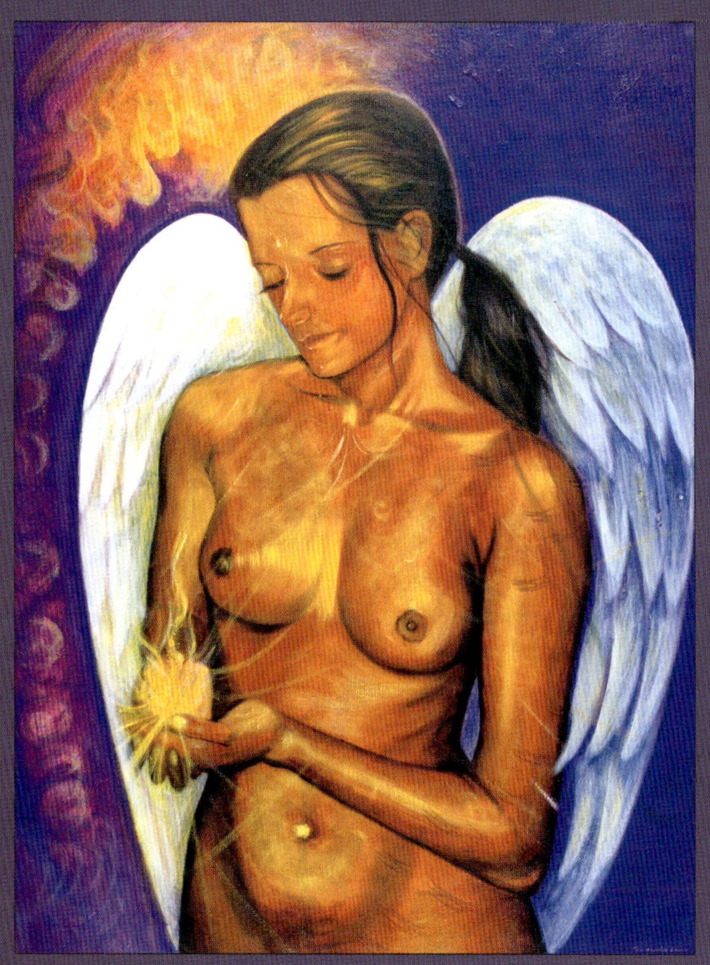

"Alchemy" Acrylic on canvas

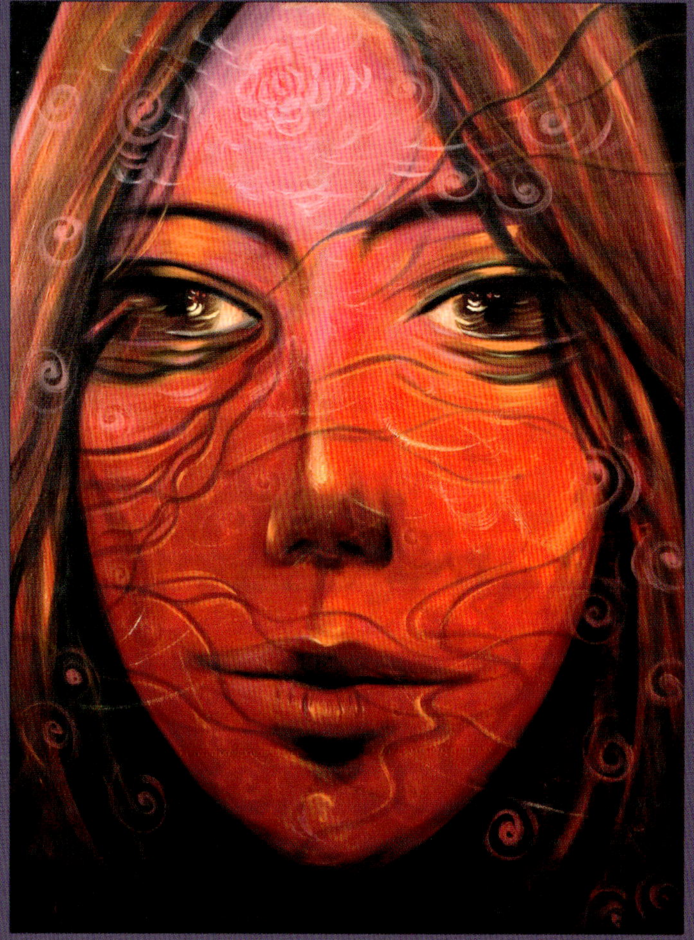

"Tapestry Of The Human Heart" Acrylic on canvas

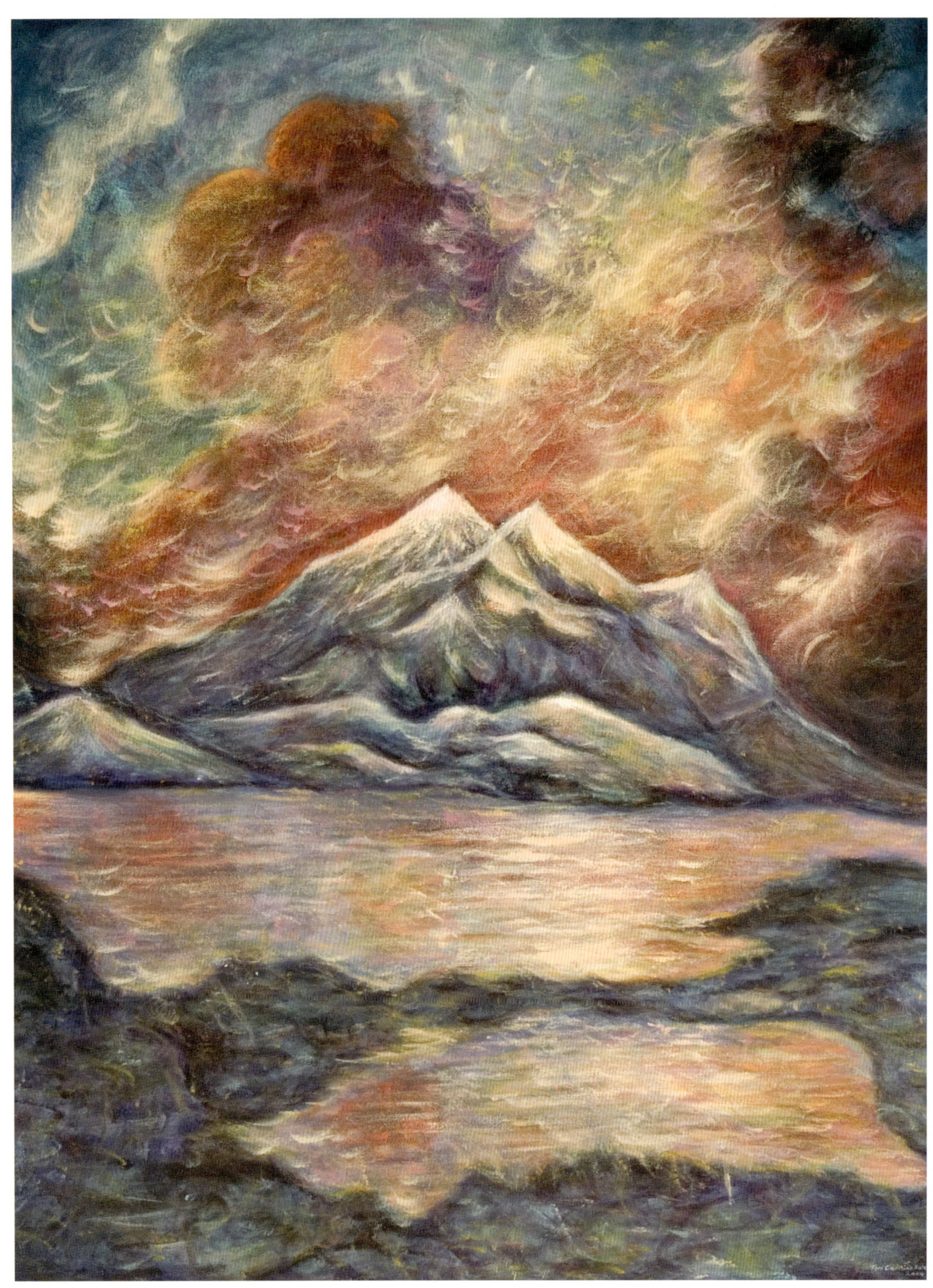

"Colour" Acrylic on canvas
Next page: "Moon Tree" Oil on canvas

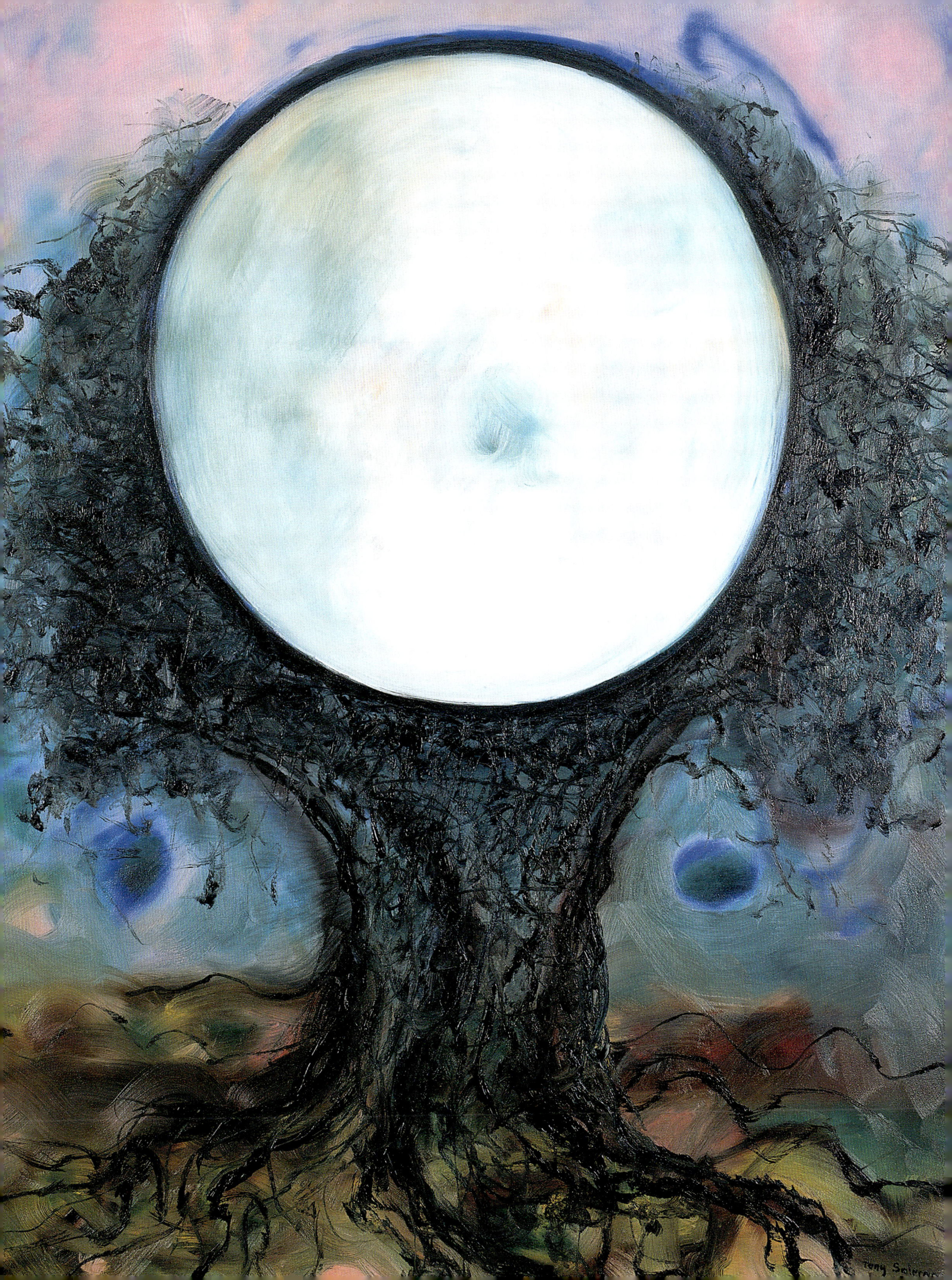

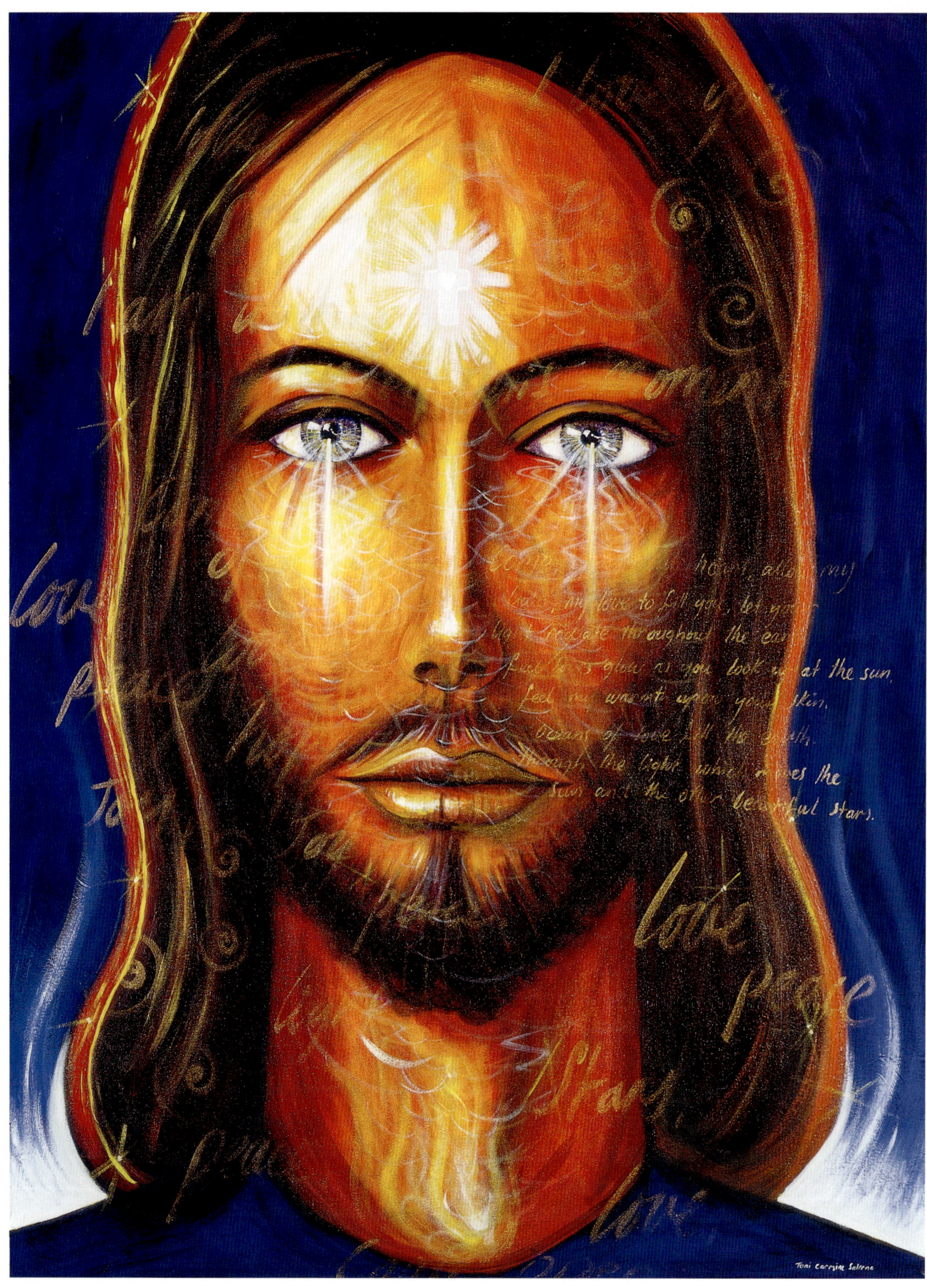

"Jesus 2000" *Acrylic on canvas*

Next page: *"The Mystic"* *Acrylic on canvas*

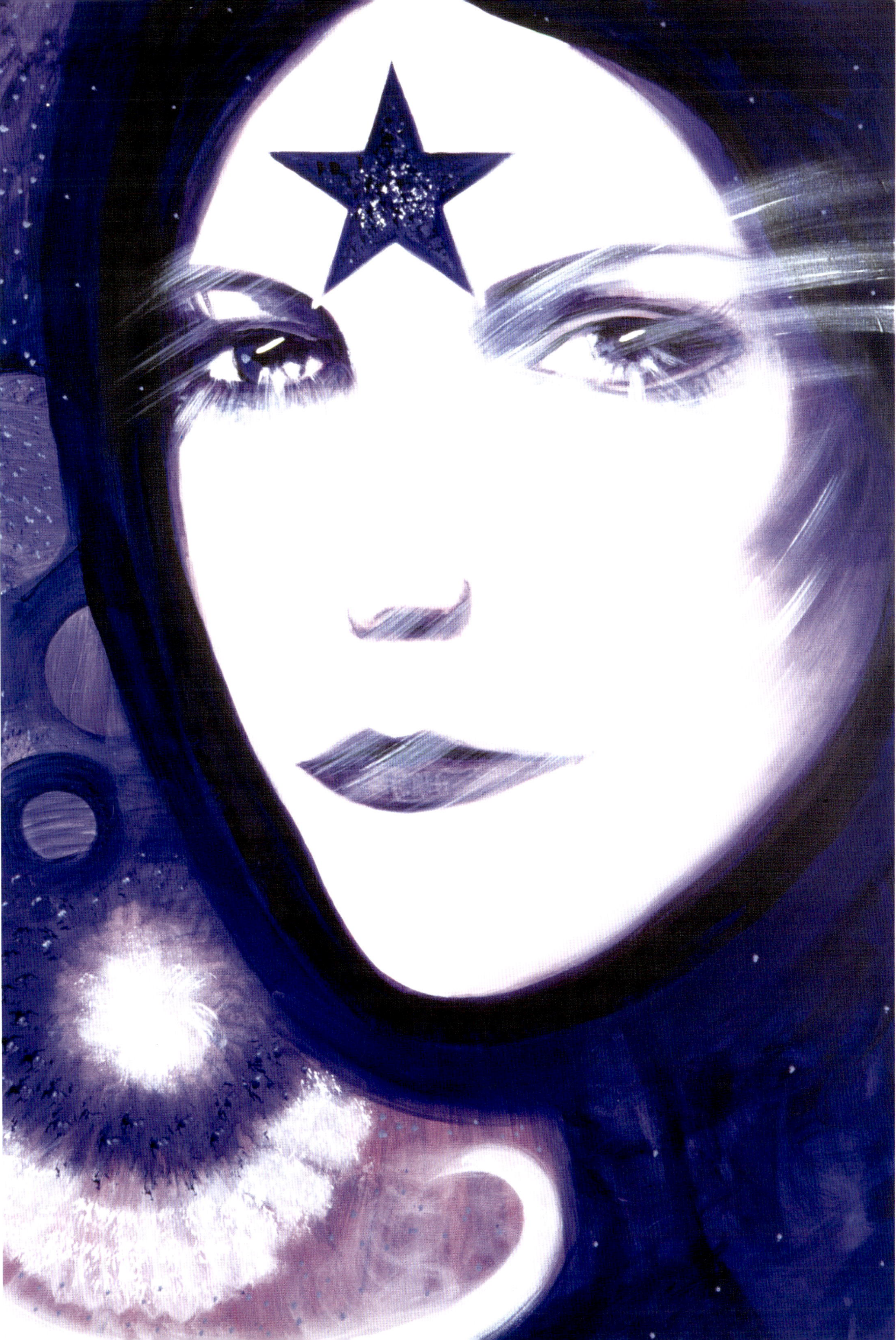

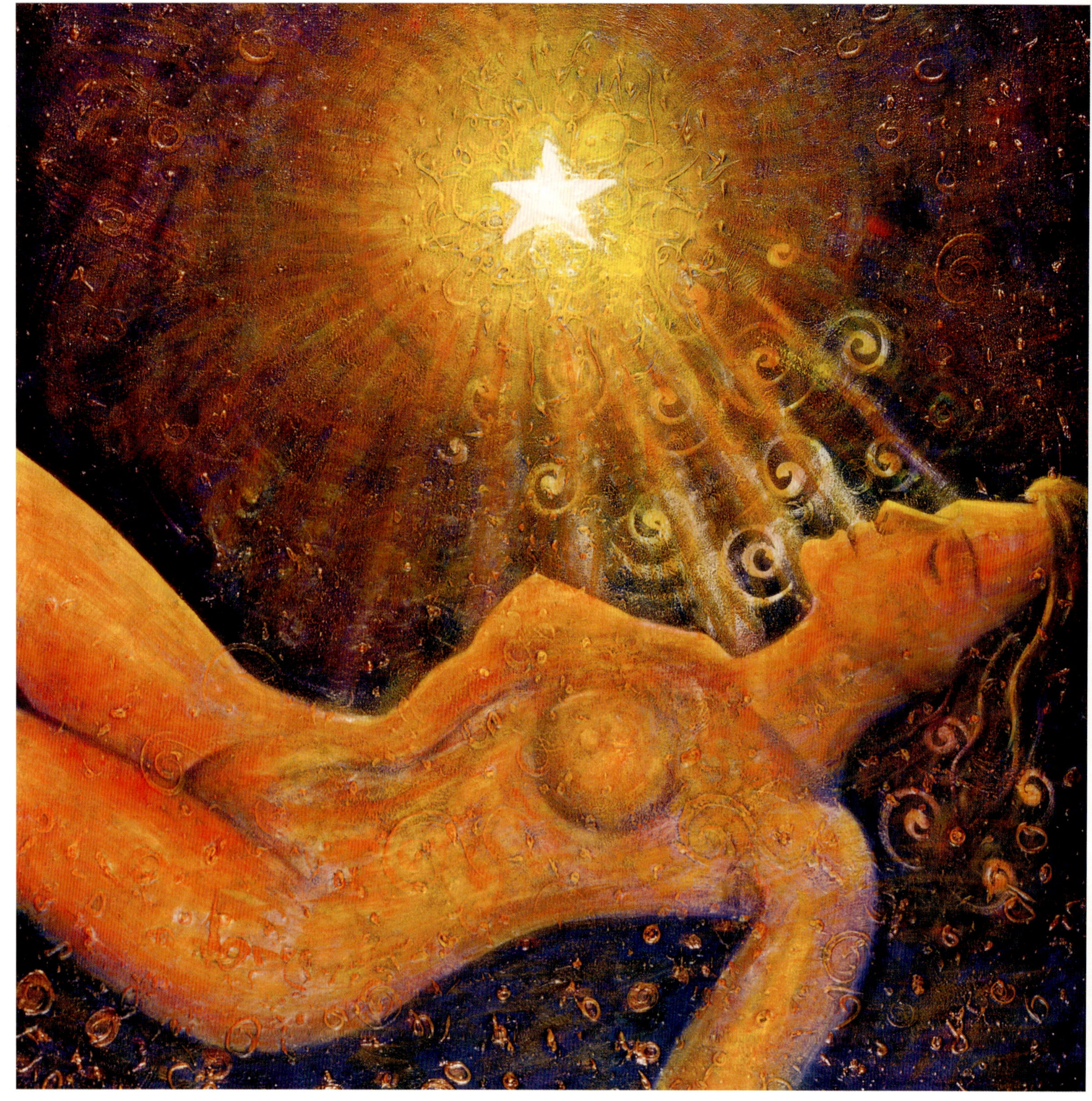

"Venus" *Acrylic on canvas* / *Next page:* *"Primordial Goddess"* *Acrylic on canvas*

Before the dawn of time
All was but a speck of light
Through a super-luminous event
We were born
And to this very day
We remain in essence... Light

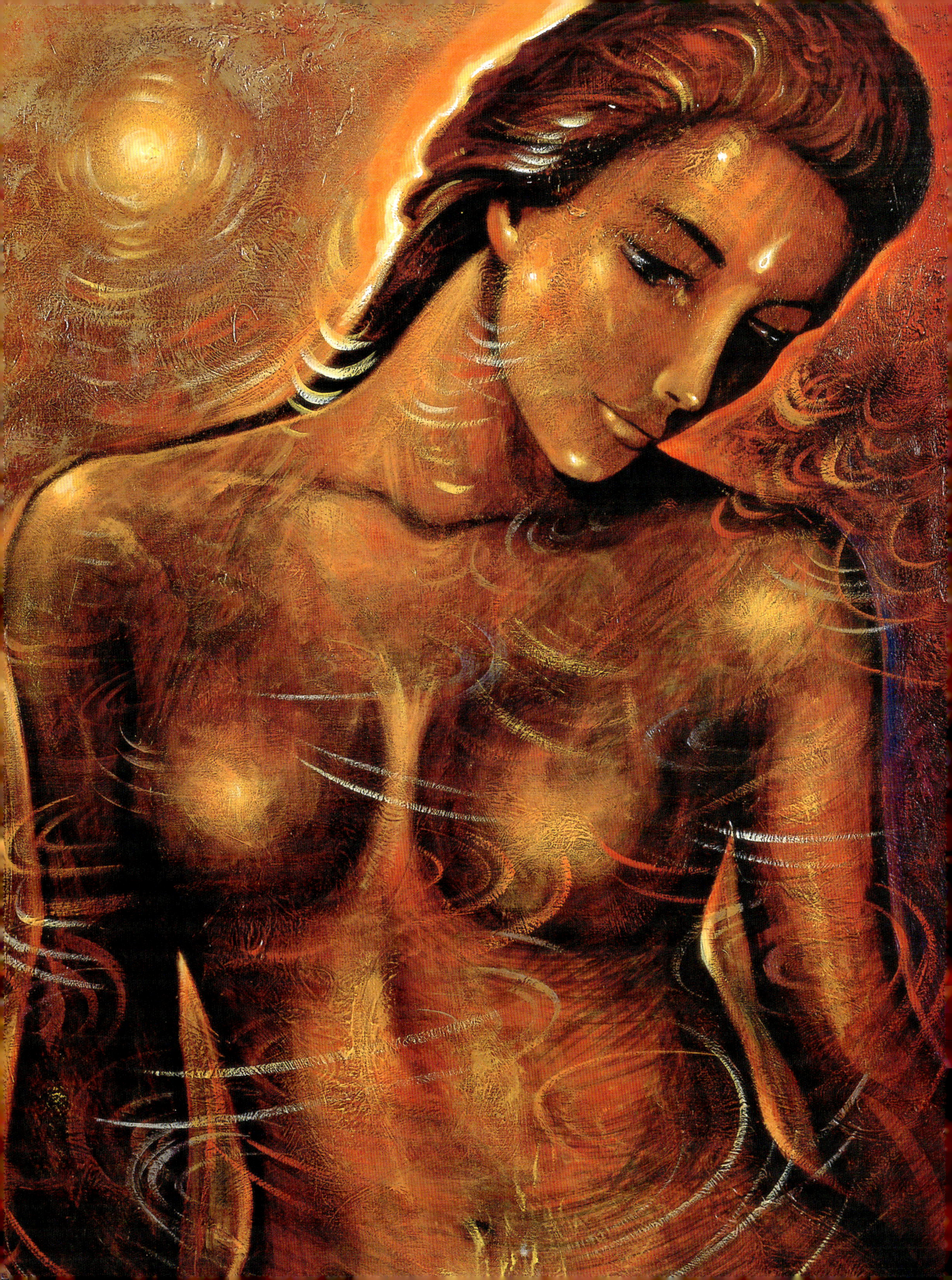

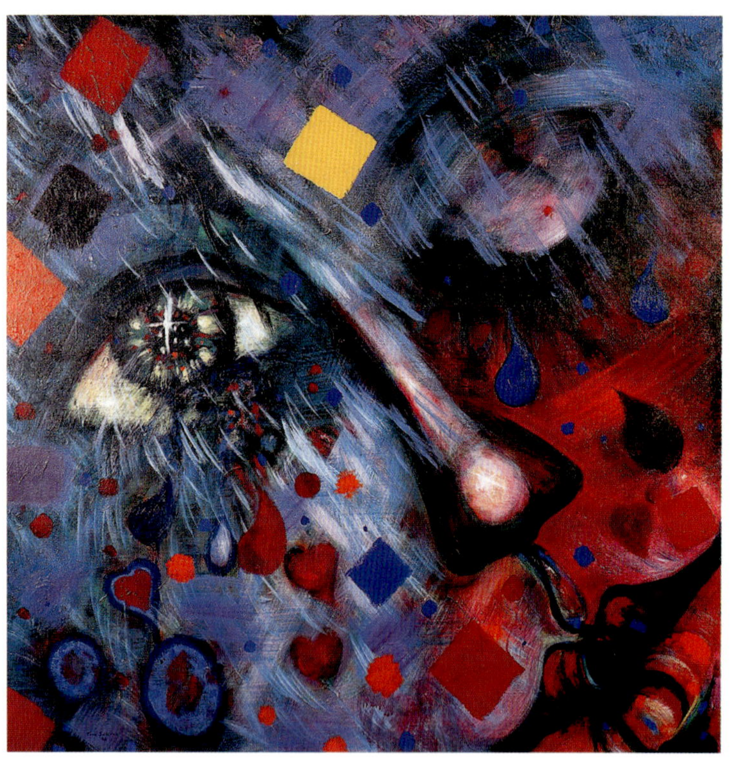

"Blue Tear" Acrylic on canvas

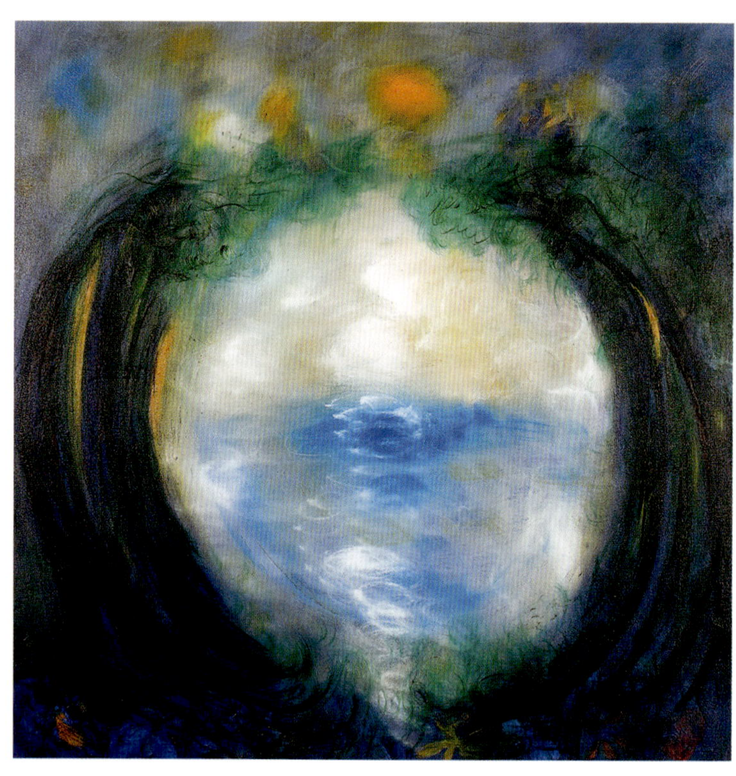

"Earth Song" Oil on canvas

We are all fragments of one whole.
All is energetically interconnected.

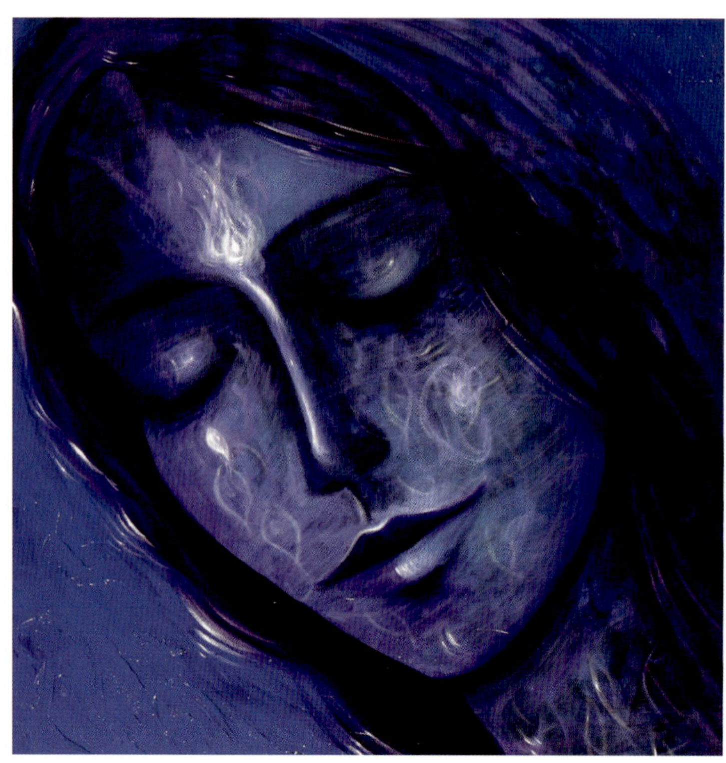

"Angel Of Relaxation" Oil on canvas

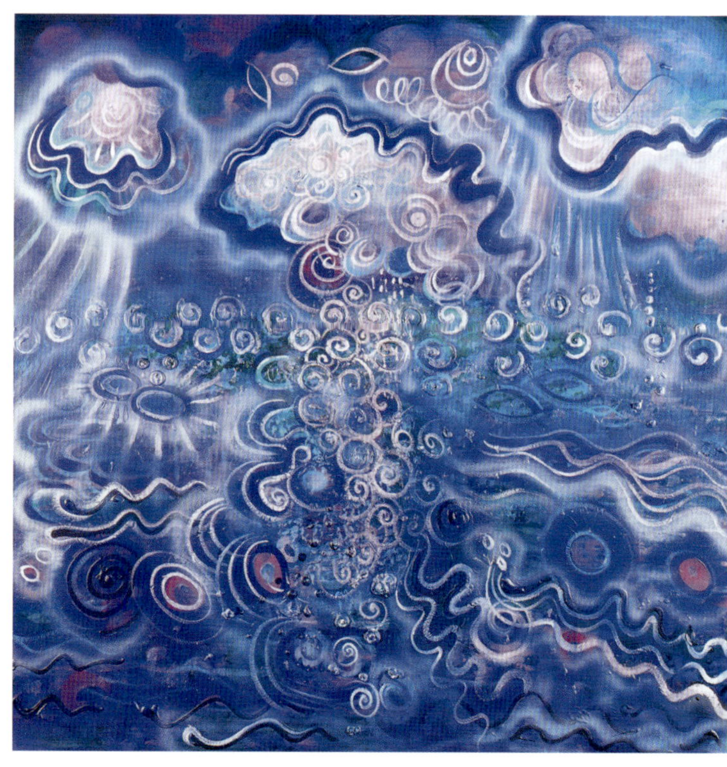

"Silver Vibrations" Acrylic on canvas

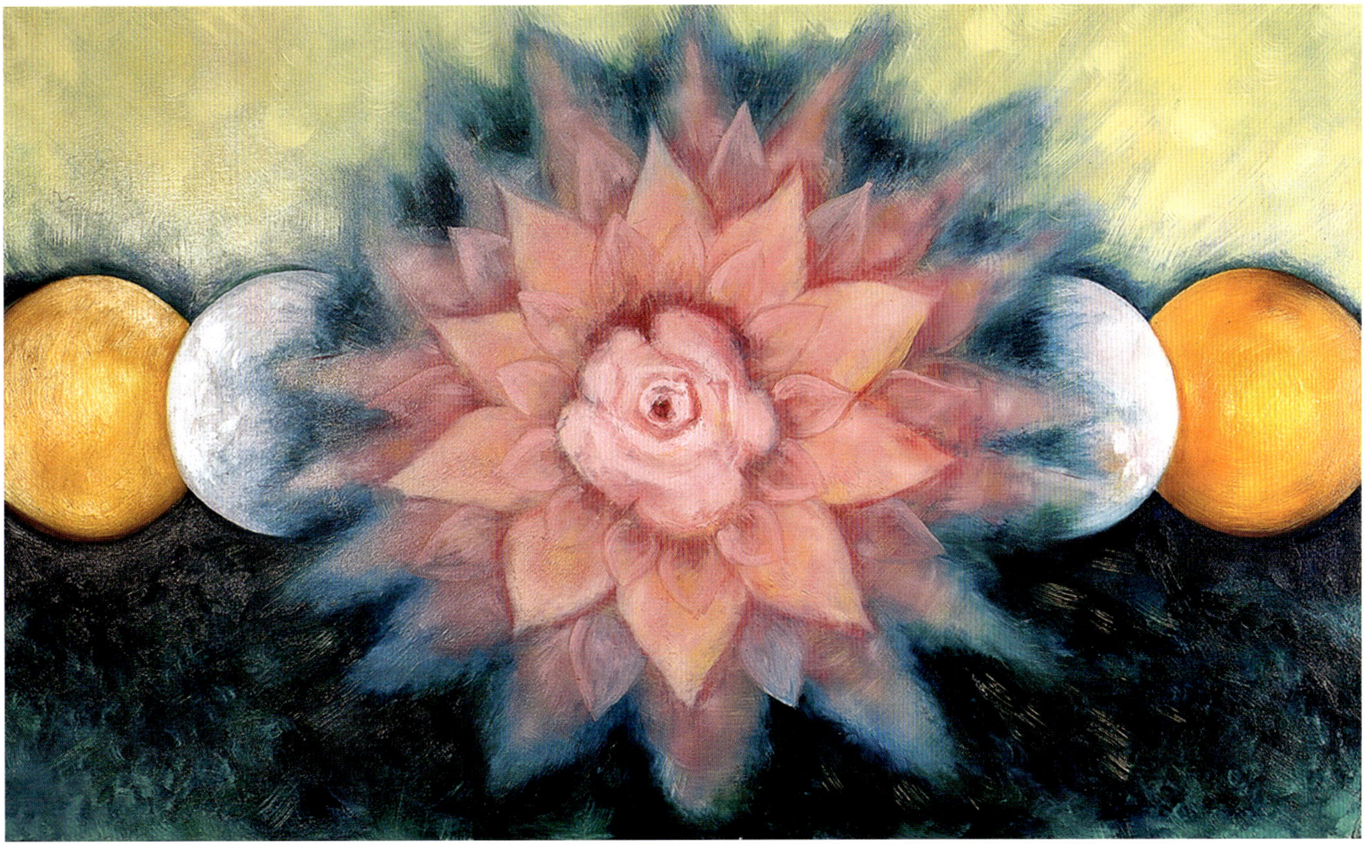

"Lotus Rose" *Oil on canvas*

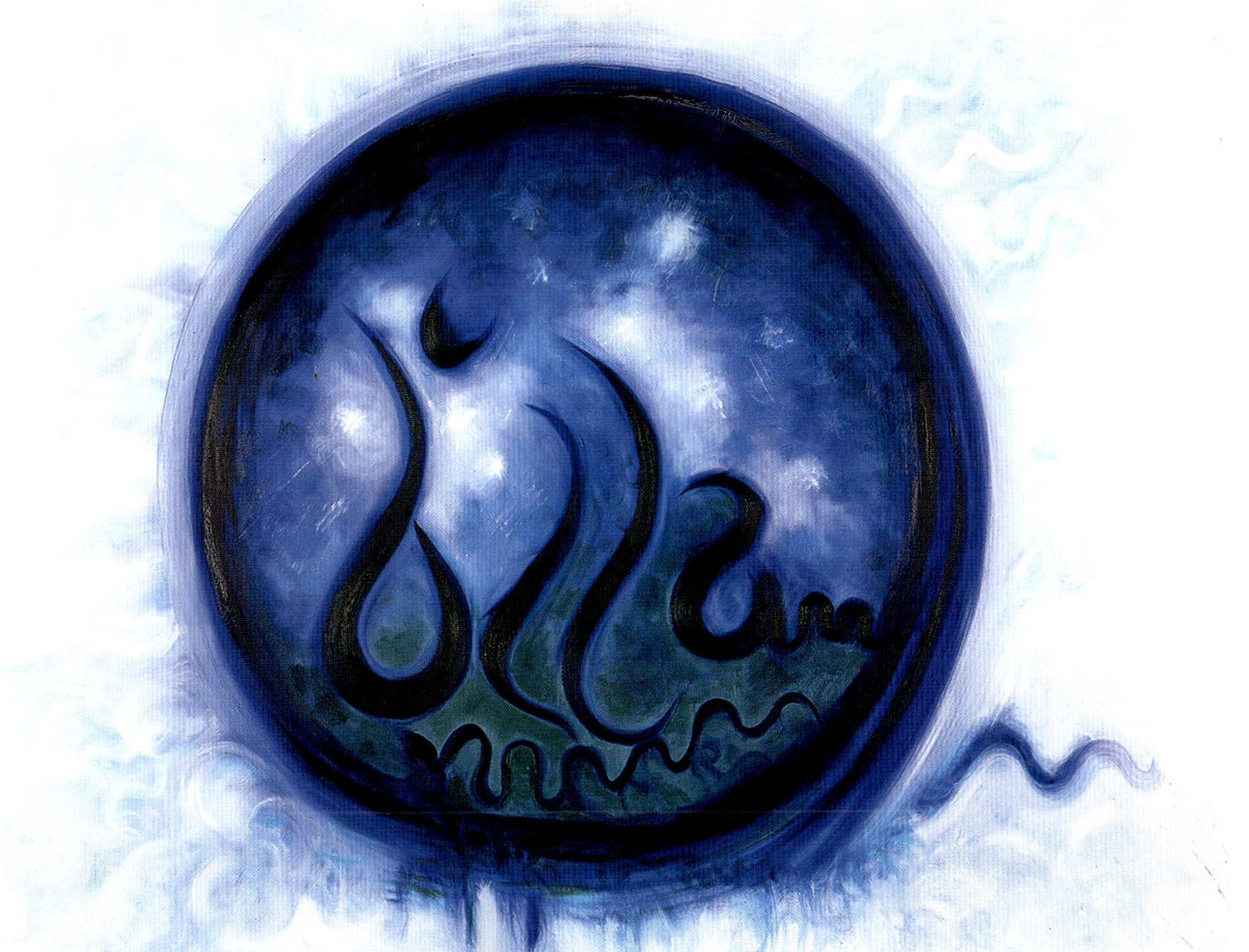

"Om" *Oil on canvas*

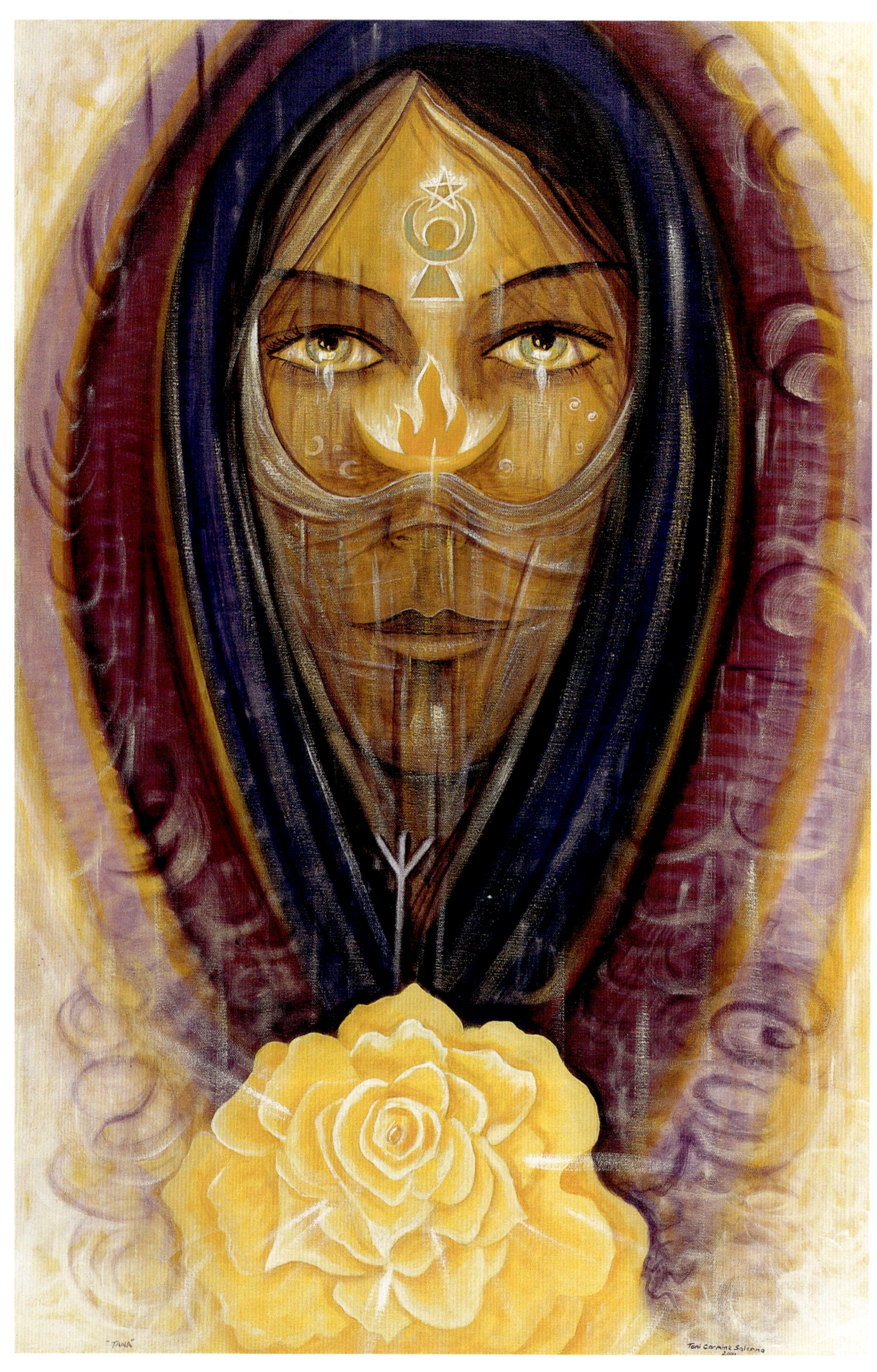

"Sanskrit Rose" Acrylic on canvas

Next page: *"Autumn Leaves"* *Acrylic on canvas*

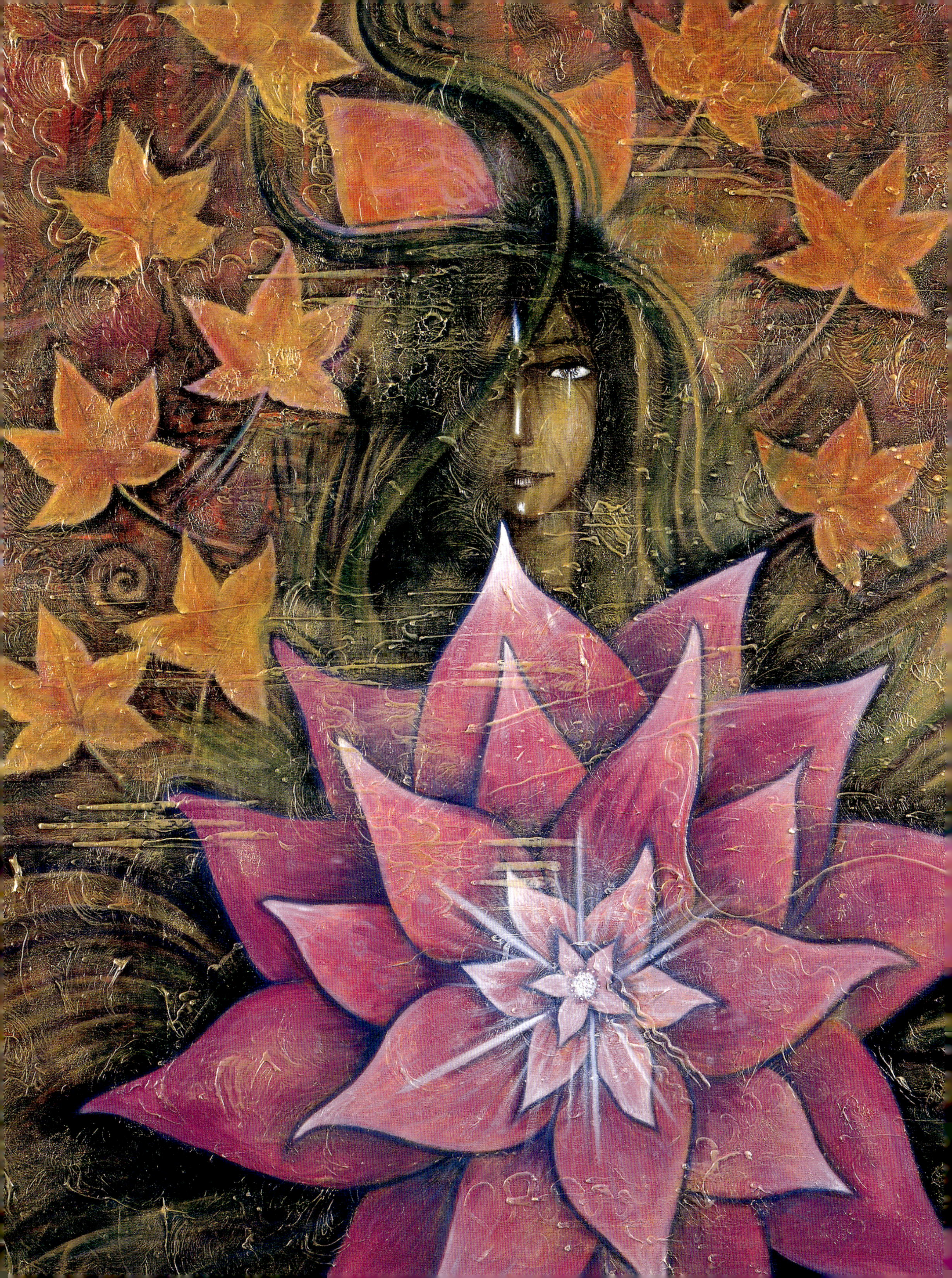

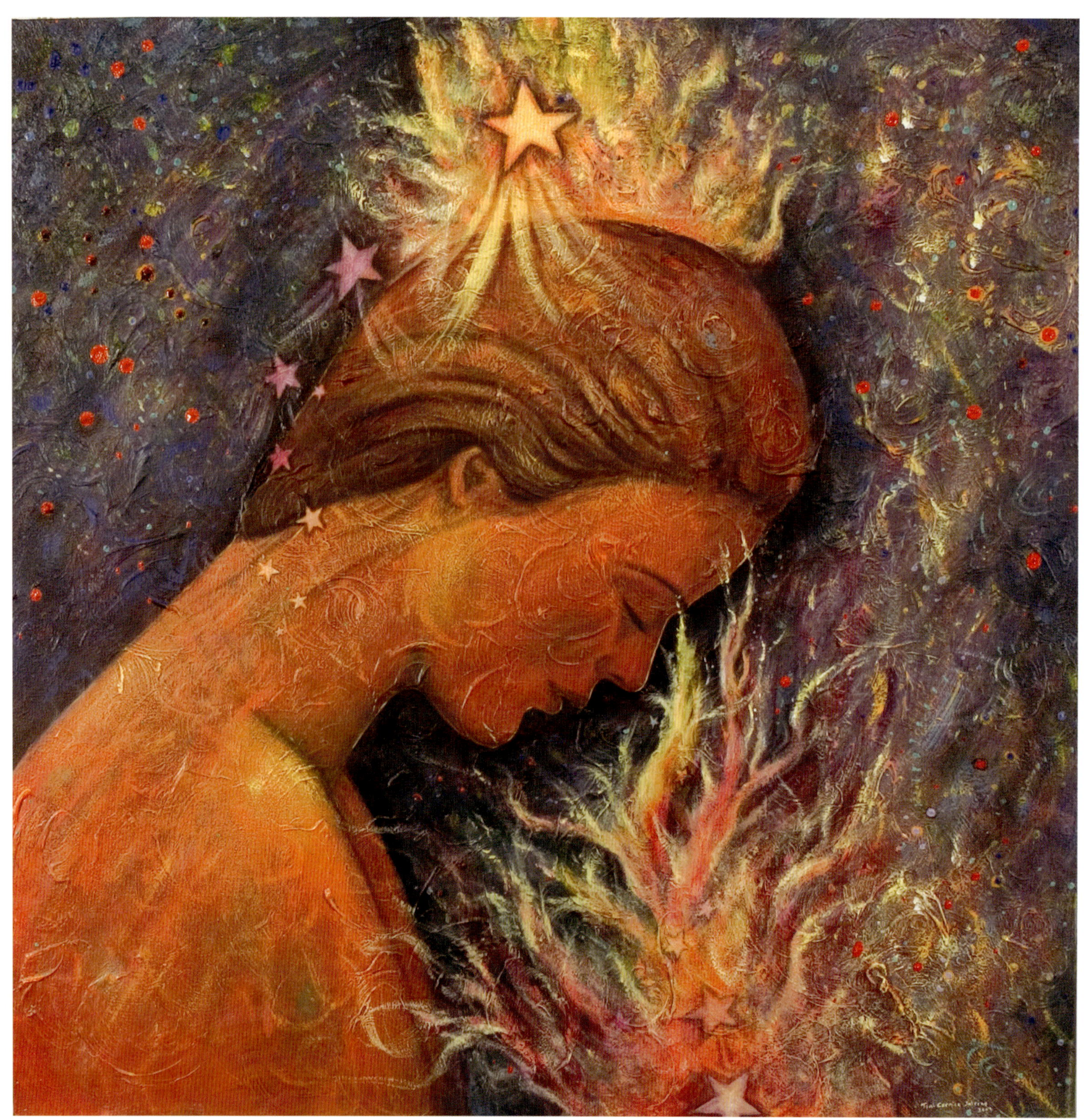

"Initiation" *Acrylic on canvas*

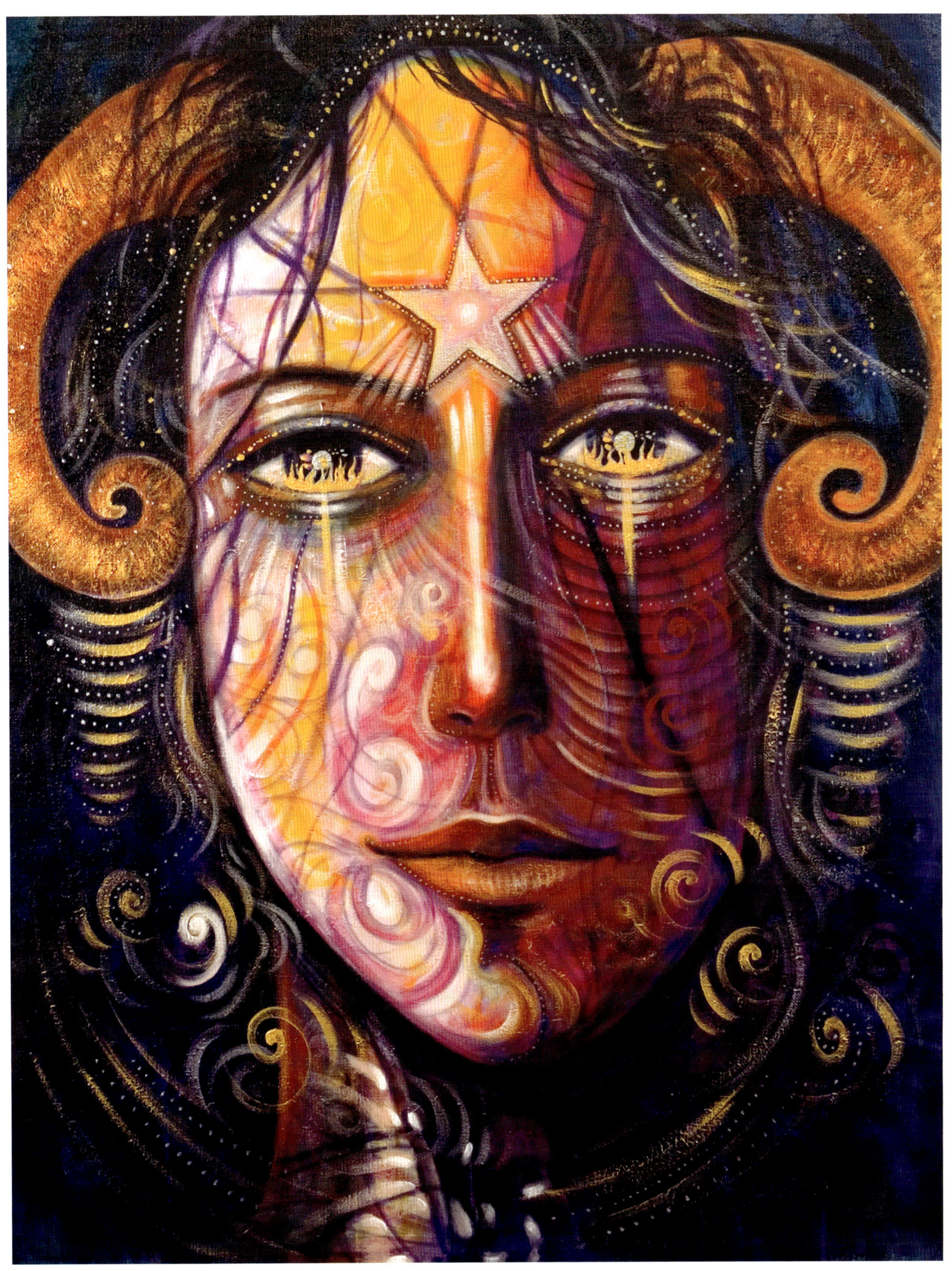

"There Is No Sorrow Without Its Joy" Acrylic on canvas

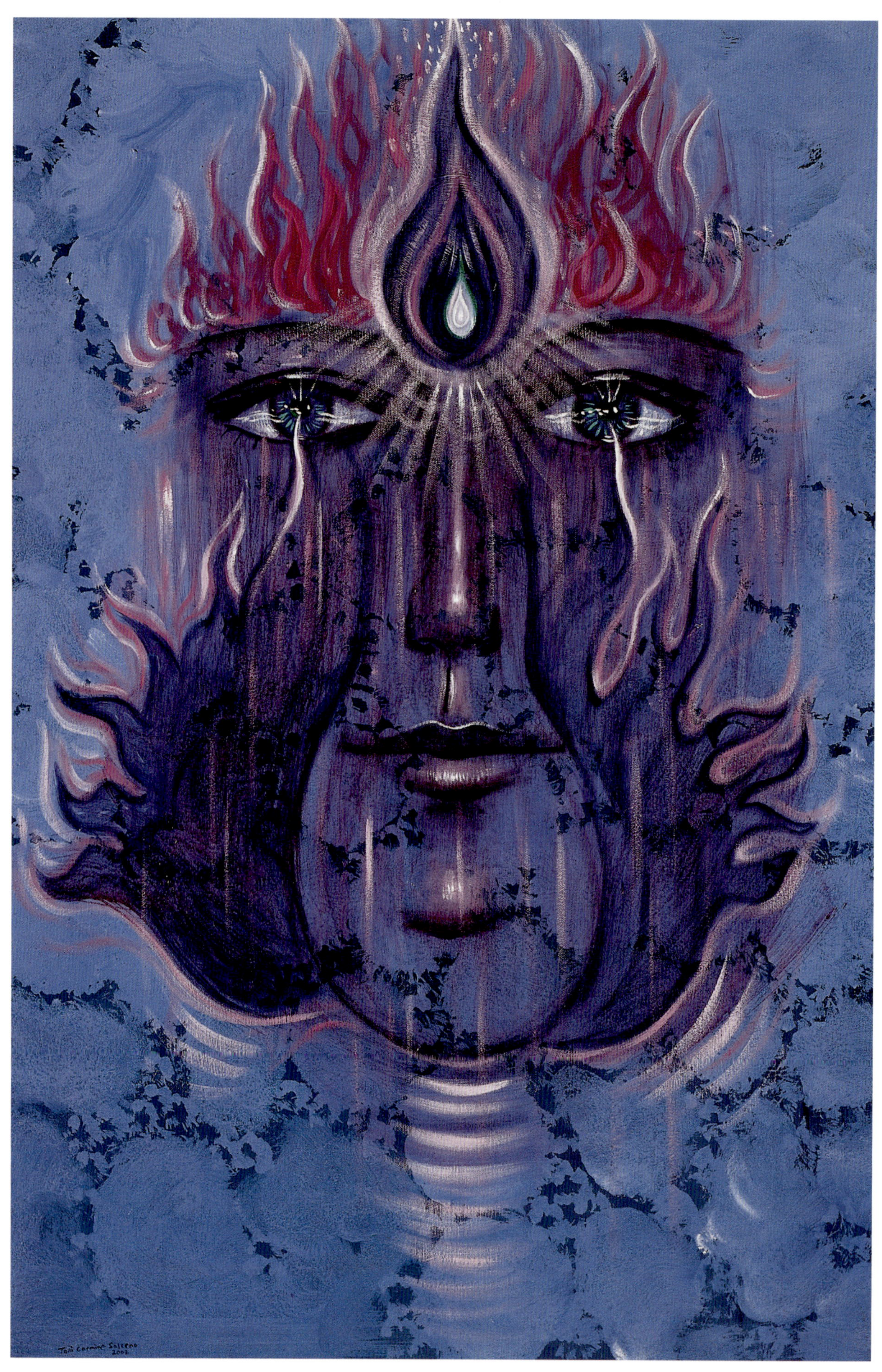

"Cosmic Flame" *Acrylic on canvas*

Next page: *"Breath Of Life"* *Acrylic on canvas*

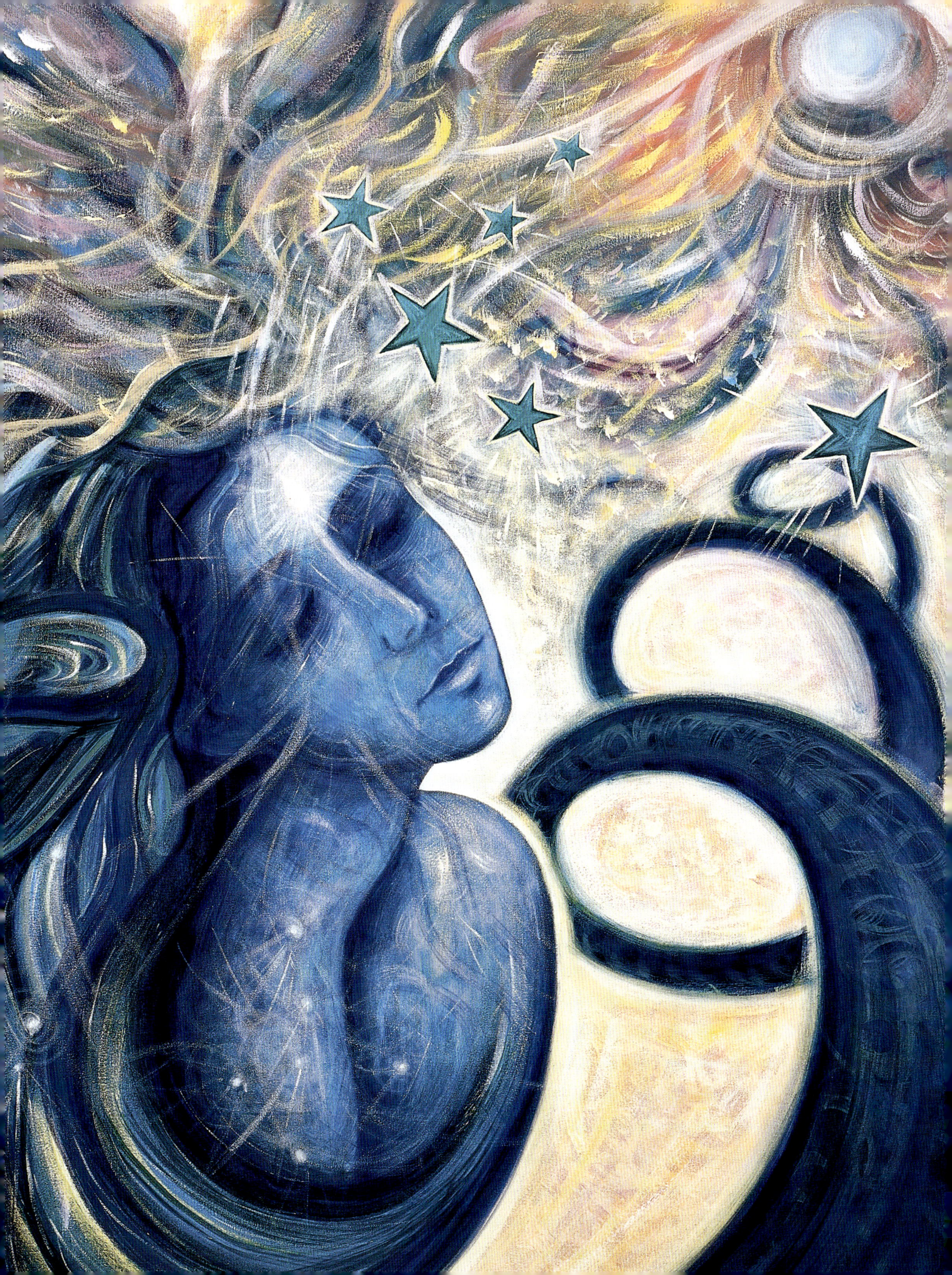

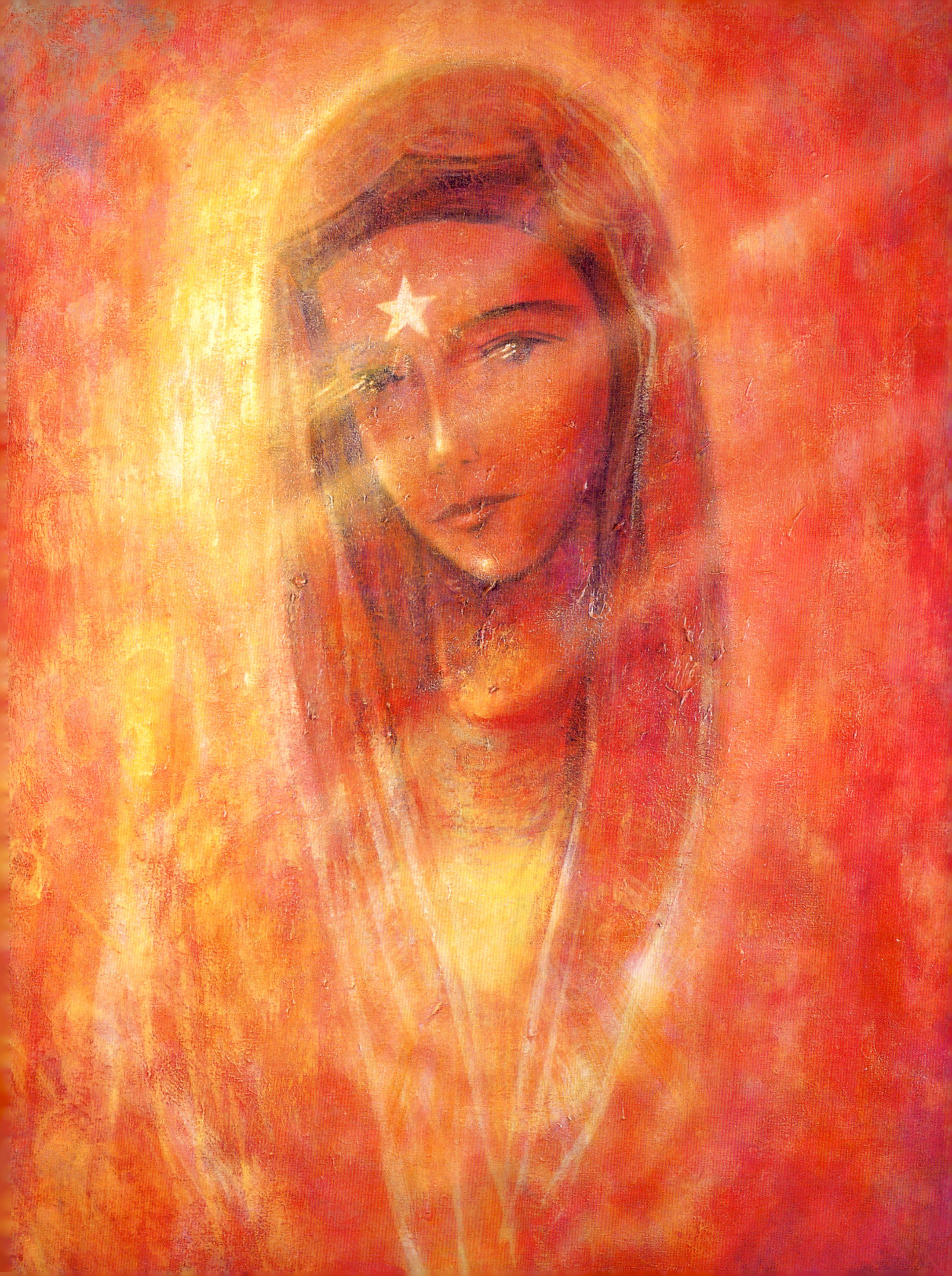

Creativity is spiritual energy
that fills the space
between each thought.

Creativity is a light
beyond the horizon
of our dreams.

It stems back
through the ancient mists
of time,

yet moves forward
beyond the tomorrow.

Toni Carmine Salerno

"Catherine Of Siena" Acrylic on canvas

INDEX OF PAINTINGS

097. Wisdom
098. The Universe
099. Willingness To Love
100. Blue Lit Flame
101. Mask Of Joy
102. Turquoise Sea
103. Lost In Our Own Equations
104. Blaze
105. Luna
106. Moon Glow
107. Forgiveness
108. Crystal Wave
109. Jo
110. Moon Goddess
111. Expectancy
112. Diavolino
113. Martine
114. Anima Animus
115. Eye Of God
116. Cara
117. Higher Self
118. Sacre Coeur
119. La Natura
120. The Poetry Of Space
121. Mont St. Michel
122. Anima
123. Alchemy
124. Tapestry Of The Human Heart
125. Colour
126. Moon Tree
127. Jesus 2000
128. The Mystic
129. Venus
130. Primordial Goddess
131. Blue Tear
132. Earth Song
133. Angel Of Relaxation
134. Silver Vibrations
135. Lotus Rose
136. Om
137. Sanskrit Rose
138. Autumn Leaves
139. Initiation
140. There Is No Joy Without Its Sorrow
141. Cosmic Flame
142. Breath Of Life
143. Catherine Of Siena

www.tonicarminesalerno.com

ine forever -

forth now - be strong

e - and forever within

that you stay - protected

night not fear - you will

now what to do -

the fears have stopped they

will not return to haunt

any more -

be aware that life is

onward and onward to a

new day - and you will

ask you to do - for you

ne and will have no doubt

ithin the stillness of my heart
ou will move with love -
you are ripe now -
your heart is ripe for love
or my work.
your waiting will stop - th
you will claim my day
as I said before you will
me forever -
forth now - be strong
ne - and forever within
eart you stay - protected
o do not fear - you will
know what to do -